To Joe

with warmest affection

Jim

Tennyson's Major Poems

TENNYSON'S MAJOR POEMS

The Comic and Ironic Patterns

James R. Kincaid

New Haven and London, Yale University Press

1975

Designed by John O. C. McCrillis
and set in Baskerville type.
Printed in the United States of America by
The Colonial Press Inc., Clinton, Massachusetts.

Published in Great Britain, Europe, and Africa by
Yale University Press, Ltd., London.
Distributed in Latin America by Kaiman & Polon,
Inc., New York City; in India
by UBS Publishers' Distributors Pvt.,
Ltd., Delhi; in Japan by John Weatherhill, Inc., Tokyo

To Arthur A. Adrian

Contents

Preface

The pleasures of writing—certainly of reading—prefaces seem to have deteriorated considerably from what they once were. Now one is obliged to dish out honeyed thanks to an indifferent family, to suggest without apparent irony that one's colleagues compose themselves into an academy of selfless readers-of-each-others'-stuff, to offer lavish appreciation to whoever it is holds the copyrights for *ELN* or some such, and to praise one's dean—all to keep a job and avoid a lawsuit. But once it was possible to exercise valuable hostilities in such places; witness Byron: "What Mr. Southey's deserts are, no one knows better than Mr. Southey: all his latter writings have displayed the writhing of a weakly human creature, conscious of owing its worldly elevation to its own debasement (like a man who has made a fortune by the Slave-trade, or the retired keeper of a Gaming house or Brothel), and struggling convulsively. . . ." One wonders what Byron would have to say about the benefits to scholarship presented by spouses and children, the Board of Regents who own the copyrights, one's dean?

In this spirit, then, I should like to thank the many people who have helped me in various ways with this project. My colleagues John Muste, Christian Zacher, and Richard Martin all ripped their way through long sections of the work, offering valuable comments of all sorts and tones and many suggestions I eagerly adopted. Gerald Bruns usefully mixed an attitude of stunned piety toward Tennyson with one of bemused tolerance toward me, telling me more about Tennyson's poetry than I could ever have learned elsewhere. Joan Webber provided not only direct criticisms of the material but a liberal and free participation in the patterns of thought I was trying to form. Richard D. Altick worked his way through nearly every sentence with great charity for me and none at all for the argument. My rapidly compounding debt to him in matters large and small is embarrassing to think about but gratefully acknowledged all the same. Each of these readers has in one way or another made it clear that he was in fact dissociated from the argument, and it only seems fair to let them all range free from errors and distortions in the work. My wife, who many times read all this and Tennyson too, encouraged not only the writing of *a* book but supported *this* book, *this* thesis, and therefore really deserves no dissociation. If I could say that she is responsible for all errors, *et cetera*, without appearing craven, I would. This book is dedicated to the man who taught me Tennyson and, along the way, provided me with a firm image of what a wholehearted and generous immersion in teaching and scholarship could, at its very best, provide.

I should also like to thank the National Endowment for the Humanities for the Younger Humanist Fellowship which gave me the time and money to do the work. I owe a special thanks to the people at the Tennyson Research Centre in Lincoln, especially Mrs. Nancy Campbell, for their great kindness to me while I was there and also for permission to refer to and quote from materials in their collection. Dr. J. M. Gray gave me during this period the benefits of his remarkable knowledge of Tennyson, Arthurian materials, and public houses in Lincoln, as well as his friendship. The Ohio State University College of Humanities provided free time and also a grant-in-aid to help this project along in every sense. Earlier versions of a part of chapter 4 and the section on "Gareth and Lynette" in chapter 8 were previously published in *Philological Quarterly* (Spring 1974) and *Texas Studies in Literature and Language* (Winter 1972), respectively. They are included here with the kind permission of The University of Iowa and The University of Texas Press.

Abbreviations

All quotations from Tennyson's poems are from Christopher Ricks, ed., *The Poems of Tennyson* (London: Longmans, 1969), cited throughout as Ricks.

BJRL *Bulletin of the John Rylands Library*
HLQ *Huntington Library Quarterly*
JEGP *Journal of English and Germanic Philology*
L&P *Literature and Psychology*
MLQ *Modern Language Quarterly*
MP *Modern Philology*
N&Q *Notes and Queries*
PLL *Papers on Language and Literature*
PQ *Philological Quarterly*
QR *Quarterly Review*
RMS *Renaissance and Modern Studies*
SAB *South Atlantic Bulletin*
SEL *Studies in English Literature*
SoR *Southern Review*
TSE *Tulane Studies in English*
TSL *Tennessee Studies in Literature*
TSLL *Texas Studies in Literature and Language*
UTQ *University of Toronto Quarterly*
VN *Victorian Newsletter*
VP *Victorian Poetry*
VS *Victorian Studies*

1

Introduction

In a famous passage, the narrator of *Middlemarch* expresses the central point of nineteenth-century irony: "We do not expect people to be deeply moved by what is not unusual. That element of tragedy which lies in the very fact of frequency, has not yet wrought itself into the coarse emotion of mankind; and perhaps our frames could hardly bear much of it. If we had a keen vision and feeling of all ordinary human life, it would be like hearing the grass grow and the squirrel's heart beat, and we should die of that roar which lies on the other side of silence." [1]

When every life becomes tragic and the element of the special case is removed, human existence itself becomes ironic. Catastrophic disillusionment and destruction are not the lot of the godlike hero, invoking by his stature the terrible laws of retribution, but of every ordinary person going about the business of common life. There are, consequently, no heroes; there are no cosmic laws to be broken; there is no possibility of fixing our pity and fear on the suffering hero. We are all victims, incapable of being "deeply moved" by what is common, uncaused, and without meaning. The tragic emotions are not released but focused and contained, and we are forced, in ironic art, to see ourselves as victims of the trivial, both trapped and released into the "illimitable inane" ("Lucretius," l. 40). We are all caught in the same incoherence, experiencing, as Melville's Ishmael says, the contradictory ironic states, floating isolation and total bondage ("And what are you, reader, but a Loose-Fish and a Fast-Fish, too?"). Increasingly in the nineteenth and twentieth centuries, we find a myth that stresses the two images of man as caught, wriggling on the deterministic pin, or loose, accidental, with only a vague hope "that nothing walks with aimless feet."

1. George Eliot, *Middlemarch*, ed. Gordon S. Haight (Boston: Houghton Mifflin, 1956), p. 144.

But this is not the only myth. There was, after all, the world of Mr. Pickwick, of Jane Austen, and much of Wordsworth: the world of liberated order, settled and humane values, sanctified and full life. The comic vision stood as an alternative to the ironic, dissolving the unrelieved tension of irony by reaffirming the dignity and power of the human will, the possibility of joy, and the continuity of all life. Comedy offered a means of surpassing the insistent "facts" of irony. Against the ironic insistence on the isolation of man, comedy posed the symbol of marriage; against the contrary insistence on bondage, it posed the symbol of the dance or the party: Christmas at Dingley Dell or Bob Cratchit's, the Mad Tea Party, cucumber sandwiches with Ernest Worthing.

The comic vision gradually becomes more difficult to sustain, perhaps, but it never dies entirely. The nineteenth century was much closer to Eden, and even its irony contains within it always the clear picture of what is lost. As Matthew Arnold says, the pain of isolation is not just increased, it is partly caused, by the memory or at least the legend of a union that once had been: "Who order'd, that their longing's fire / Should be, as soon as kindled, cool'd?" ("To Marguerite—Continued," ll. 19–20).

The comic thus stands against and enriches the ironic myth. Just so, irony begins to move to dominate all art, not necessarily because artists chose that myth, but because for serious writers of the last century or so, "irony is . . . much less often a rhetorical or dramatic strategy which they may or may not decide to employ, and much more often a mode of thought silently imposed upon them by the general tendency of the times." [2] But, by a striking further paradox, those artists most conscious of the advancing prevalence of the ironic view were precisely those who most aggressively resisted it. Those most sensitive to the present were also most deeply sensitive to the past: they saw that the comic life was lost but still remembered it most vividly. They continued to ask, with Hardy, "And why unblooms the best hope ever sown?" because they in part believed in—or at least remembered—the grand artistic, religious, and political hopes of the past.

The most crucial problem for these artists was contained in the perception that the present, the only thing really alive, is void of meaning, while the past, which is dead, alone contains the meaning

2. D. C. Muecke, *The Compass of Irony* (London: Methuen, 1969), p. 10.

that can give life. The past is both immediate and beyond reach. The comic vision refused to yield completely to the ironic, and we find, in artist after artist, these forms existing side by side. One could argue, in relation to the past, from full and resonant comic grounds: "The Present is the vassal of the Past: / So that, in that I *have* lived, do I live, / And cannot die, and am, in having been— / A portion of the pleasant yesterday" ("The Lover's Tale," ll. 115–18). Here our bondage to the past is made cause for an extension of personality throughout time, so that our being "a portion of the pleasant yesterday" helps define us in relation to time and insures that we "cannot die," implying not only that we have life in the past but that we will, by irrational but very compelling analogy, continue to live in the time that has defined us.

But "portion of the pleasant yesterday" recalls nothing so firmly as the grim lines from "The Lotos-Eaters": "All things are taken from us, and become / Portions and parcels of the dreadful past" (ll. 91–92). It is not just that this "pleasant" past has become "dreadful"; time the protector has become time the ravager. This transformation locates for us the center of Tennyson's major poetry: the interplay and conflict of the comic and ironic modes. No other nineteenth-century writer is more responsive to the intense presence and distance of comic life, the memory that seems to make life possible in its promise of continuity and yet turns it into a mockery of genuine life, a literal death-in-life.

Tennyson's career can be seen as a strong and courageous resistance to the demands of ironic art, an art he had, moreover, mastered very early. If one sets aside his minor poems—the political and public verse, his English and domestic idyls, and his dialect and humorous poems—something like a semicircular pattern may be traced. The *Poems by Two Brothers* and the volumes of 1830, 1832, and 1842 all contain a few comic poems but show, in the main, a steady development toward more compact and rich ironic statement. Beginning with *The Princess*, however, and continuing through *In Memoriam* and *Maud*, Tennyson tries various and often unique comic strategies, only to return to irony in the late poems, and particularly in *Idylls of the King*, surely the major ironic work of art of the century. This development is neither simple nor pure—comic and ironic forms are used throughout his career—but the main outlines seem reasonably clear.

This suggested pattern differs markedly from that implied by what was once critical orthodoxy: the view that Tennyson and his poetry could best be apprehended by a series of contraries. Harold Nicolson made an admirably strategic division of the lyric, morbid, and mystic Tennyson from the public bard,[3] and we have had, since, a good many developments and refinements of this view.[4] At present, critics frequently deny the dualism and assert one or another unity in its place.[5] It is, however, surely just as dangerous to ignore the tension in Tennyson's poetry as to go on inventing new labels for it. One can, of course, see how apt and expressive descriptions such as "life-weariness," "despair," "frustration," or "melancholia" [6] are in explaining the basis of Tennyson's art. Even more basic, it seems to me, is a larger formal battle carried out in his poetry between two alternate myths. One of these, irony, does express itself in the form of balanced, but unreconciled, opposites; the other, comedy, takes a firm, single direction. The first myth has often been approached indirectly by means of the dualistic view mentioned before; the second has largely been ignored.[7]

3. *Tennyson: Aspects of His Life, Character, and Poetry* (London: Constable, 1923).

4. Most notable are Arthur J. Carr's fine essay, "Tennyson as a Modern Poet," *UTQ* 19 (1950): 361–82 and E. E. Smith's *The Two Voices*, which is organized around various paralleled opposites in Tennyson's outlook and poems.

5. See Carl Robinson Sonn, "Poetic Vision and Religious Certainty in Tennyson's Earlier Poetry," *MP* 57 (1959): 83–93, and Jerome H. Buckley, *Tennyson: The Growth of a Poet*, p. 255. An extreme view is presented by John R. Reed, *Perception and Design in Tennyson's "Idylls of the King,"* who argues that Tennyson developed a single moral design which "he exploited . . . time and again" (p. 30). William Brashear sees unity springing from Tennyson's "awareness of doom"; see *The Living Will*, p. 60. The most recent assertion of unity is made by Ward Hellstrom, *On the Poems of Tennyson*, who claims that Tennyson "consistently endorsed the choice of life over death and involvement over isolation" (p. 4).

6. These phrases belong, in order, to the following: Robert Langbaum, *The Poetry of Experience*, p. 89; Brashear, *The Living Will*, p. 67; Carr, "Tennyson as a Modern Poet," p. 381; and W. H. Auden, Introduction to *A Selection from the Poems of Alfred, Lord Tennyson*, p. x.

7. One book, Valerie Pitt's *Tennyson Laureate*, does *not* ignore the second generic direction, nor does it insist on any simple dualism in Tennyson. Her statement on the central position of Tennyson's poetry seems to me exactly right: "There is in his work a true dialectic, a tension between the insight of the solitary and the sense of the common and the social. An awareness of the romantic wastes, the fluent and unshaped, appears through, and sometimes is imposed upon, an intense realisation of normal activity and order" (p. 18).

If one substitutes "comedy" and "irony" for Pitt's "sense of the common and the social" and "insight of the solitary," respectively, he will find a rough correspondence to what I have been trying to say. I can only express my admiration for *Tennyson Laureate*—it seems to me far and away the best critical book on Tennyson—and add the disclaimer that my emphasis is quite different: Pitt sought really to deal with Tennyson's public poetry and his public role, asking, as her central question, "How did the poet of a purely private emotion become the poet of a public order?" (p. 15). That she has answered this question so well is reason enough not to ask it again.

Tennyson's Irony

The narrative pattern of irony, what Northrop Frye calls "the mythos of winter," [8] has frequently been characterized in discussions of "open" or "general" irony and distinguished there from the "specific" or "closed" irony that is more properly thought of as a technique. This general irony is noncorrective, presenting, like all irony, some conflict but insisting always that the conflict cannot be resolved. This is the irony of the impossible situation, an irony that includes us all as victims—characters, readers, even the ironist.

Art rooted in "unidealized existence" (Frye, p. 223) is likely, then, to formulate its structural principles and its narrative patterns in reference to general irony. There are no heroes and no heroic action; worse, there is no coherence to support any purposeful action whatever. Such heroism and such coherence are, however, often recalled in this irony in order that they may be parodied. In fact, parody seems to be the basic principle of this narrative irony. It feeds on the affirmations contained in the other traditional patterns: romance's idealizations,[9] tragedy's cathartic sacrifice, comedy's liberation. Practicing always a rhetoric of deception, this pattern forces us to anticipate resolutions that never come. Such rhetoric is deliberately unstable, seeking to disarm us, to include its audience with its victims. The characteristic themes are of disillusionment and meaningless defeat, the fall from freedom into bondage.

While there is some specific irony in Tennyson[10]—one thinks of "The Last Tournament" or the verse epistles—he is, clearly, not

---

I do think, though, that her final estimation of Tennyson and especially her reasons for that estimation suggest that new questions ought to be asked: "Tennyson does not approach the tragic resolution because, although he knew the tragic disaster, he had never realised the tragic guilt. It is perhaps this that always we seem to miss in his poetry, perhaps this which in spite of his range and his skill makes him seem at times less than the really great" (p. 246). The hidden assumptions about generic rankings (tragedy, naturally, being best) are as distorting as the overt trick of basing final judgments on such standards as the presence or absence of "tragic guilt." I agree that Tennyson did not deal with tragedy at all, but that fact should imply no value judgment.

8. *Anatomy of Criticism*, pp. 223–39. Further references will be given in the text.

9. Frye, in fact, argues that this "parody of romance" is the central structural principle of irony (p. 223), but it does seem that the generic principle of parody applies equally to all myths; if anything, we meet it most frequently in reference to comedy, not romance.

10. Jerome H. Buckley, in "Tennyson's Irony," *VN*, no. 31 (1967), pp. 7–10, makes as good a case as can be made for Tennyson as a verbal or specific ironist.

Donne. But he does utilize extensively the more general narrative pattern, especially in the depiction of dominant opposites which cannot be coordinated or made to cancel, but which demand equal and contradictory responses. The tension between the religious, hopeful symbol on the one hand, and the tragic or melancholic symbol on the other, marks the center of Tennyson's poetry, the point being that his irony is not merely gloomy, almost never simply macabre. The contraries exist together, as brothers, an early poem says, stealing "symbols of each other" ("Song [Every day hath its night]").

The result is that no emotion can flow outward from us. The comfort of comedy and the perverse comfort of decisive negativism are alike denied, and the reader is suspended between alternate emotional and intellectual responses to alternate, unreconciled themes. Whatever Tennyson may have meant by his cryptic remark that "what the public do not understand is that the great tragedy is all balance throughout," [11] the "balance" he achieves and transmits is the ironic one presented in *Moby-Dick*, where the *Pequod*, tilting dangerously to one side under the weight of a whale's head lashed to it, hoists another on the opposite side, thus regaining her "even keel; though sorely strained, you may well believe." Ishmael goes on to point out the usefulness of this image as a symbol for the human mind, poised and paralyzed and unable to "float light and right." Irony, it may be said, causes so much horizontal strain that it makes any free forward movement impossible.

At its most obvious, Tennyson's ironic vision did insist directly and openly on the alternate truths: death is all, life is all—"All Things Will Die," "Nothing Will Die," as the poems from 1830 put it. But we find the unresolved oppositions in much less dramatic and ostentatious form throughout his career. In the beautiful poem, "To the Marquis of Dufferin and Ava" (1889), for example, he deals with both the greatness of the Indian Empire (Lord Dufferin had been governor-general of India) and the sense that India was the treacherous fate that drew his son Lionel to his death. Toward the end of the poem, these views coalesce as Tennyson dwells on the terrible fact that his son died so far from him, with strange rites and in a strange sea: "Not there to bid my boy farewell, / When That

11. Quoted in Hallam Lord Tennyson, *Alfred Lord Tennyson: A Memoir* (New York, 1898), 2:226. This work will hereafter be cited as *Memoir*.

within the coffin fell, / Fell—and flashed into the Red Sea, / Beneath a hard Arabian moon / And alien stars" (ll. 42–46).

The strong romantic associations packed into "Arabian moon" and "stars" are juxtaposed against the brutality of "hard" and "alien." But the romantic associations are not canceled by the adjectives, just as the speaker's belief in the Indian enterprise or in the continuation of life through death is not shattered. The lines describing the death are, after all, contained in a tactful public utterance, which celebrates first the virtues of a good colonial ruler and ends in a vision of love in this life and the next. The poet—and the reader—perceives both visions with equal force: the private, despairing clarity of the image of a remote death, suggesting the alien universe and the absurd, causeless nature of life, along with the public, hopeful vision of reasonable and kindly political activity and a religion of love. Neither wins. It is the great virtue of Tennyson's art that, as he matures, the diffuse and obtrusive "All Things Will Die"—"Nothing Will Die" dichotomies become compacted into phrases as suggestive and haunting as "hard Arabian moon."

Irony does not dominate all of Tennyson's poetry, but it does control the early poems (up to 1842) and many of the late ones, most prominently *Idylls of the King*. In the great middle period, the period of *The Princess, In Memoriam*, and *Maud*, Tennyson searched for means to transcend the ironic tension of vividly presented but unreconciled opposites. Transcendentalism helped, of course, and we find lively statements of it attributed to him: "Nothing worthy proving can be proven" or "Poetry is truer than fact," [12] for instance. But transcendentalism is likely only a small part of the major cause of Tennyson's liberation, which is the discovery of the possibilities of comedy. In fact, it could be argued that transcendentalism was convenient not primarily for its doctrine but for its ability to provide a happy surprise behind every false appearance, exactly paralleling the ending of comedy, where the disguises come off and reveal familiarity and promise. In any case, Tennyson spent the central part of his career writing comedy, imaging the very form he could also parody so completely. The movement from liberty to bondage was for a time reversed, as Tennyson sought to forge a unique and lasting comic vision.

12. The first statement is from "The Ancient Sage," l. 66; the second from *Memoir*, 2:129.

TENNYSON'S COMEDY

"Comedy" here is taken to mean the mythic pattern, not that which is funny. In this sense it duplicates in quality our sense of the term "irony"; that is, it is a narrative pattern, supported by an appropriate formal but unstated convention (or conventions). It clearly emphasizes liberation, freeing the ego from traps which are external and, especially, internal so that it may find, in its rejuvenation, a more or less exuberant social and personal life. Comedy finds its source at the close of the basic myth, in the resurrection of the dead god and his restoration of fertility and happiness to the community. It transforms an inhibiting condition, usually a social condition—symbolized by an unjust king, law, parent, personal vice or illusion—to a clarified and liberated one: from "law to liberty," as Frye says (p. 181).

Comedy is especially satisfying because of its sense of complete-ness, its location at the very end of the myth, but also because of its magical way of solving problems that hinge on the contrary demands of the private self and of society. It takes as its hero a figure who confronts an unjust law boldly and endures a period of neglect or even hostility in order finally to overcome injustice and gain recognition and reward from his society. By means of a focus on the liberation and rewarding of the hero, comedy feeds the isolated egos of us all. At the same time, by attacking relentlessly all misanthropic and overtly egoistic tendencies and by regarding all extroverted and social traits as laudable, comedy supports commu-nity.

This union of the personal and the communal is effected partly because we can easily identify both with the egoistic hero and with the society he redeems, but it is also true that comedy works very carefully to keep that heroic ego within certain bounds. One must, it suggests, be expansive in one's joy and, above all, charitable. Charity and forgiveness take the place of tragedy's iron justice and retribution and often stand in conflict with them. Comedy empha-sizes the miraculous and improbable; tragedy the necessary and inviolable. Thus, the hero is rewarded with gifts that will tend to social expression: marriage, which supports and prolongs the social order, and money, which is seen almost entirely in terms of its allowing the hero to give gifts, hold parties, and the like. In other words, if we are willing to define ourselves socially and accept certain minor restrictions on our pride and our tendencies toward tyrannical or blind behavior, we can be rewarded with gifts that are both social and personal. After all, in comedy marriage implies a beautiful lady.

Comedy thus works against social definition seen broadly and impersonally (i.e. in terms of modern social science or the nineteenth century's political economy) and supports social definition seen narrowly and personally. Finally, comedy's position at the end of the myth means that, with the shadow of death and sacrifice behind it, it retains a very strong feeling about the preciousness of life itself and is always dedicated to it.

It is not often recognized that Tennyson's poetry contains a large element of this zest for experience, usually expressed indirectly but often coming to the surface in lines like, "One only joy I know, the joy of life" ("Life," l. 14). As Georg Roppen very perceptively argues, "Tennyson's obsessive preoccupation with death is the negative aspect of an insatiable life-zest which informs a considerable part of his poetry and seeks expression in various directions. His craving for immortality . . . is not an aspiration to beatitude, but to continued, happy life." [13] But the comic sense that controls the major poems of the middle period is often realized in ways both puzzling and unique. The comedy is maintained only in the midst of difficulties so large that the form and even the values must be continually won and re-won. The conventional certainties of comedy are very difficult for Tennyson to accept, despite the fact that he had a strong artistic—and certainly personal—instinct to do so.

As a result, we have comedies which are not only highly specialized but which are haunted by their inverse: very sophisticated parodies of that comedy. The comic vision is never as purely expressed as is the ironic, and its tentative quality checks the resounding confidence that is usually necessary to bring off comedy's miraculous, nonlogical leaps. I am not suggesting that ordinary comedy can work only by establishing a mindless euphoria, but it seems clear that very little comedy is as dubious of its own affirmations as is Tennyson's. This very distrust, however, can make the affirmations all the more striking. Easy as it is to make jokes about Queen Victoria's comparison of *In Memoriam*'s comfort to that

13. "Alfred Tennyson," in *Evolution and Poetic Belief,* p. 79.

of the Bible, no one can doubt that the queen spoke sincerely and out of the depths of real need. It is no small thing to offer hope in the face of death; comedy has always tried to do just that.

But the tentativeness of Tennyson's great comedies helps to explain why he was never fully comfortable in that form. Despite the fact that *In Memoriam*, for instance, is a finer poem than "Rizpah," the latter is more unified and generically resonant. Tennyson could growl on with "grim affection" about "Bones" [14] —it is a fully finished and formed utterance—but he apparently disliked talking of *In Memoriam*—partly, I suppose, because he was so close to it, but also because it is so highly complex, almost generically mystifying, offering various directions for our emotions, only to pull them together at the end with a resolution that has not seemed fully satisfying to many. *In Memoriam* is Tennyson's version of *The Divine Comedy*, but it lacks entirely the total confidence and the resultant easy coherence of Dante's poem. Tennyson, one feels, could have written ironic poems like "Rizpah" forever. It is a wonder and perhaps a clue to his greatness that he tried with such skill and against such odds to write a poem about a world that could be rescued for sense, loyalty, and love.

It is a great wonder principally because Tennyson seemed unable to delude himself, except in minor poems. Even Dickens could bluff—witness John Harmon and Bella Wilfer in *Our Mutual Friend*—if the genre so demanded. But Tennyson, in his major poems, is always turning over the comic coin, seeing if the affirmation can stand its own negation. This ironic tendency in his comedy is both remarkable and unsettling. Every comic generalization stands, but not on very steady legs.

First of all, while Tennyson could accept completely the necessity and even the beauty of a social or domestic life—"Come down, O maid," for instance, is one of the most complete lyric expressions of domestic comedy in our literature—he perceived at the same time that this vision could operate as a trap, killing the spirit of man and encasing him in deadly trivia. There is a strong sense of this opposition in *The Princess*, "Ulysses" is a full statement of the problem, and *Idylls of the King* explores the pressures of the social life as subtly as *Middlemarch* and with very much the same view.

Second, Tennyson felt most uneasy about the principle on which

14. According to Sir Charles Tennyson, *Six Tennyson Essays*, p. 189.

comedy reverses tragedy: time's renewal. Time triumphs not only in *The Winter's Tale* but in every comedy, by having its linear march expose the false, restricting society, by its realization of a transcendent joy that lies outside time, or by its denial of time's dominion: they lived happily *ever after*. Tennyson's ambiguous attitude toward the past has already been mentioned; it seems, however, that there was a larger ambiguity, involving change, which he could see both comically and ironically. For instance, the comic expression asserts that change is comfortable, that it is for the better, and, most important, that it does not alter our real being: "We are all changed by still degrees, / All but the basis of the soul" (" 'Love thou thy land, with love far-brought,' " ll. 43–44). The comic view of stasis and change takes as its symbols, respectively, eternity and regeneration. Turned about, however, these assurances become the two ironies that dominate much of Tennyson's poetry: comfortable change is transformed into meaningless flux; solid and unchanging being becomes an image of man trapped and unable to help himself.

Further, though comedy always has managed its defeat of time by a projection into the future, it has generally done so successfully only by convincing us of the powerful happiness realized in the present. "They lived happily ever after" has meaning only if they are happy now. Tennyson seemed constitutionally unable, however, to imagine genuine and full comic happiness materializing for a long, long time; sometimes, one gathers, not until a few eons have passed. It is a peculiar comic satisfaction that one can obtain from waiting for evolution to solve problems. Evolution is not nearly as rhetorically persuasive as, say, sex. Still, this is to oversimplify a more complex issue that involves what Spedding called Tennyson's "almost personal dislike of the present, whatever it may be." [15] Existentialism is a modern term, but all effective comedy has contained more of it than Tennyson could muster.

Tennyson's tendency to complicate the comic mode is apparent even in very minor issues. His use of repetition, for instance, is, on the surface, highly appropriate to comedy, where the recurrence of events gives us a sense of the deep continuity of life and growth. In Tennyson, however, the lulling reassurances contained in the repetitions of "Come down, O maid" can just as easily become the

15. Quoted in *Memoir*, 1:154.

compulsive, desparately negative "Let us alone" of "The Lotos-Eaters" or "Tithonus," where the suggestions of life, ever awakening in similar patterns, are made hideous by burlesque. Similarly, there is in Tennyson a distrust of the comic principle of prodigious abundance, of wild, almost uncontrolled generosity. He spoke of being appalled by "the lavish profusion . . . in the natural world . . . from the growths of the tropical forest to the capacity of man to multiply, the torrent of babies." [16]

Still, though it is complicated and even tortured, comedy is central to Tennyson's vision, so remarkably strong that it could be maintained and find long and continued expression despite ironic pressures from without and within. It is the interplay of these two forms that I wish to examine. Tennyson mediates between the two great myths that have become the dominant modes of modern artistic expression.

THE MINOR POEMS

There are, of course, other forms and other developments in Tennyson. It is a given that he wrote some extraordinarily interesting poems and some quite uninteresting ones, not that many would agree on which are which. It is not important to draw exact lines, though it is important to attempt an explanation of why poems like "The Spinster's Sweet-Arts" or "English Warsong" affect us as they do: with irritation or not at all. Most of these minor poems are striking for their simplicity, their grim single-mindedness and relentless narrowing of emotion and focus. They stand in marked contrast to the complexity, suggestiveness, and expansiveness of the other poems. One way to think of them is as a relaxation from the great tensions of irony and the difficult sort of comedy Tennyson wrote. It may seem odd to speak of "tensions" being produced in this way, but we have seen for some time that Tennyson was caught between the worlds of *Pride and Prejudice* and *Hyperion*,[17] between the practical, novelistic world and the visionary, mythical world. The tension I am discussing, though not coincident with the other, lies over it and surely makes it understandable that simple poetic reductions might occasionally be inevitable. In any event, those poems which seem to me reductive fall into three

16. Quoted in *Memoir*, 1:314.
17. The wonderfully bizarre matching, I must admit, is Frye's, *Anatomy of Criticism*, p. 59.

groups: the political and public poems, the domestic idyls, and the humorous and dialect poems.[18] Some of these poems are excellent in their way, but they do not, I think, constitute the major part of Tennyson's achievement, nor do they contribute a great deal to his present reputation.

When Tennyson's first child died at birth, the poet wrote to John Forster, describing the event with his strange and characteristic mixture of the naïve and the sophisticated, the immediate and the detached:

> The nurse dressed up the little body in pure white. He was a grand massive manchild, noble brow and hands, which he had clenched in his determination to be born. Had he lived, the doctor said he would have been lusty and healthy, but somehow he got strangled. I kissed his poor pale hands and came away and they buried him last night in Twickenham churchyard.[19]

Notice how Tennyson uses the typical locutions associated with nineteenth-century sentimentality—"the little body," "pure white," "poor pale hands"—while suggesting the very opposite of sentimentality. The "core of toughness" [20] always discernible in Tennyson's best poetry here controls and mutes the potential sentimentality by encasing it in accents of reserve and detachment. The bleak and naked quality of "but somehow he got strangled" or "they buried him last night in Twickenham churchyard," the staccato sentences, and the use of coordinations that simply string statements together, give the impression of artlessness, the refusal to rearrange, subordinate, and heighten—in fact, to interpret at all. The major impression is that of inexplicable awfulness temporarily mastered, of unbearable grief not overcome but suspended. The mixture of tones, in other words, provides a subtle and moving irony.

One way to look at the domestic idyls, the humorous poems, and the political poems is in terms of a dislocation of this ironic conjunction. The "core of toughness" is exaggerated into the uncontrolled energy and exhibitionistic release of the political poems; the tenderness and sentimentality become the humorous

18. See the Appendix for a fuller discussion of the minor poems.
19. Quoted in Sir Charles Tennyson, *Alfred Tennyson*, p. 262.
20. G. Robert Stange uses this fine term in relation to "Demeter and Persephone" in "Tennyson's Mythology, *ELH* 21 (1954): 80. It has, I think, general application to his poetry.

poems or the static and hazy idyls of the hearth. All represent a relaxation from the strain and difficulty of the ironic or comic modes one finds in the major poetry. One notices, for instance, that Tennyson seemed to find it necessary to write the domestic idyls *only* during periods when his major poems were ironic in form. The domestic idyls begin to appear in the 1830 volume, there are some dozen of them in the *Poems* of 1842, and he begins writing them again in about 1860, just one year after the publication of the first installment of *Idylls of the King*. During the comic period, between *The Princess* and *Maud*, these poems virtually disappear.[21] There was apparently no need then for this therapeutic exercise, but they increase in direct proportion to the seriousness and dominance of his ironic vision.

Setting aside these minor poems, then, we are left with the poems that constitute Tennyson's claim to our attention, along with some revealing and interesting preliminary work. From *The Devil and the Lady* to *Idylls of the King*, the poet worked with irony and comedy, testing, reordering, and trying new combinations in an attempt to find an adequate form. In one of those irresponsible but penetrating remarks with which W. H. Auden filled the famous introduction to his edition of Tennyson's poems, he calls Tennyson "the great English poet of the Nursery." There is not much truth in this, but there is some. Tennyson's poetry hardly seems to "deal with human emotions in their most primitive states," [22] but it does express our most fundamental plights and hopes with an intensity and honesty that only a half-asleep Auden would ever call "stupid."

21. There is one exception: "The Brook" appeared in the *Maud* volume of 1855. There were one or two added to later editions of the 1842 poems too, but except for "The Brook," none was written in the "comic period," i.e. between *The Princess* and *Maud*.

22. Introduction to *Poems*, p. xvi.

2

The Early Poetry

While Tennyson's earliest poems are not unsophisticated, they are usually very uncomplicated, almost as if the poet had established for himself in each poem a single structural, thematic, or technical problem.[1] It is remarkable how deliberately and continuously these poems use the clichés of irony and, to a lesser extent, comedy. Tennyson here serves his generic apprenticeship in public and presents a programme of his later progress in irony, where he will take the themes and techniques, isolated here, and combine them, reworking the clichés into poems that form the center of the developing conventions of irony.

As for comedy, he appears to have needed no apprenticeship. *The Devil and the Lady*, written when he was fourteen, is so assured in style and so easy in development that it is, as everyone who mentions it says, "astonishing." There are youthful excesses, certainly, but also a surprising maturity,[2] particularly in the poetic vision that could produce such a troubled and potentially dark comedy. This is no piece of high-spirited merriment or confident satire. It begins in the Jonsonian manner, but Tennyson seems quite uninterested in corrective satire, even at this early stage, and the comedy soon moves beyond correction to a more unsettled and complex form.

With *Poems by Two Brothers*, comedy is made clearly subordinate, as the young poet begins to develop the materials of irony. Anyone reading through his contributions to this collection is bound to be struck by the poems' nearly uniform grimness. In only about one-fourth of them is any sort of comic spirit evident, and even

1. W. D. Paden, in his *Tennyson in Egypt*, has demonstrated what highly idiosyncratic patterns may be observed in these conventional poems. Paden's book is also the most extended and interesting study of Tennyson's earliest poems.

2. Sir Charles Tennyson also remarks on the poem's maturity (*Alfred Tennyson*, p. 40), though he regards it as mature only in "skill and ease of versification," not in its outlook.

there it is often rather bizarre. All the others, I think, are deliberate and careful exercises in the ironic mode.

To cite just one example, "The Dell of E——" demonstrates Tennyson's experiments both with structural reversal and with the inversion or burlesque of comic principles. Exactly half of the poem asserts a unification of man and nature which is flatly denied by the other half. The first stanza describes objectively the beauty the dell once possessed; the second moves us closer to its restorative, calming powers. There is then an abrupt switch to an image of desolation. Man, it turns out, has destroyed what he needed most. The final stanza goes on to climax this irony, suggesting that the trees may have been cut to build warships, that what once gave men joy now functions as their killers, bearing "terror round / The trembling earth" (ll. 51–52).

This double climax or "capping" is very common in Tennyson; he often adds a final and unexpected twist that brings the theme into focus abruptly and with a shock. That men set out to ravage their greatest friend is one irony; that they have transformed this friend into an instrument of death complements and intensifies the point. But the poem is quick to block any moralistic renderings of this perception. In fact, the real point of the poem is that there is no point. We are not asked to reflect that we ought not to do such things but to accept how sad and horrible it is that we do. The poem ends not with admonition, nor even with the ironic shock discussed earlier, but with the understated reflection that the trees really served better in their previous state, that, instead of being used to kill, it would have been "lovelier, had they still / Whispered unto the breezes with low sound, / And greenly flourished on their native hill" (ll. 52–54). The delicacy and simplicity of *lovelier* are deliberate, and they contain most of the force of the poem. This is decidedly not corrective irony. It sees simply the loveliness of Paradise and the absurdity of its loss; it never suggests that this loss can be recovered. While such themes are less blatantly announced and such reversals generally less sudden in Tennyson's mature poetry, the basic principles are developed here in *Poems by Two Brothers*.

Poems, Chiefly Lyrical (1830) and *Poems* (1832) are both more sophisticated and much more varied than Tennyson's contributions to *Poems by Two Brothers*, but in the major[3] poems of these two

---

3. I recognize that "major" is a rather too convenient term in this assertion, but the poems

volumes[4] are the same dominance of the ironic mode and curious persistence of the comic that marked the earlier poems. What had been simple, however, now becomes more complex, and the deliberate separation of themes, images, and techniques now yields to combination and compression. Tennyson has mastered the rudiments of irony and begins in these volumes to experiment with the various technical and thematic possibilities it allows him. Though many of these poems are imperfect, a few are as successful as any poetry Tennyson was to write. Already with these early volumes, Tennyson reaches maturity in that form. His later ironic poems tend to become more subtle and even more experimental; they expand the genre itself by challenging its limits. These 1830 and 1832 volumes, however, do more than just prefigure Tennyson's major ironic work; they contain some of it.

But not much. That the apprenticeship stage of *Poems by Two Brothers* has not been left entirely behind is apparent in poems like "A Dirge," which deals starkly with the superiority of death to life, not in religious but in naturalistic terms. According to this view, life is so horrible that the coffin seems like freedom and the gnawings of "the small cold worm" (l. 9) comfortable. Though the poem somewhat confusedly mixes this startling perception with incongruously comic lines that suggest the unification of the body with nature, the urgent rejection of life overrides any assurances. The desire for escape from the tangled ugliness of the world to the peace of death is voiced over and over in Tennyson: those most sensitive to life's promise, he says, are those who are forced to reject what now passes for life. The apparent simplicity of "A Dirge," then, covers a very remarkable and extreme appeal, the same one that we recognize later, in its full development, in such poems as "The Lotos-Eaters."

I include under that heading seem to me to represent conventional choices; they are, in any case, generally the poems that are fixed by the tradition of anthologists as most popular, representative, and interesting.

4. Some of the most important poems originally published in the 1832 volume—"The Lady of Shalott," "Oenone," "The Palace of Art," and "The Lotos-Eaters"—are discussed not here but in the next chapter. Roughly half of the *Poems* of 1842 is made up of poems reprinted from the 1830 and 1832 volumes, sometimes with very extensive and crucial revisions. Where such revisions seem to me to make basic changes in the poem's structure, theme, or especially genre, I have treated it along with the 1842 poems; where the revisions seem less important, I have left the poem in its original position. I acknowledge that such decisions are arbitrary; I hope they are reasonable.

Somewhere between the simplified ironies that carry over from earlier work and the rich unity of the major poems in these volumes are poems like "The Ballad of Oriana," which combines a rather bald ironic narrative with a more sophisticated ironic characterization. Tennyson is clearly less interested in ballad simplicity here than in the vision of entrapment. The story of the man who meant to shoot an enemy but instead sent an arrow through the heart of his fiancée contains the suggestion, proper to irony, that major catastrophes are essentially uncaused. But here the necessary sense of grim absurdity threatens to shade over into the near-humorous sense that all this is a silly accident, due not to a cosmic imbalance but to inaccurate marksmanship.

The poem is rescued from this almost ludicrous melodrama by the fine stroke of changing the lady Oriana from a dear memory to an oppressive fear, a horrifying threat. The repetition of her name in nearly every other line supports this transition from devotion, to hypnotic adherence, to something like terror. Caught in the trap of memory, the narrator soon finds himself in the typical ironic position, with a "breaking heart that will not break" (l. 64). In this anguish, he would seek the release of death, but that "I dare not die and come to thee, / Oriana" (ll. 96–97). The narrator is not worried that his beloved is removed too far from him but that she may not be far enough away. The romantic vision of a union beyond the grave is parodied by asserting its simple undesirability. In a similar reduction of tragic dignity, the narrator's anguish becomes mere fatigue: "A weary, weary way I go, / Oriana" (ll. 89–90). The obvious and melodramatic situation thus begins to move toward more profound irony.

No such qualification is necessary for at least three of these early ironic poems: "Supposed Confessions," "Mariana," and "A Dream of Fair Women." Though not all successful to the same degree, they are the first full expression of Tennyson's mastery of the ironic form.

"Supposed Confessions of a Second-Rate Sensitive Mind Not in Unity With Itself" is, in point of fact, the confession of a first-rate sensitive mind experiencing what is finally a terrible unity. The only real weakness in the poem is in its title, which has at least two obvious and important defects: the first is the hedge implied by "Second-Rate"; if one really attends to this qualification, the irony dissolves under the hint that a mind which was not second-rate could escape the dilemma. The second weakness is contained in the

"Not in Unity" phrase (which, incidentally, was removed from the title when the poem was reprinted in 1884). Though the mind presented is, in a special sense, disunified, the title may suggest to us that we are viewing simply a mind in conflict: one unable to decide, or one which is merely sidetracked from a true course. This would not matter much if the inaccurate suggestions were not picked up and reinforced by the last line of the poem: "O damnèd vacillating state." Vacillation suggests mechanical elasticity; it has no relevance at all to the mind presented here.

The narrator of this poem is incapable of any movement, mechanical or otherwise; for he is caught in a state in which life and death are the same. The intellectual endeavor which he prizes as proof of his humanity—"It is man's privilege to doubt" (l. 142)—is precisely what causes his misery; he is mocked by the joy and simple unity available to the life of a stupid sheep. He is trapped between his inability to find comfort and his knowledge that comfort is available. He believes in and even sees peace quite vividly; if he did not, the tension would disappear. But this peace is inaccessible to him, not so much because he has grown away from religious faith, though that is part of the problem, but because the use of his intellect has made him separate, isolated from his kind. Irony always pictures "growth" as a movement toward disharmony and alienation: the growth of the personality that frees us also imprisons us in our isolated selves.

Thus the poem concerns something more than the loss of religious faith; it deals with the loss of comic vision. The narrator sees that the final victory over death is to be found in the simple, unintellectual harmony of community: "How sweet to have a common faith! / To hold a common scorn of death!" (ll. 33–34). He sees just as clearly that the source of this trust is the wonderful security and unity of mother and child: "Thrice happy state again to be / The trustful infant on the knee! / Who lets his rosy fingers play / About his mother's neck, and knows / Nothing beyond his mother's eyes" (ll. 40–44). These remarkable lines define the Edenic impulse in exact psychological terms; they further suggest that the speaker understands his own development in terms of the growth out of the possibility of comedy—or infancy—into an ironic vision. Tension is guaranteed by his unwillingness to relinquish absolutely the comic view. Unable, then, either to accept or reject, he can only *doubt*. This is certainly the central word in the poem; it is perhaps the central word to describe the most prevalent motive of nine-teenth-century irony. By redefining man as the creature with the power to suspend certainty, irony created the rootless man, not undefined but defined only by the trap he is in, caught between equally unavailable or unattractive alternatives.

It is not, then, a thematic conflict between belief and disbelief that is presented so much as the state of suspension caused by that conflict. Tennyson displays here at its perfection a technique he will often use to demonstrate that suspension between alien worlds. In the climax of the poem the speaker begins a prayer to God for mercy and enlightenment. At its start the prayer is graceful and undisturbed: "Let thy dove / Shadow me over, and my sins / Be unremembered, and Thy love / Enlighten me" (ll. 180–83). As the prayer goes on, however, the comic hope gradually modulates to bitterness, as the imagery becomes harsher and grimmer: "O teach me yet / Somewhat before the heavy clod / Weighs on me, and the busy fret / Of that sharp-headed worm begins / In the gross blackness underneath" (ll. 183–87). The prayer thus contains its own hopeless antithesis and mirrors the stasis of the narrator's mind. Hope and despair are held together in the ironic suspension of doubt.

Adding to this tension, finally, is the rhetorical distance that is maintained.[5] Though the subject matter of the poem and much of the language are highly charged and highly personal, there is an extreme self-consciousness at work that keeps the narrator himself at a curious remove from the personality examined. The narrator's capacity for self-criticism almost certainly separates him from us and establishes a rhetorical tension between the strong quality of emotion and our sense of distance from it. Thus, much like the speaker, we are ourselves poised and unable to find an adequate release for the emotion raised.

"Mariana" likewise portrays and engenders a suspended position. The poem is, in the first place, remarkably adrift from its presumed Shakespearean source. As John Stuart Mill said, "There is no mere amplification; it is all production, and production from that single germ." [6] It is certainly "all production," developing from an intense

5. William Cadbury's "Utility of the Poetic Mask," *MLQ* 24 (1963): 374–85 provides a fine analysis of this point. His contention that the poetic mask draws attention away from the speaker and toward the conflict, however, seems to me only half right.

6. Review of *Poems, Chiefly Lyrical*, in *Westminster Review* 14 (1831): 219.

and single-minded imaginative speculation on the short and evocative phrase, "Mariana in the moated grange." By separating Shakespeare's character so completely from the play, Tennyson achieves the intense focus that also makes the desolation seem uncaused. There is no point in looking to *Measure for Measure* in order to find out *why* "he will not come," much less to determine that he will, as he does in the play, come after all. Here there is no narrative movement at all, the whole point being that Mariana's love is senselessly denied, that her fruition is cut off without reason. At least, by restricting the poem to her baffled ignorance, Tennyson makes it clear that any *reasons* are radically disproportionate to the implications of pointless imprisonment. "He cometh not" is all that matters, and the poem thus develops the purity of a cosmic statement of irony.

For though the poem is often treated as a picture of sheer desolation, a "giving in" to melancholy,[7] our response is surely not so simple and very definitely not so easy and relaxed as the word *melancholy* would suggest. The poem seems to move to a climax, but it actually mocks climactic structures. The picture of a bondage that cannot be broken is created and reinforced by all the details of the poem: the thick, clogged opening lines, for instance, or the metrics of the refrain, where the quick, regular movement of "She only said, 'My life is dreary, / He cometh not,' she said" is interrupted by the unexpected sluggishness of the next line—"She said, 'I am aweary, aweary' "—a line which not only suggests the very hopelessness and weariness it is talking about but also retards and thus emphasizes the decisive last line of the refrain—"I would that I were dead!"

One should also note the brilliant way in which Mariana's heightened sensitivity is suggested: she both sharpens small details and obliterates the distinction between large ones. She knows all about the patterns on the bark of the single poplar tree but confuses waking and sleeping states (ll. 30, 61). The distortion here

---

7. There is something closer to mere melancholy in "Mariana in the South," which is certainly not just "Mariana" transplanted to southern France. The religious emphasis, particularly at the end, gives the poem a kind of grim upbeat, which changes the refrain and dissolves the ironic tension: "The night comes on that knows not morn, / When I shall cease to be all alone, / To live forgotten, and love forlorn" (ll. 94–96). I am not suggesting that this pathetic longing for death leads to comedy, but it does allow us to relax from irony into the easy, masked self-pity of melancholy.

resembles that of nightmare, with its horrifying clarity of detail and its absolute lack of boundaries, its absence of familiar context. Similarly, her stasis is supported even by the slight ambiguity of "she only said," repeated in every refrain and suggesting either that this was all she *said*, or that all she *did* was to say this. It is an arresting ambiguity that goes nowhere. There are no choices to be made; either meaning is equally appropriate, or equally inappropriate. The notion of her doing nothing all day except saying this, *or* the notion that the terror of her situation evoked only this minimal response, strike us as uncoordinated but equally applicable meanings.

But the image of desolation and weariness finally is balanced by the poem's remarkably strong support of Mariana's associations with youth, growth, and hope. The poem's irony is defined by the pressure of the undeniably just claims of love and comic promise against the equally undeniable fact of denial. The positive side is, of course, implied very strongly by the enveloping situation: Mariana's youth and hope are supported by the fact that she is waiting for a lover, as they are also by her connection with a pastoral landscape (somewhat distorted, of course) and with romantic terms like "casement."

Primarily, though, the positive level is presented by inverting the usual images of comedy and the pastoral. The poem is filled with references to beauty, order, and hope—all, of course, bitterly distorted but nonetheless there. The opening lines give a parody of a beauty that is ordered and controlled. Man's capacity for both enjoying and arranging nature is mocked in the image of sluggish decay overcoming the flower-plots, rust and disorder invading the carefully controlled growth of the ornamental pear tree. The image of man as master of nature's beauty is thrown against that of man as victim of nature's anarchy.

Mariana, it must again be insisted, is not caught by this last image only; she is caught between the two. On one hand there is the "blackest moss" but on the other is the poplar tree, one of the poem's most important symbols. In the midst of the dark and stagnant waters of the marsh grows a single poplar tree, "all silver-green" (l. 42), the only relief in "the level waste, the rounding gray" (l. 44). One entire stanza (ll. 49–60) is devoted to the shadow of this tree and the implications of this teasing symbol of the growth

and promise[8] that are denied her but are *ever* present to her, falling
"Upon her bed, across her brow" (l. 56), and making itself a part of
her mind. It is a symbol of genuine hope that can be neither
claimed nor forgotten; it stands for all that makes release impossible
for Mariana. Also supporting this mocking, positive side of the
poem is the recurrence of the day's cycle, with each morning
bringing a renewal of the bitter knowledge of what is not there and,
more important, the taunting reference to "the sweet heaven" (l.
15), a heaven of which she is constantly aware, even though it is
closed to her.

This same conjunction of illusory hope and a knowledge of
hopelessness is mirrored in the intricate structure of the poem. The
only motion is the merely apparent one within actual stasis.
Though the refrain does suggest a genuine development in its
change from "He cometh not" to "He will not come," we recognize
that these are not really separate perceptions, that they simply state
the tension that defines her entire existence, the waiting with the
certain knowledge that there is no point in waiting. And we see, too,
that this poem is narrated from such a distant perspective as to
describe not a climactic movement but a slice of life, a typical day
with its recurrent hopelessness, rising to a finality that will be
dissolved by the renewed hopeless hope of a new day. The action,
then, is ironically recurrent, not tragically complete. The tragic
simplicity of a climax is distorted to a conclusion that consists only
of a mouse squeaking and a fly buzzing. The tragic sensibility has
now only these materials; only trivia surround her.

This poem is a prototype of Tennysonian irony, formulating

8. Ward Hellstrom, *On the Poems of Tennyson*, argues that the tree is a symbol of death, and
he alludes to a broad range of "classical and folk traditions" which make that association (p.
156). Aside from Euripides's story of the sisters of Thathaon and the reference in *The Odyssey*
to the poplar at the mouth of Calypso's cave, I can locate only various mythological
dictionary references to the black poplar as a funeral tree in ancient Greece; it stands more
generally for a loss of hope. Frankly, I do not know what this adds up to. On the other side
are the more "natural" associations connected with the tree, its contrasts with the rot and
decay surrounding it in this poem, and its suggestions of assertive masculinity. This last point
is developed by G. O. Gunter in "Life and Death Symbols in Tennyson's 'Mariana,'" *SAB*
36 (1971): 64–67. He argues that the tree here "denotes a cosmic life force," more
particularly "a phallic symbol" (p. 65). However that may be, I suppose the most sensible
solution is an appeal to the context, where the mocking, tantalizing image is most readily
associated with a life that is absent. Some confusion or ambiguity in the image, however,
would clearly not be inappropriate and might be seen as reinforcing the general instability of
Mariana's situation and perception.

many of the techniques and attitudes that appear later, but it is also a highly instinctive form of a vision which, even in later poems, is often put more obtrusively. When the ironic dilemma is stated more overtly, the poetry appears more obviously thematic, sometimes even thematically "divided." Because of this, it is easy, but I think wrong, to approach it as merely dualistic. Such an approach ignores the potential unity provided by ironic tension. Tennyson is not on one side of the argument or the other; like all ironists, he is on neither side—and both.

A good example of a poem that appears to be but is not a "thesis poem" is "A Dream of Fair Women," which establishes its irony partly in reference to its apparent source, Chaucer's *The Legend of Good Women*. Tennyson's poem resembles Chaucer's only superficially; the earlier poet's comforting, stable framework is removed,[9] and the cosmic resonance of the tales, comforting or not, is implicitly denied. Taking the place of Chaucer's coherent series of portraits of faithfulness, love, and tragedy, Tennyson's group emphasizes the discontinuity of history and the pointlessness of presumed grandeur. The catastrophes here are either paltry or uncaused. The ironic conjunction is put immediately in the deceptively limpid introductory lines: "In every land / I saw, wherever light illumineth, / Beauty and anguish walking hand in hand / The downward slope to death" (ll. 13–16). What ties the portraits together is the "hand in hand" union of beauty and anguish. There is no further thematic point.

The dream itself takes place in the mocking familiarity of the narrator's memory, a continual symbol in Tennyson for comedy, here used to create a distorting framework: "The smell of violets, hidden in the green, / Poured back into my empty soul and

---

9. It is interesting to note that there *was* in the first version (1832) of Tennyson's poem a sort of undeveloped moral point that could have given some stability:

> In every land I thought that, more or less,
>   The stronger sterner nature overbore
> The softer, uncontrolled by gentleness
>   And selfish evermore:
>
> And whether there were any means whereby,
>   In some far aftertime, the gentler mind
> Might reassume its just and full degree
>   Of rule among mankind.

Tennyson dropped these lines in later editions.

frame / The times when I remember to have been / Joyful and free from blame" (ll. 77–80). And all this happy nostalgia prefaces a nightmare. The first figure, Helen, begins by putting in clipped, disconnected, and very dramatic phrases the essence of her ironic function. Because she was beautiful, carnage resulted: "Where'er I came / I brought calamity" (ll. 95–96). Though the narrator naïvely tries to twist this into a romantic framework, claiming that he too would have died for such a face, such escapes are disallowed. He is soon overwhelmed by the march of hideous and meaningless deaths: Iphigenia relates the grim, realistic details of the knife moving "through my tender throat" (l. 115)[10] in a sacrifice which led only to further desolation; Cleopatra reduces her potentially tragic position to ludicrous capriciousness, saying that death really is not so bad except that "I have no men to govern in this wood: / That makes my only woe" (ll. 135–36). She turns her grand suicide into an act of petty revenge: "Of the other [Caesar]: with a worm I balked his fame. / What else was left?" (ll. 155–56).

Jephtha's daughter, who follows, is the most complex case of all. Her sacrifice had depended on a grisly kind of gambling, her father having promised God that for victory over the children of Ammon he would kill the first person he saw leaving his house to meet him. Though she continues after death to defend her father and to proclaim the rightness of God's law, the narrator ignores all this and responds only to the monstrousness of the situation: "My words leapt forth: 'Heaven heads the count of crimes / With that wild oath'" (ll. 201–02). The absurdity of Jephtha's sacrifice is that perceived by Browning's Caliban, for whom divine justice is represented by the decision to murder every twenty-first crab: "Let twenty pass, and stone the twenty-first, / Loving not, hating not, just choosing so." The girl's pathetic defense of her murderer is further undercut by a long simile comparing her voice to the sound of a "holy organ" in a cathedral. The Christian context mocks the Old Testament ruthlessness without offering any further hope, for the last sad portrait is of the Christian Rosamond, "whom men call fair" (l. 251).

The poem ends with a typical ironic capping: the naïve narrator adds that he unfortunately woke before the good part of the dream,

---

10. Tennyson later came to believe that this description was "too ghastly realistic" and softened it to "The bright death quivered at the victim's throat." See Ricks's note, p. 446.

before he was able to see Margaret Roper, Joan of Arc, or Edward
I's wife, Eleanor, "who knew that Love can vanquish Death" (l.
269). The ingenuous persona blandly makes the point that all
heroic and comic aspects of death are denied. The last gruesome
twist is his complaint that poetic language is insufficient to describe
his dream. Such language is too pure; it fails to provide adequate
tension, particularly "to give the bitter of the sweet" (l. 286)—as if
the terrible vision we have just seen has been "sweet."

Accompanying this irony is a persistent strain of comedy, which
is found here in many poems, most of which are deliberately
understated, self-conscious, and very light in touch. The self-paro-
dying "O Darling Room" seems simply an extreme of this, not, as
Croker assumed, too ridiculously self-indulgent and self-centered,
but rather too detached, self-aware, and apologetically trivial. Just
as specialized and partial is the comic impulse behind a poem like
"Lilian," which plays off against the slavish adoration implied in
most of the poems in this extended female gallery—"Isabel,"
"Adeline," "Madeline," and so forth—by treating the tinkling
laughter of the cruel "Airy, fairy Lilian" (l. 1) as a cause for
irritation rather than romantic languor. Instead of being mastered
by her gay coquetry, the lover adopts a masterful tone himself,
warning her that he is becoming so bored with her laughing that if
praying won't stop her he will stomp on her, "crush" her. There is a
limited but genuine comic satisfaction provided here, not only in
the burlesque of the essentially ironic lover-slave tradition, but in
the bolstering of the human (especially the male) ego by suggesting
that the will can control any emotion.

There are instances of much fuller and genuinely liberating
comedy in these volumes, most notably in the lovely paired poems,
"The Mermaid" and "The Merman." These poems confront
explicitly the image of the isolated self and move to the celebration
of joy and union. Both poems open with a brief stanza that is part
invitation, part pure song, emphasizing both the beauty (thrones,
golden crowns or curls) and the loneliness ("Sitting alone, / Singing
alone") of the magical state enjoyed by the mer-creatures. The
second stanza not only admits the isolation but emphasizes it,
carefully restricting it, however, to the daytime, to the rational,
dutiful part of the merman's life, and the self-absorbed alienation of
the mermaid. This admission out of the way, the full force of the

poem can fall on the nighttime life, the life of the complete imaginative self, of irrational fulfillment: "Oh! what a happy life were mine / Under the hollow-hung ocean green! / Soft are the moss-beds under the sea; / We would live merrily, merrily" ("The Merman," ll. 37–40).

It is true that the merman and mermaid envision somewhat different nighttime paradises: his is free, open, promiscuous—"I would kiss them often under the sea, / And kiss them again till they kissed me" (ll. 34–35)—while hers is quieter and more controlled— "But the king of them all would carry me, / Woo me, and win me, and marry me" (ll. 45–46). But there is no real conflict here; the discrepancy is part of the gentle joke, bringing up the extra force of the comedy-of-manners sexual battle to support the principal Edenic comedy. More important, this compartmentalization of the solitary from the communal self is an important strategy and an important part of comedy's answer to irony. The poems here admit the argument that all men are isolated, but they see that isolation simply as a part of a multiplicity of conditions, a multiplicity, furthermore, which contains not only isolation but happiness and freedom. The ironic strategy is to focus and solidify; comedy's is to expand and free, to reject entirely the absolutism of irony.

But comedy is just as susceptible to attack from irony, and it is certainly more usual in Tennyson to find the comic solution subverted. The ironic poems are often generically pure; the comic poems very seldom are. One may offer plausible biographical or sociological reasons for this fact, but simpler reasons are implicit within the forms. Irony is based on parody and thus is, in a way, parasitic. It is, further, defensive and hides its premises; comedy, at its best, is expansive and exposes all its secrets. When the two modes are competing, as in Tennyson, it is difficult for comedy to survive. Irony with a comic twist results in the sheer peculiarity of "Mariana in the South"; comedy transformed to irony results in the uniform power of "Mariana."

This ability of irony to attack comedy is more clearly illustrated in the contrasting poems, "The Poet" and "The Poet's Mind." "The Poet" is certainly a comic poem, though exclusively public and social in its emphasis. Still, it provides a strong and effective image of the force of poetry, expressed in the specifically comic terms, "hope," "youth," "spring." The grand object is to recapture Eden, not just for the poet but for the entire world: "Thus truth was multiplied on truth, the world / Like one great garden showed" (ll. 33–34). It would be an Eden ruled by the expansive goddess of comedy, "Freedom" (l. 37).

But "The Poet's Mind" shows a garden that is shrunken and delicate, threatened by a very dangerous enemy: the rational mind, the dry and shallow wit of the "dark-browed sophist" (l. 8). The flowers "would faint" (l. 15), the plants would be blighted, the "merry bird" would be killed (ll. 22–23) if the sophist were to enter. Most important, the source of all this life and joy, the large fountain in the center, fed "from the brain of the purple mountain" (l. 29) and recalling the great symbol for poetic energy in "Kubla Khan," would itself "shrink to the earth if you came in" (l. 37). Great images of power, lightning and thunder, are associated with this fragile and threatened fountain—"In the middle leaps a fountain / Like sheet lightning, / Ever brightening / With a low melodious thunder" (ll. 24–27). But there seems to be only an illusory union of power and beauty, only a faint echo of the confident and unendangered voice of Wisdom set loose by the garden in "The Poet": "Her [Wisdom's] words did gather thunder as they ran, / And as the lightning to the thunder . . . / So was their meaning to her words" (ll. 49–50, 53). "The Poet's Mind" is thus an inversion of "The Poet"; it suggests the ironic trap that may await the too-certain vision of comedy.

Though comedy never entirely disappears and though it later reaches full expression in Tennyson's poetry, it is irony which came to dominate his writing of this period. It controls *Poems by Two Brothers*, the volumes of 1830 and 1832, and, to an even greater extent, *Poems* of 1842.

3

Poems (1842)

Whatever else may have been happening during the famous "ten years' silence" from 1832 to 1842, it is clear that Tennyson was refining his ironic techniques. There is, in his work, a strong movement away from elaboration toward compression and understatement, from amplification of a clear situation toward obliquity and spare indirection. Further, having mastered the presentation of ironic theme, Tennyson now turned to experiments with ironic rhetoric. The 1842 volume is filled with poems that create a subtle bondage within for their characters and an equally subtle bondage without for their readers. The general agency of this imprisoning rhetoric seems to be what can crudely be termed "ambiguity," and the means of achieving it are various: often the ironic formula of saying as little and meaning as much as possible is applied; often structural parallels are allowed to develop and reinforce meanings that are not explicitly stated.

But the most important technique is the removal of moral or ethical context. Poem after poem presents a situation which seems to demand a judgment or a series of judgments and which, at the same time, either makes secure judgment impossible or makes contradictory judgments necessary. The greatest poems of this volume are those which inevitably project a moral or social dilemma without suggesting the means for solving that dilemma; they work equally hard to bring forth and to render doubtful our judgments and our decisive responses. They not only present but engender an ironic position. There are further treatments, in this volume, of ambiguities in theme and situation, as in poems like "Break, break, break" and "The Lady of Shalott," but Tennyson does seem to have become increasingly interested in making his traps work outside rather than inside the poem. He is even willing to allow his characters to escape in order to build walls around the reader.

But this rhetorical irony depends upon the compression he developed in presenting the usual "impossible case" of irony, the ironic theme. "Break, break, break," for instance, is a bitter poem on unrecompensed, pointless loss, but it achieves its power and makes its point very indirectly, largely through structural implications. The direct statements are deliberately localized and simple, making concrete the emotion of the poem without stating its implications. Because the poem is so indirect, a good many competing interpretations have been advanced, but all are based on perceptions of the poem's structure. The middle part of the poem—the image of the children's happiness and of the stately ships—is framed by an address to the sea. The explicit terms of the address change a great deal, of course, between the first and the last stanza:

> Break, break, break,
>   On thy cold gray stones, O Sea!
> And I would that my tongue could utter
>   The thoughts that arise in me.
> . . . .
> Break, break, break,
>   At the foot of thy crags, O Sea!
> But the tender grace of a day that is dead
>   Will never come back to me.
>
> [ll. 1–4, 13–16]

The original desire for poetic utterance ("I would that my tongue could utter") is fulfilled, it seems, and the unnamed, unformulated "thoughts" crystallize into one final summarizing thought. Though it has been argued that the last lines represent for the speaker a kind of acceptance, even a positive resolution,[1] they seem to me not to release tension or to solve a real dilemma but to state an agonized perception. That is, the original problem of achieving speech yields to a greater, genuinely impossible problem. The *and* which begins the third line of the first stanza implies an imagined bond with the sea; the speaker searches for union with the blank, monotonous continuity of the indifferent, smashing waves.

1. This point is made most directly by Bert G. Hornback, "Tennyson's 'Break, Break, Break' Again," *VN*, no. 33 (1968), pp. 47–48. It is also implied by T. J. Assad ("an impression of man's resiliency which enables him to absorb the shocks of life"), "Tennyson's 'Break, Break, Break,'" *TSE* 12 (1962): 80; and by Clyde deL. Ryals (the tone of the ending, he says, is almost matter-of-fact), *Theme and Symbol in Tennyson's Poems to 1850*, p. 107.

The middle two stanzas of the poem, however, present a vision of joy and assured life so alien to and distant from the speaker that, by the time he returns to the immediate focus of the rocks and the breaking sea in the last stanza, he senses, not fundamental unity—not even a unity with the sea's unconcern—but fundamental disjunction. The *and* is replaced by *but:* instead of nature's participation in his grief, he sees nature's absolute impersonality. He is mocked not only by the joy of the laughing children at play but by the bleak harshness of the sea as well; for he is denied even the continuity of memory. "The tender grace of a day that is dead" is as finally absent as the "vanished hand" (l. 11).[2] The speaker's self-indulgent, romantic communion with the rocks and the indifferent sea whips back on him, and he is left only with the certainty that there is no continuity and no meaning in time, memory, or death. He is left in pointless, unheroic isolation.

The development of the ironic situation is even more elaborately indirect in "The Lady of Shalott." It is possible to discuss the poem in terms of rhetorical irony, emphasizing the problem of whether or not we are made to approve of the Lady's isolation or of her leaving. But this is a problem externally imposed by critics, probably by analogy with most of the other poems in this volume, where the means and terms of judgment are indeed key issues. Here, however, the ironic situation is balanced in such a way as to suspend judgment absolutely. Unlike, say, the Soul in "The Palace of Art" or the mariners in "The Lotos-Eaters," the Lady presents no arguments and has no real choices. She is in isolation; she is lured away; she invokes the curse. Artistic withdrawal is neither condemned nor approved. The necessity for judgment is just what marks the difference between rhetorical irony and the complex but basically contained thematic irony in this poem.

One might, interestingly enough, have made a good case for rhetorical irony in the 1832 version of the poem. At least it would have been a better case, since the revisions for the 1842 volume almost all act to broaden the focus of the poem by removing our attention from the Lady herself and directing it to her environment.

2. This argument was advanced as early as 1872 by R. H. Hutton, "Tennyson," *Macmillan's* 27 (December 1872): 147–48. It is developed further by Phyllis Rackin, "Recent Misreadings of 'Break, Break, Break,'" *JEGP* 65 (1966): 225–26, and by James Kissane, "Tennyson," *ELH* 32 (1965): 93. These fine analyses are echoed in several places in my own reading.

The changes emphasize the sense of a determined situation and deemphasize the image of a personality making a decision. To take one of many instances, lines 24–26 are changed from "A pearlgarland winds her head: / She leaneth on a velvet bed, / Full royally apparellèd" to 1842's "But who hath seen her wave her hand? / Or at the casement seen her stand? / Or is she known in all the land?" It is this "land," the external world of Camelot, that emerges in the 1842 version as a major force and symbol in the poem, suggesting the principal lure and promise that draw the Lady out of her isolation. But active terms like "draw" are misleading; for the movement is only apparent, not real. The broadest, most general irony of the poem is that the Lady simply exchanges one kind of imprisonment for another; her presumed freedom is her death.

The Lady is most commonly seen as a form of the artist, and doubtless her absorption in weaving the beautiful web suggests that. But her story also, as in "The Book of Thel," symbolizes the birth of the soul, the movement out of childhood protection into adulthood, the development from innocence to experience, the promise of social and unified being to the isolated ego.[3] All these possibilities coalesce around the central ironic pattern: the carefree but incomplete self, imprisoned in that self and cut off entirely from any direct experience, is drawn by the lure of sexuality, beauty, growth, and change—life itself—not into freedom and expression but into obliteration. The real dilemma is one that can be neither judged nor solved. The Lady must obey and must defy the curse.

The opening of the poem quickly establishes the ironic contrast, setting up a picture of the world that is both true and false, true in objective fact but with terribly misleading implications:

> On either side the river lie
> Long fields of barley and of rye,
> That clothe the wold and meet the sky;
> And through the field the road runs by
>   To many-towered Camelot;
> And up and down the people go

"On either side" of the Lady is the promise of fruitfulness and warmth, gentleness and motion. The abundance of nature is

---

3. Hellstrom, *On the Poems of Tennyson*, pp. 11–12, sees the Lady as choosing mortality, but he does argue that the poem is quite un-ironic.

connected to heaven and to man, the grain *clothes* the field, joining
the earth both to man and to heaven, and the field contains the
road on which all human activity takes place. The center of this
microcosm is Camelot, many-towered as a temple, the source of the
apparently benign and unified activity. In contrast, the Lady lives
on a "silent isle" (l. 17), imprisoned within "four gray walls, and
four gray towers" (l. 15). It is true that within this tomblike home
there is a "space of flowers" (l. 16) and that her song "echoes
cheerly" (l. 30) from it, but the force of this contrast between her
island and the outside world is so strong that such contradictory
details are nearly swept aside. Even the suggestive revelation that
the curse is connected not to isolation but to life, that she is not
cursed now but will be if she chooses to live, is submerged in the
continuous development of the basic ironic contrast.

Part 2 (ll. 37–72) creates an image of life at Camelot, the
irresistible world of "realities," as Tennyson so enigmatically puts it,
that "takes her out of the region of shadows." [4] The main reality
presented here is motion itself. In contrast to her stasis, the pictures
of the world she sees are "moving," "winding," "whirl[ing]",
"ambling," "riding." This static-dynamic dualism is crucial: she
believes the lying promise of the mirror, progressing from her
death-*like* isolation into the whirl of movement that is literal death.
The most important of these perceived images of dynamic eternal
life makes her "half sick of shadows" (l. 71) and prepares her for the
final destructive lure:

> For often through the silent nights
> A funeral, with plumes and lights
> And music, went to Camelot:
> Or when the moon was overhead,
> Came two young lovers lately wed;
> "I am half sick of shadows," said
> The Lady of Shalott.
>
> [ll. 66–72]

Notice the indiscriminate *or* that connects the funeral and the
lovers. Life offers funerals or marriages; both are equal: love is
equivalent to death.

The next section (ll. 73–117) is dominated by the image of

4. *Memoir,* 1:117.

Lancelot. For the Lady, he is the symbol of personality and
fulfillment in the vast scene of the world's growth and beauty. He
seems to her to provide an even more specific promise: the
achievement of individual identity. He is the first person to be
named in the poem, and he seems to guarantee the validity of
names and their ability to give permanence and meaning to the self.
He comes, riding "between the barley-sheaves" (l. 74), with all the
abundance of nature. Lancelot carries with him a shield, in which
"A red-cross knight for ever kneeled / To a lady" (ll. 78–79), an
image of perpetual promise, invoked in terms of courtly love. The
emphasis in Tennyson's lines on "for ever kneeled," however, also
implies that it is only the promise, not the fulfillment, that is
perpetual. The "blue unclouded weather" (l. 91) in which Lancelot
appears conspires to make this image as beautiful and blinding as
possible: like a "meteor, trailing light" (l. 98) he "flashed into the
crystal mirror" (l. 106).

The first "reality" the Lady actually meets after invoking the
curse is the truth of this mocking nature, which is no longer blue
and unclouded but dark, with a "stormy east-wind" and a heavy
low sky over the "pale yellow woods" (ll. 118–21). Images of
oppression and waste surround her. Pathetically, she still tries, by
writing her name on the prow of a boat, to claim the promise of
personality Lancelot had held out to her. But her personality is not
confirmed, even by her death, and the tragic assertion of being is
burlesqued. As she floats by Camelot, the knights "read her name"
(l. 161) but respond only with misunderstanding: "Who is this? and
what is here? / And in the lighted palace near / Died the sound of
royal cheer; / And they crossed themselves for fear, / All the
knights at Camelot" (ll. 163–67). She manages to create only a
flurry of superstition.

Lancelot, however, is presumably differentiated from this confu-
sion and muses quietly a moment—only to exhibit how undifferen-
tiated he actually is: "He said, 'She has a lovely face; / God in his
mercy lend her grace, / The Lady of Shalott' " (ll. 169–71). "She
has a lovely face" is absurdly inadequate to the mystery and
potential tragedy of the Lady's story. We move only from one level
of incomprehension to another. Lancelot is a structurally height-
ened parody of those figures at the end of a tragedy—Horatio is an
example—whose duty it is to interpret, clarify, and keep alive the
story of the tragic action, thus ensuring the institution of a new

order. Here the death is uninterpreted because there is no context to give it meaning and no interpreter. Lancelot turns from the Lady after a perfunctory benediction, dismissing her and thus permanently fixing the absurdity of her death.[5] This, then, is what the parable of growth and development amounts to: not criticism of the Lady, or Lancelot, or "isolation," or the world; only an ironic equation of development with decay. The Lady is born into death.

Perhaps "The Lady of Shalott" marks the limit of this form of Tennyson's indirect, thematic irony; not that he was to abandon it, but it was to be subsumed in the search for more inclusive ironies, ones that would contain even the reader. Surprisingly, he found the means for this subtle rhetorical irony not in the further dissolution of his readers' judgment but in an insistence on judgments. The secret of this extension was not in the abolition of old certainties but in the reinforcement of them. Still, and it is a large qualification, these certainties are never unopposed, they are never adequately supported, and they never provide solutions. They are certainly present and we are asked to make judgments based on them, but these judgments are either contradictory or, more commonly, trivial. They go nowhere. They never answer the questions that are raised in the poem, though they do create others. Most of all, these judgments do not provide comfort or release; they construct the ironic prison.

This rhetoric clearly involves a refinement of irony's traditional control of perspective and distance. It is nothing new for irony to vary our perspective abruptly, asking us to see as immediate and painful what we had supposed was comfortably distant and secure. Still, though the reader is often moved against his will, he always knows where he is. In the 1842 volume, however, Tennyson is striving to project the state which irony embodies, to create the suspension and discomfort the poems discuss. Previous poems had been made ambiguous by structural or thematic means; here the ambiguity is achieved rhetorically, by making our perspective on the poem uncertain. He removes the solid position from which we

5. This new ending is one of the major revisions in the 1842 version. The original had presented the same irony, but rather crudely, referring to "the wellfed wits at Camelot." It had also redundantly drawn attention to the Lady's futile attempts to establish her personality: "this is I, / The Lady of Shalott" had concluded the first version (see Ricks, p. 361). John Stuart Mill called the first ending "a lame and impotent conclusion" (*London Review* 1 [1835]: 413), which indeed it was.

can make judgments and then urges on us both the necessity for judgments and their futility.

The most radical form of this uncertain perspective is found in the dramatic monologue, where the removal of context makes it extremely difficult not only to know how to judge but to be sure if one should judge at all. Certainly, the creation of a solid position from which one can observe how the speaker "contradicts himself" or is subject to the poet's satire is a critical fiction, a convenience that distorts the effects of the poem.

Robert Langbaum's *The Poetry of Experience*, a brilliant discussion of the problem of perspective in the dramatic monologue, uses a very open appeal to our *experience* in the poem to demonstrate that an overtly satiric reading of a dramatic monologue is a possible, but rather crude and uninteresting response. To see that Ulysses's comments on Telemachus are contemptuous is one thing; to argue that this contempt acts to condemn Ulysses is something else. There is no way we can find within the poem a morality that allows for such certain judgments. By removing rhetorical securities, the dramatic monologue does, as Langbaum insists, force us to experience the speaker himself, not a meaning which is external to him.

Still, the tendency of this form to find the extreme case, in fact to be generally effective in direct proportion to the outrageousness of its argument and the distance of the speaker and action from conventional moral and social norms, means that our instinct to make judgments is very strongly activated. Langbaum argues that the tendency to the extreme case and the bizarre subject reduces judgment to absurdity and further indicates the widely accepted need of the poet to resuscitate, to drive through customary associations and revivify life.

One can grant these arguments but see them as subservient to another principle he mentions but then seems, in particular analyses, to ignore: the tension between sympathy and judgment. It seems to me that, contrary to what I take to be the implications of Langbaum's argument, judgment is not an attendant or superficial response but an immediate and powerful one. But it is also given no place to rest, no terms with which to deal, and this very fact accounts for the ironic rhetoric. We are asked to respond simultaneously on two contradictory levels: that of distant critical judgment and that of absorbed, direct experience. We must and we cannot do both; and we realize, therefore, the tension between the now disjoined meaning and experience.

The dramatic monologue manifests a special form of the ironic rhetoric, which works to suspend the ease of judgment by making perspective unstable. Though many of the poems that follow in my discussion here are not pure dramatic monologues but uncertain mixtures of monologue and soliloquy, they contain the essential features of the rhetoric of the dramatic monologue: the uncertainty of context, the demand for judgments, and the absence of support which makes judgments significant.

To begin with the least complex of these poems, "Oenone," is to be presented at once with a picture of an ironic dilemma that seems very much like earlier ones: Oenone is trapped by her own fruitless passion, left in desolation, and forced to regard death as a victory. The constant reiteration of "Dear mother Ida, harken ere I die" comes to indicate to us how bound she is by circumstance and her own emotions.[6] But there is something new here, a further irony connected with point of view. Though the dominant current of the poem is Oenone's lament, a passionate song that involves us strongly, there is, at the same time, an inner contradiction that is crucial but that can be perceived only by suspending our involvement. Put briefly, the contradiction is this: Oenone's surrender to her emotions begins to look like that of her ostensible betrayer. Thus we see her as something other than a simple victim of Paris or the arbitrary power of the goddesses. She is also victimized by her own passions, perhaps finally by the absurdity and irrationality that rule in human affairs.

Despite our participation in her cry of pain and injustice, then, we see that she too has been denied the gift of "self-reverence, self-knowledge, self-control" (l. 142). Pallas's offer, we are led to believe, is clearly the proper one for Paris or any other human being to accept: her appeals are the broadest and most conventionally moral; she appears to disdain using any deceptive rhetoric to persuade Paris; her offer of law and freedom combines all basic human aspirations; and, most crucially, she has Oenone's direct support: "and I cried, 'O Paris, / Give it to Pallas!' " (ll. 165–66).[7]

6. I am indebted for this point to Martin Dodsworth's "Patterns of Morbidity," *The Major Victorian Poets*, ed. Isobel Armstrong, pp. 30–33. See also James Walton, "Tennyson's Patrimony," *TSLL* 11 (1969): 746–48.

7. For an interesting contrary view on Pallas Athene in this poem and others, see Gerhard

But the acceptance of Pallas's offer seems, in the end, both necessary and impossible, as Oenone herself goes on to demonstrate. Oenone reacts to Paris's decision by echoing exactly the unreasoning feelings that had controlled her false lover. She does not rise to Pallas's counseled self-control but competes on the same grounds as the love goddess Aphrodite: "Fairest—why fairest wife? am I not fair? / My love hath told me so a thousand times . . . . Ah me, my mountain shepherd, that my arms / Were wound about thee, and my hot lips prest / Close, close to thine" (ll. 192–93, 198–200). Instead of adopting Pallas's "wisdom in the scorn of consequence" (l. 148), she submits to and is ruled by consequence. Instead of self-reverence, she feeds on thoughts of self-destruction; instead of law, she thinks of revenge. The ironic climax comes when she stirs herself to live, not to change and repent but to experience the grim consolation of seeing others go with her: "I will not die alone" (l. 253).

This is clearly a reading to which only a part of us attends; it ignores much of the poem and distorts our full response, but it is, I think, an approximation of our critical, judgmental reaction. That judgment is in constant tension with the vision of Oenone as a completely innocent victim. There is no way we can blame her for her passion; passion is all that works, and she has, in any case, no choice in the matter. The poem acts to deny us the comfort of a solution by making us live with the desolate and bewildered Oenone, who, like us, senses the rightness of Pallas's answer but who proves by her pathetic life the irrelevance of "self-reverence, self-knowledge, self-control." We can be neither completely absorbed by the pathos of her life nor comfortably detached from it.

The tension is even more marked in "The Lotos-Eaters," another poem in which the removal of adequate or certain context makes judgment very difficult. The extreme argument presented, however, the attempt to persuade us that death is the ecstatic completion to any sane and sensitive life, seems to demand some kind of judgment. The result is a poem about release, the effect of which is to increase tension. We are unable to resist the appeal of the mariners and equally unable to yield to it. They "argue us out of any speck of reserve that may linger," says Langbaum,[8] but one is

---

Joseph, "Tennyson's Concept of Knowledge, Wisdom, and Pallas Athene," *MP* 69 (1972): 314–22.

8. *The Poetry of Experience*, p. 90.

bound to wonder if this is not overstated, if we really give up our inclination to judge so completely. Admitting the hypnotic power of the mariners' escape plan and the fact that we are likely these days to find an argument from ironic premises very apt, one can still acknowledge the barriers the poem erects against the complete surrender of the critical faculty.

There is, in the first place, at least the conscious repugnance one feels to having the attractive argument for lassitude pushed so hard and so far; there is also our awareness of the overall context of the mythic source in *The Odyssey* and that poem's celebration of impulses exactly the opposite to those encouraged here; there are possible moral contradictions or at least signals that alert moral judgment in the mariners' argument, particularly in their confession that it is *unpleasant* "To war with evil" (l. 94); there is a pervasive allusion to the argument of Despair in book 1 of *The Faerie Queene*,[9] which also creates a context for judging the mariners' actions as specifically blasphemous or un-Christian; there is the revised ending, whose bitterness is so strong that some feel it condemns the mariners;[10] there is, finally, the first word of the poem, "Courage," which rings through the subsequent lines and perhaps modulates their arguments. The final irony is that both the courageous Ulysses and the mariners who eat the lotos have an easier time of it than the reader; they, at least, can make choices and dissolve the tension.

The balance of sympathy and judgment is carefully controlled throughout the poem. Despite all the negative indications, it is, at the same time, difficult to resist an appeal which is so shrewdly grounded in a comic impulse: the desire for peace and order. That the mariners are so fully aware of what they are doing and of the implications of their argument—"Give us long rest or death, dark death, or dreamful ease" (l. 98)—makes their quest seem only an extension, not a perversion, of comedy. They very deliberately reject a world of absurd and impersonal change for one of sameness, even if that sameness means death.

But it is not only quiet that they seek. The landscape is one "in which it seemed always afternoon" (l. 4), "a land where all things

---

9. The parallels between the argument of Despair and that of the mariners, and some of their implications, are discussed in an article of mine, "Tennyson's Mariners and Spenser's Despair," *PLL* 5 (1969): 273–81.

10. See, for example, Jerome H. Buckley, *Tennyson*, p. 71.

always seemed the same" (l. 24). The use of *seemed* here develops the interesting suggestions that they are purposefully deceiving themselves and also that they are attaining a new level of apprehension, where what seems is what is: "And deep-asleep he seemed, yet all awake" (l. 35). This new state embodies not only lassitude but "ecstasy." [11] From this point of view, the mariners are simply leaving behind the world of trivial care and objective reality, learning to "harken what the inner spirit sings" (l. 67). The Lotos-land is their Innisfree, and they are not cowardly suicides but imaginative poets, courageously giving form to what they hear "in the deep heart's core." This argument can be carried only far enough to be suggestive, but the hint that, in some ways, the mariners are not beneath, but above, common concerns is strong. They are both advancing and retreating, condemned and admired.

The same uncomfortable mixture is stressed in the curiously appealing conjunction of the tendency to isolation and to union. Though the state the lotos-eaters attain seems to be that of the total solitary, and though "if his fellow spake, / His voice was thin, as voices from the grave" (ll. 33–34), they sing in chorus and they consistently use plural pronouns. The lotos allows complete self-absorption, yet somehow communion as well. The last line of the poem, with its appeal to "brother mariners," seems both sardonic and compassionate. They are, in one sense, guilty of the ultimate social insult, and they give very short shrift to the appeal of home and family (ll. 114–25); but their argument is put in such general and extrapersonal terms that it seems to be a generous act, a sharing of the secrets of a new perception and new solutions. They reject a community of activity, turmoil, waste, and life for one of quiet, consummation, and death. It is a strange fellowship, but one that is difficult to deny.

By far the dominant appeal of the poem, of course, is to the other half of the comic equation: the magnification of the isolated self. The major argument is that the self can here experience a perfect fruition: "The flower ripens in its place, / Ripens and fades, and falls, and hath no toil, / Fast-rooted in the fruitful soil" (ll. 81–83). This positive appeal to a subtle and luxurious self-indulgence is supported by strong negative arguments, a chorus with variations

---

11. The term and this part of the argument are borrowed from Alan Grob, "Tennyson's 'The Lotos-Eaters,'" *MP* 62 (1964): 124.

on the theme of bondage: first, that man, the supposed apex of creation, is the only creature who knows the sorrow and pain of toil (l. 69); second, that life as they know it is death (and, by implication, the death they are choosing is genuine life); third, that challenges lead nowhere since nothing is cumulative: "Is there any peace / In ever climbing up the climbing wave?" (ll. 94–95); finally, that their destination is here in any case, since their families view them as they now are—shadowy, imaginative beings sung of by minstrels (ll. 121–23).

The decision at the end to "lie reclined / On the hills like Gods together, careless of mankind" (ll. 154–55) is not, then, stated as a justification but as the most coherent explanation of the order they perceive and the ironic solution to man's place in it. They meet cosmic indifference with an indifference of their own; in the face of nothingness they become nothing. What had begun as a local and particular sense of their own peculiar surroundings—"the wandering fields of barren foam" (l. 42)—becomes a general vision of all life, expressed in the same metaphor of waste and pointlessness: "an ill-used race of men that cleave the soil, / Sow the seed, and reap the harvest with enduring toil, / Storing yearly little dues of wheat, and wine and oil; / Till they perish and they suffer—some, 'tis whispered—down in hell" (ll. 165–68). The final line of the poem is more than an appeal to the "brother mariners"; it is a direct appeal to the readers. It is the balance of the ironic rhetoric that ensures our being unable either to accept or to reject this invitation.

Of all these poems, "Ulysses" seems to come closest to breaking this ironic tension. Though there is more to the poem than the "need of going forward" [12] Tennyson offered as his motive in writing it, the central power to which we respond is that of romantic heroism. There are complex modulations in tone, certainly, but for most readers the poem moves toward an expression of serene confidence: "Though much is taken, much abides; and though / We are not now that strength which in old days / Moved earth and heaven; that which we are, we are" (ll. 65–67). But Ulysses is much more than another indomitable superman, beyond the reach of time and death. He, in fact, grants the power of circumstance, even of age and physical weakness. He does not stand above these forces but is caught by them, and he knows it.

12. *Memoir*, 1:196.

Yet he refuses to see himself as a victim and thus provides an answer to irony: the undefeated will.[13] The will accepts its own condition unflinchingly—"that which we are, we are"—but does not allow the force of external terror to negate it. In the face of death, the comic will asserts an irreducible ego; the acceptance of reality amounts to a triumph over it. The great modern hero is this old man, who has already had his heroic adventures and who now achieves his personality and defines the hope of ours simply by refusing not to be. The comic and heroic will is the poem's subject; its primary motive is the relaxation of ironic tension.

But the tension is relaxed only within, not outside, the poem; for Ulysses, but not for us. The view of heroism is made comprehensive as well as intense, and it is this completeness that causes the escape to be closed to us. The force of the will projected here is enormous, but it is also, we sense, highly specialized. The poem lacks entirely comedy's usual sense of inclusiveness. "Ulysses" deals just as powerfully and rigorously with what the hero cannot accept as with what he can; nearly half the poem is devoted to sloughing off the encumbrances that stand in the way of this narrow solution. Because the poem is so explicit about this pruning, we can see the magnitude and variety of the human spirit being sacrificed for its heroic but naked endurance. The result is the only heroism and the only solution to irony now possible, both compelling and impossibly restrictive. Despite the resounding, positive conclusion, the poem has worked to deny us the ability to participate in it uncritically.

Though apparently an alternative to "The Lotos-Eaters," then, "Ulysses" operates in much the same way; it presents an answer that dissolves tension for the speaker and increases it for the reader. The two poems also seem to have similar strategies for attacking the ironic dualism by heightening one-half of it: they both magnify the isolated, individual ego. Though the means of satisfying the ego are very different, perhaps even opposite, in the two poems, both solutions are equally exclusive and equally extreme. Some commentators, in fact, argue that these extremes meet, that Ulysses's desire for life is rooted in a desire for death.[14] This reading, perhaps,

13. See Charles Mitchell, "The Undying Will of Tennyson's Ulysses," *VP* 2 (1964): 87–95, for a reading that emphasizes this point.

14. Langbaum (*Poetry of Experience*, pp. 90–91) is most notable. Though he also adopts this response to the poem's tone, R. F. Storch's "The Fugitive from the Ancestral Hearth," *TSLL* 13 (1971): 281–97, is far more subtle in treating the complexity of the poem. His essay

sacrifices too many important distinctions for this striking similarity, but it is true that both poems are very uneasy with social demands, especially the sense of social acceptance that is central to comedy. In place of this society they are forced to offer substitutes: the extraordinary fellowship of death in "The Lotos-Eaters" or, in "Ulysses," what appears to be some highly dexterous faking.

For "Ulysses" seems to insist absolutely on the final separation of the individual from communal values: the only hope for the existence of the self is in isolation. The rejection of community begins at once:

> It little profits that an idle king,
> By this still hearth, among these barren crags,
> Matched with an agèd wife, I mete and dole
> Unequal laws unto a savage race,
> That hoard, and sleep, and feed, and know not me.
>
> [ll. 1-5]

The values associated with unity, order, and harmony, with love, family, and nation, are treated with lofty and imposing contempt. "Little profits" catches exactly the sneer of aristocratic understatement that is so disarming and so insusceptible of argument or reproof. What strikes us here is the control and the breathtaking rapidity with which all these civilized values are swept aside by the rush of the demands of the primitive self. The correctives we might apply are based on moral and social values that have been made irrelevant.

Ulysses proceeds in the next lines with an expansive, positive tone that provides us with a kind of rhetorical breather. His affirmations of a life-hunger act as a form of flattery, emphasizing the indiscriminate richness and value of simple experience. But the real work of this second section (ll. 6–32) is to reinforce the independent power and value of the ego: "I have enjoyed / Greatly, have suffered greatly, both with those / That loved me, and alone" (ll. 7–9). Love and all other mere externals are flattened and reduced to insignificance. The affirmations are all on the surface; under-

---

discusses in a rich and interesting way many of the same conflicts in the poem noted here, tracing both their cultural and literary associations. Also see William E. Fredeman, " 'The Sphere of Common Duties,' " *BJRL* 55 (1972): 380–82.

neath, the paring away continues as we approach nearer to the pure, undisguised self.

When he turns to Telemachus,[15] there is little disguise left. The naked scorn of the opening lines has simply changed to a more confident, if bored, patronizing. Ulysses "accepts" Telemachus and his duties, certainly, but he accepts them as inferior, hardly deserving of his attention. This sense of casual superiority is carried largely by his diction, which is weary, cliché-filled, "official" language. The tinge of parody is most apparent in his compliments: Telemachus is "most blameless" (l. 39)—that is, most mediocre. Ulysses's evident relief at having dismissed this tiresome subject— "He works his work, I mine" (l. 43)—emphasizes the enormous elevation he has attained. The key is "I mine." Ulysses has by now accomplished his own goal: the rigorous and careful definition of the heroic self.

The final section completes the pattern, presumably, by incorporating the triumphant ego of Ulysses into the fellowship of his mariners. From another point of view, he must now turn to the reader and include him in his plans. It is all rhetoric, both in the best and worst senses: it is eloquent persuasion and also mere cajolery. In these lines we hear most clearly the echo of Dante's sinner,[16] who, after a stirring call to his comrades—"Ye were not form'd to live the life of brutes, / But virtue to pursue and knowledge high"—turns and with a different voice entirely proudly announces the issue of his persuasive powers: "With these few words I sharpen'd for the voyage / The mind of my associates, that I then / Could scarcely have withheld them" (see Ricks, p. 561).

There is more than a touch of this self-assured rhetorician in Tennyson's figure. Master of all experience and, by this point in the poem, master of his own situation, Ulysses proceeds to overpower his men—and he nearly overpowers us. But we sense the great

15. Or merely turns to discuss Telemachus. Whether or not Telemachus is there could be important, but it is not a soluble problem. I think it is consistent with the outrageousness of Ulysses's appeals that he should say these things in public with his son present; I think the formal introduction, "This is my son, mine own Telemachus" (l. 33), suggests a public statement. But I realize that arguments like these cannot be final.

16. The most interesting examination of the influences on the poem is by B. J. Leggett, "Dante, Byron, and Tennyson's Ulysses," *TSL* 15 (1970): 143–59. Leggett views the influence of Byron as extremely important and notes briefly a parallel that supports the reading of the poem advanced here: "It is evident that in both the Byronic Hero and Ulysses the identification of the self with the external world is qualified by the exclusion of the remainder of mankind" (p. 153).

control and assurance in his language, the uniform public rhythms
so very different from the jagged, varied movement earlier. Lines
like, "It may be we shall touch the Happy Isles, / And see the great
Achilles, whom we knew" (ll. 63–64), are striking partly for their
quality of heroic understatement, but also for the self-consciousness
of this understatement. We apprehend the exhilaration of the lonely
and triumphant ego behind all this, and the very magnificence of
the language alerts our critical sense and heightens the tension
between sympathy and judgment.

Ulysses finally offers not comic union but absorption into his own
ego. Everything in the poem has demonstrated how resistant he is to
being reduced to "one equal temper of heroic hearts" (l. 68). The
heroic will can triumph only by cutting itself off from the very
values it now seeks to affirm. He has defined himself by casting
away all communal, ego-reducing ties, and he thus leaves us with
no real solution. The final lines sadly reinforce both the greatness
and the inaccessibility of the hero. With a finer irony even than the
lotos-eaters' appeal to their "brother mariners" to join them in
oblivion and death, Tennyson shows the existential hero able to
create by his supreme will a unity he cannot join simply because his
will is supreme. Ulysses leaves irony behind, but he pays a great
price for his escape. And he makes it impossible for us to go with
him.

No one, I assume, has ever consciously wanted to join Tithonus,[17]
though the essential force of the dramatic monologue makes us live
for a time with his dilemma. Tennyson talked of this poem as a
"pendent" to "Ulysses,"[18] but it is more than a companion or even
a contrast to the heroic poem; it is a bleak parody of its impulses.
"Tithonus" gives an embittered view of what lies "beyond the
sunset" Ulysses had so grandly proposed as the heroic destination.
It is, in fact, a total comic parody, not only of the proud defiance of
"Ulysses," but also of the opposite pole, the regressive urge to be
warm and protected expressed in "The Lotos-Eaters": instead of a
luxuriant sensual escape, Tithonus laments, "I wither slowly in
thine arms" (l. 6).

17. I acknowledge that the 1842 version of the poem, entitled "Tithon," was really a
shorter version of the famous "Tithonus" (published in 1860), which I am discussing here. I
hope the reader will pardon the discrepancy on the grounds (1) that the essential ironic
vision—if not the rhetoric—of both versions is the same, and (2) that the poem presents an
interesting contrast to "Ulysses" and is thus conveniently treated here.

18. *Memoir*, 1:459.

Jacob Korg argues convincingly that "Tithonus" "demonstrate[s] the danger of fulfillment" [19] itself. Thus, this complete inversion of comedy is instructive as a purified form of Tennyson's ironic art. The symbols of imprisonment, cosmic treachery, and death-in-life form the bases of his main ironic themes. The predicament is a variation on one the poet had worked out quite early: man is caught between his precisely equal needs to live and to die. In a further darkening of this point, Tithonus is made a slave to life, not death, suggesting the grotesque argument that man is born to shun the single friendly act of nature, his destruction.

Such an argument calls up very strong instinctive resistance, and the major artistic problem here is to generate sympathy in order to bypass our urgent need to judge. Most generally, Tennyson manages to do this by making the poem one of the most impassioned and self-absorbed of dramatic monologues. The speaker has very little perspective on his own situation and is mastered by his single obsession with release. Thus, we are not ourselves encouraged to find the detachment that more self-control or variety would allow. Even more important, perhaps, is the effect of the fine opening, where the "pure" poetry of incantation subversively draws us into the poem. The repetitions, the regular iambs lengthening into anapests, the very sense of natural accept-ance implied in the repetitive *ands*—all tend to mask the subject of these lines and set us up for Tithonus's violent argument: "Me only cruel immortality / Consumes" (ll. 5–6).[20] The basic inversion has by now been accomplished, and Tithonus can proceed.

The tension between sympathy and judgment is further increased by incongruous echoes from the comedy of manners. The whole poem is cast as a lovers' quarrel, filled with bizarre flattery and sly wheedling. The simplest logic behind Tithonus's argument is the strategy of pure pressure: keeping up a steady stream of words, even the same words, until the opponent yields from exhaustion. The ending lines can be seen, in this light, as a grotesque bribe, combining flattery and an implied promise to keep still:

> Release me, and restore me to the ground;
> Thou seëst all things, thou wilt see my grave:

19. "The Pattern of Fatality in Tennyson's Poetry," *VN*, no. 14 (1958), p. 9.

20. This metrical change and its effects are discussed by Mary Joan Donahue, "Tennyson's *Hail, Briton!* and *Tithon*," *PMLA* 64 (1949): 410.

> Thou wilt renew thy beauty morn by morn;
> I earth in earth forget these empty courts,
> And thee returning on thy silver wheels.

[ll. 72–76]

The echo of the comedy of manners and its accompanying comfortable and assured values jars horribly with the genuine sound of Tithonus's anguish. He is forced to plead for precisely what cannot be granted, and he is subject to a caricature of renewal and growth, a daily reminder of his loss. He is tauntingly placed at the center of comedy, with sexual beauty, promise, light, energy, and eternal renewal. Of course these hopes do exist in the well-meaning and quite real Eos, but comedy here is the source of torment. "Tithonus" is Tennyson's purest irony: it confronts comedy directly and argues that the comic vision is itself the final trap.

"St Simeon Stylites" represents the extreme of this rhetorical irony. Even the tendency of commentators, from Leigh Hunt on, to treat it as a satiric poem, acting in one way or another to condemn its speaker,[21] is expressive of the strength of the ironic tension in the poem and our desire somehow to resolve it. For the poem deals with a monstrous parody of Christianity, a parody that is both ludicrous and profound. "St Simeon Stylites" may present a blatant self-advertisement, but it is also a lament or confession, depending on our angle of vision. There is no single or easy response allowed. St Simeon is, of course, both disgusting and funny; the ways in which he gives himself away are so numerous and obvious they need not be recounted. But the absorbing energy of the poem and the great intensity of its speaker urge a sympathy and association that combat the satiric or judgmental response. The basic problem seems to be that St Simeon is not only bizarre but typical; he exists both at the end of the spectrum of human impulses and at its exact center. to view the poem as satiric twists it into a petty attack on a target

21. Hunt called it an "appalling satire on the pseudo-aspirations of egotistical asceticism and superstition" (review of *Poems* [1842], *Church of England Quarterly Review* 12 [October 1842]: 361–76; quoted in Ricks, p. 542). Valerie Pitt says its theme is "the corruption of self-cultivation" (*Tennyson Laureate*, p. 122), a notion pursued at length in William E. Fredeman's " 'A Sign Betwixt the Meadow and the Cloud,' " *UTQ* 38 (1968): 69–83. Robert Langbaum, as usual, presents the other side of the coin, the case for "sympathy" and identification (*Poetry of Experience*, p. 87). The tensions between the poem's "existing moment and its unmentioned outcome" are discussed by Christopher Ricks, *Tennyson*, pp. 107–11.

that is trivial and far too easy. It also oversimplifies by responding to the pride, the confidence, and the monstrous in St Simeon and ignoring the humility, the painful doubt, and the voice of simple humanity. The whole poem is a tortured utterance as well as a smug one.

To take just one example, the chief characteristic of St Simeon's language is enumerating excess: "Patient on this tall pillar I have borne / Rain, wind, frost, heat, hail, damp, and sleet, and snow" (ll. 15–16). There is a clear, naïve delight expressed here, a proud ticking off of torments. He has a childish faith in quantities, a belief that he can prove his case by sheer weight. He displays throughout an absurd dependence on numbers: "Then, that I might be more alone with thee, / Three years I lived upon a pillar, high / Six cubits, and three years on one of twelve; / And twice three years I crouched on one that rose / Twenty by measure; last of all" (ll. 84–88). There is no end to his belief in the power of arithmetic. Or almost no end, for behind the jejune confidence is both a note of doubt—"I think that I have borne as much as this— / Or else I dream" (ll. 91–92)—and, even more important, a tone of petulant anger, as if the mere thought that all his trials might not be rewarded fills him with rage: "O Jesus, if thou wilt not save my soul, / Who may be saved? who is it may be saved?" (ll. 45–46).

There is an incipient sense of injustice, then, that pervades his argument and lends a poignant and serious note, even to his enumerations. St Simeon is isolating and exposing to view a central tendency of Christianity, the exaltation of pain: "Show me the man hath suffered more than I" (l. 48). He expresses the terrible logic of injustice that, as Camus says,[22] pervades Christianity: rather than erasing or explaining irrational torment, God demonstrates, by suffering Himself, that He too is subject to absurd pain. Suffering becomes a sign of sanctity, and beneath St Simeon's humorous surface is his dim perception of the fact that the comic symbol of mercy and forgiveness also becomes the ironic symbol of uncaused torture, the "life of death" (l. 53) that St Simeon typifies.

As is usual with the dramatic monologue, the ending of the poem climaxes this theme and its careful balance of the humorous and awful, the detached and immediate. This time there is not a single

22. *The Rebel: An Essay on Man in Revolt*, trans. Anthony Bower (New York: Knopf, 1967), p. 34.

ironic capping but a series of them. First, there is the reestablished image of the ludicrous side of St Simeon, now heightened by his assumption of the crown of Paradise and his exultant confidence (ll. 205–08). Then he is suddenly struck with a flash of pathetic doubt, a perception of impending trickery: "Ah! let me not be fooled, sweet saints" (l. 209). The immediacy of pity is soon qualified as St Simeon returns to his old habit of exact totting up, even in regard to his own death: "I prophesy that I shall die tonight, / A quarter before twelve" (ll. 217–18). In the very last lines he turns to the audience with a grotesque benediction and comment on his own rhetoric: "Let them take / Example, pattern: lead them to thy light" (ll. 219–20). On one hand, we certainly cannot accept this "example"; on the other, we cannot avoid recognizing it as the inescapable "pattern" of our lives. The case is both absurd and ironically true.

These ironic poems are accompanied by a new and very interesting development in comedy. The 1842 *Poems* presents Tennyson's first extended attempts to mix the two genres within a single poem. More and more, the comic resolution arises from—or is placed upon—an ironic situation, so as to provide a kind of negative comic catharsis. The sense of freedom is almost solely a sense of release from irony, produced not by the power of a comic narrative but by the mere snapping of tension. The feeling is not so much one of recapturing Eden as having been released from prison.

This is the general effect, I think, but there are, in fact, so many variations in the use of comedy to combat irony that our responses are bound to be more complex. There is even in these volumes at least one poem, "The Day-Dream," that is entirely free from irony. It seems completely pure, gentle, and untroubled, despite the fact that it rests on just the comic notion that is parodied in "The Lotos-Eaters," a notion now, of course, disguised:

> Well—were it not a pleasant thing
>   To fall asleep with all one's friends;
> To pass with all our social ties
>   To silence from the paths of men;
> And every hundred years to rise
>   And learn the world, and sleep again.
>   [L'Envoi, ll. 3–8]

The individualistic extremism of "The Lotos-Eaters" is masked by the insistence on "all one's friends" and "all our social ties"; the earlier argument for the dark fulfillment of death is modified to a wish for long intervals of quasi death to do away with boredom. The real appeal, of course, is clear: one wakes seldom and briefly and then, happily, is able to "sleep again." "The Day-Dream" is fully successful in its aims, but it strives only for the quality called "charming." It is, in any case, a very rare instance of undisturbed comedy in this stage of Tennyson's work.

Much more common is the form of "The Palace of Art," which is poised between comedy and irony. Though the poem deals with a dilemma, it is rendered as a comic dilemma and therefore not the proverbially impossible one. The main body of the poem does seem to deal with a vision of life that is both wonderful and impossible: the life inside the palace is not condemned, but it cannot be maintained. Instead of the familiar ironic rhetoric, however, a new device and a new way out of the trap are introduced by the ending: the sudden arrival of an unexpected perspective that has few or no roots in the preceding matter but gives new possibilities, though not a solution. The new perspective simply leaves doors opened, suggests that the bondage is not complete, and thus releases the irony without really completing the comedy.

The concrete basis of the dilemma in "The Palace of Art" is clear, though there are many ways to characterize the impulse that is embodied in the description of the palace and its rooms, and the contrary impulse that finds expression in the recoil from the palace: art vs. life, pride vs. humility, "private sensation vs. vitalism," stasis vs. movement, isolation vs. communion with others.[23] I put these views in this simplistic form not to depreciate them but to show how complementary they are and how, to my mind at least, they point to a problem within comedy itself. As in "The Lotos-Eaters" and "Ulysses," the drive toward gratification of the individual ego is made incommensurate with a public definition of self.

The disjunction of these once-joined public and private drives obsessed Tennyson, as it did many other artists. The *Henry IV* plays, for instance, are statements on this comic problem, just as many of

23. The first reading is common to many critics; the others belong, in order, to Joseph Sendry, " 'The Palace of Art' Revisited," *VP* 4 (1966): 149–62; William R. Brashear, *The Living Will*, p. 74; William Cadbury, "Tennyson's 'The Palace of Art,' " *Criticism* 7 (1965): 23–44; and Valerie Pitt, *Tennyson Laureate*, pp. 55–57.

Tennyson's poems are. The "soul" in this poem is striving for the comic satisfaction of self-indulgence, which is pushed to the point where it not only lacks social resonance but can thrive only insofar as its distance from social concerns is marked and definite. Just to the extent that the demands of the primitive self are met, the demands of social being are ignored. The trap, of course, is created from the fact that the exclusive indulgence of egoistic demands leads not to satisfaction but to poverty of spirit.

But the separation strategy nearly works, and the initial irony of the poem depends absolutely on our perceiving the apparent perfection and convincing richness of the palace and the vision it embodies. The poem opens on an image of near anarchy, a life of ease, sensuality, and lawlessness. But the disorder is brought under control by the emphasis put on the power of the palace's builder and by the tone: the key words, "all is well" (l. 4), give the sense that chaos yields to order. In fact, the life in the palace is remarkably integrated,[24] carefully working against stagnation and excess: "Reign thou apart, a quiet king, / Still as, while Saturn whirls, his stedfast shade / Sleeps on his luminous ring" (ll. 14–16). The image is one of motion so unobtrusive and perfect that it gives the impression of stillness; it is perfectly disciplined motion but not stasis.

The theme of discipline and control runs throughout; the palace stands finally as a symbol of the life of the imagination, its ability to integrate and balance. Over and over again the image combines order and chaos, art and nature. The four symmetrical courts, each with a "squarèd lawn" (l. 22), contain in their center dragons, spouting "a flood of fountain-foam" (l. 24). The regular cloisters are "branched like mighty woods" (l. 26) and echo the wild fountains. The emphasis is on presenting "a perfect whole / From living Nature" (ll. 58–59), creating, in other words, the ordered but vital world of art. Even the decorations in the palace are described so as to suggest this union of energy and quiet in the dynamic balance of arrested action: "Or sweet Europa's mantle blew unclasped, / From off her shoulder backward borne" (ll. 117–18). The alliteration emphasizes the fact of movement, but that movement is held in

24. A very skillful attempt is made by Andy P. Antippas, in "Tennyson's Sinful Soul," *TSE* 17 (1969): 113–34, to show that the images are so excessive as to subvert and ironize themselves. This is surely the best case that can be made for such a reading; even so, it seems unconvincing to me.

suspension by the erotic subject and by the skillful arrangement of the next two lines, which balance the realistic emphasis on motion with an alternate consciousness of the artificial and the stylized: "From one hand drooped a crocus: one hand grasped / The mild bull's golden horn" (ll. 119–20).

It is a world of pure and finished art. The soul's desire to include *every* landscape and *every* mood is not just the result of simple pride; it is the artist's need to rival God, to create that which, indeed, is superior to God's work in that it is not, like His, subject to decay: "Below was all mosaic choicely planned / With cycles of the human tale / Of this wide world, the times of every land / So wrought, they will not fail" (ll. 145–48). The object is a grandly comic one, as heroic as Ulysses's and equally hopeful. It is the attempt to give life to the human soul, "joying to feel herself alive" (l. 178). The grand project fails, of course; joy turns to scorn, liberty to imprisonment. At the center of the fall is the basic image of ironic frustration: "A still salt pool, locked in with bars of sand, / Left on the shore; that hears all night / The plunging seas draw backward from the land / Their moon-led waters white" (ll. 249–52).

But the ending of the poem refuses to complete this climactic irony: "So when four years were wholly finishèd, / She threw her royal robes away. / 'Make me a cottage in the vale,' she said, / 'Where I may mourn and pray'" (ll. 289–92). The movement toward repentance reveals an opening we had no idea was there. It also suggests that the trap was no trap at all, just a mistake which, in traditional comic fashion, teaches us a lesson so that we will know better next time. It may be, of course, that the alternative to isolation, the life in the vale, will create a new trap. But then it may not. The poem does not take a stand on this point, for it does not seem ultimately to be important. We have a release, and that is what counts.

This time, appropriately, there is a comic capping: the poem ends in a spirit of real generosity, tossing out yet another possibility and opening another exit: " 'Yet pull not down my palace towers, that are / So lightly, beautifully built: / Perchance I may return with others there / When I have purged my guilt," (ll. 293–96). If one extreme does not work, Eden is not lost, nor are we: we can try the other. If that does not work, combine them. There is a sort of jaunty irrationality here that is surely deliberate. No full satisfaction is given; but then, the ironic forces have been, if not defeated, at least kept at bay.

"The Two Voices" utilizes the same device exactly to find a slightly more certain release and a fuller expression of comedy. The poem is a little less tentative than "The Palace of Art," but it still works primarily to relieve the torment caused by the problem, not to solve it. The dilemma faced is again caused by the ironic perspective, but here it is put almost solely in rationalistic terms. Instead of the full imaginative life of the Palace of Art, we have only a logical argument, very shrewd it is true, but not nearly so dangerous. The voice presses on the narrator a recognition of the undeniable gulf between the grand desires of the human will and the triviality of that same individual will in the face of the boundless cosmos and teeming, wasteful life.

This is a view that appears over and over in Tennyson, most notably in *In Memoriam*, but here it can be defeated by its own weapons. The single-minded irony doubles back on itself. Purely conceptual thought, the narrator admits, can never open jails; it always builds new ones: "in seeking to undo / One riddle, and to find the true, / I knit a hundred others new" (ll. 232–34). Though this fact originally seems cause for despair, it gives him the perspective he needs to break the spell of the suicidal voice. When that voice finally reaches its climax of nihilism—"A life of nothings, nothing-worth, / From that first nothing ere his birth / To that last nothing under earth!" (ll. 331–33)—the narrator can resist with surprising ease.

By insisting on complete uncertainty and by attacking relentlessly the common assurances men live by, the dark voice has been supporting an absolute principle of doubt, a very slippery principle, of course, since it can just as well be used against the too-certain certainty of irony itself: " 'These words,' I said, 'are like the rest: / No certain clearness, but at best / A vague suspicion of the breast' " (ll. 334–36). Ironic certainty is only a "vague suspicion"; so are conclusions based on evidence from the senses. Therefore, by irony's own argument, the comic belief has just as much validity. Though there is no *more* validity for the comic solution and though there may be no certainty at all, the tension of conclusive irony is relieved.

At this point, then, the poem has reached the openness and

uncertainty with which "The Palace of Art" closes. "The Two Voices," however, goes one step further. Having established and accepted a limbo in which ironic arguments have no final power, the speaker goes on to demonstrate the independent appeal of a comic vision. He immediately turns to the most fundamental point, that comedy ministers to life: " 'Tis life, whereof our nerves are scant, / Oh life, not death, for which we pant; / More life, and fuller, that I want" (ll. 397–99). There follows an extended closing symbol, the picture of the church-going family. And though one could wish that the descriptive adjectives—*prudent, pure, grave, demure*—were done away with, there is a fine aptness in the symbol's suggestion of permanence and calm. The placid life depicted here is a deliberate contrast to the negative, climactic hysteria urged by the dark voice. The comic alternative is made a deliberate cliché, simply because clichés endure. Against the temporary exhilaration of a suicide, Tennyson throws the consciously unexhilarating domestic comedy. The symbol is made to suggest a kind of permanence denied to irony.

"The Two Voices," then, moves closer to transcendence, arguing that inward evidence is far superior to the feeble conclusions drawn from the senses. But the poem returns in the last stanzas to a more tentative state, suggesting that one may, at best, choose between the comic and ironic perspectives, but that there is no necessary finality to the choice. The tension in the poem is released by an exercise of will, as William Brashear says. He also asserts that this power of will, as shown in the ending, makes life only "endurable," not "meaningful." [25] The life contained in the closing symbol clearly does, however, have a meaning, one just as clearly transmitted to the narrator; it is just that the meaning is not fixed. The voice of despair has not been stilled, but then it is not the only voice. Further, one is not merely suspended in meaninglessness but can find analogues and correlatives that give form and substance to comic perception. If the tomb and suicide are valid symbols, so are the family and the church. The very fact that they are balanced is, in this world, cause for joy.

At least one poem in this volume uses comedy not to suspend but to master irony. "Locksley Hall" makes it very easy to solve problems, suggesting that it is best to ignore them or, even better,

---

25. "Tennyson's Third Voice: A Note," *VP* 2 (1964): 286.

never really to have them. It is, it seems to me, an almost purely
psychological poem with a purely psychological and personal
solution. Its social and philosophical solutions are trivial at best,
since the answers, though highly satisfactory for the speaker, are
very idiosyncratic ones. They are not, for instance, very rational.
"Locksley Hall" shows how irony can be mastered by an ego that is
so large it is invulnerable, easily turning back even the sharpest
attacks, and refusing to give to problems the attention that would
result in an emotion more profound than spite. The speaker never
experiences any real depression, let alone despair, but he is very
adept at ritualistic scapegoat exercises, whereby he bolsters his own
ego and sense of control by rehearsing, with obvious satisfaction,
problems that have already been solved or safely ignored. The
"raving" is all carefully controlled; more than that, it is clearly lots
of fun:

As the husband is, the wife is: thou art mated with a clown,
And the grossness of his nature will have weight to drag thee down.
. . . .
What is this? his eyes are heavy: think not they are glazed with
  wine.
Go to him: it is thy duty: kiss him: take his hand in thine.

[ll. 47–48, 51–52]

This is a thin kind of comedy, perhaps, very close in its appeals to
the childish pleasure of inflicting pain, but it is, for that very reason,
genuine comedy. The speaker is unable to assert himself beyond a
snarl, but that is enough for him. The pleasant retaliation that
satisfies him is, in its private deviousness, just like that C. S. Lewis
attributes to the arguments of Beëlzebub in book II of *Paradise Lost*:
if your mistress is lost to you, poison her dog.[26]
   The speaker of "Locksley Hall" is, in the end, entirely unselfcon-
scious (though he does once [l. 63] pause and acknowledge that he
"blusters," he quickly goes on to bluster some more), and he sprays
accusations around with joyful spite, reveling in the waspish,
imaginative pictures he can create. He finds greatest satisfaction in
the search for the "causes" of his unjust treatment, and he sees them
everywhere, particularly in the nature of Amy or of the social
system. He arranges it so that the sources of his problems are all
comic, at least in the sense that they are external and easily subject

26. C. S. Lewis, *A Preface to Paradise Lost* (London: Oxford University Press, 1942), p. 104.

to change. If irony can be connected, centrally and finally, to
something as specific as the Chartist movement or even material-
ism, there is no real dilemma.

There is, however, one genuine problem touched on here, the
relation of the individual to progressive, especially statistically
progressive, general development. The speaker's final solution, of
course, is to connect himself to the march of time, to mix with
action, and so forth, so as to spin down the ringing grooves of
change with the "world." But what does the "world" have to do
with him? There seems to be an enormous distance between the
broad generalizations about progress and the detailed particularity
of his personal problem. The narrator perceives this gap and asks,
in the most poignant lines of the poem, how he can ever be touched
by the "increasing purpose" of man:

Yet I doubt not through the ages one increasing purpose runs,
And the thoughts of men are widened with the process of the suns.
What is that to him that reaps not harvest of his youthful joys,
Though the deep heart of existence beat for ever like a boy's?

[ll. 137–40]

His famous generalization on this point—"Knowledge comes, but
wisdom lingers, and I linger on the shore, / And the individual
withers, and the world is more and more" (ll. 141–42)—is not so
general after all. The center of the lament is: "I linger on the
shore," the image of the lonely solitary, alienated by the impersonal
and useless ("wisdom lingers") progress of time. If the individual
withers in the process, the highly individual speaker can hardly
hope for a solution from a development that annihilates all he seeks
to preserve.

But he is not really touched very deeply by this or by any other
contradiction. His comrades happily call to him in the midst of his
troublesome musings on progress, and he is able to regain his
driving, egoistic shallowness. Fittingly, the poem does not close with
a "solution" but with an image of petty vindictiveness, the real
motive and principle that have guided things throughout: "Comes
a vapour from the margin, blackening over heath and holt, / Cram-
ming all the blast before it, in its breast a thunderbolt. / Let it fall
on Locksley Hall, with rain or hail, or fire or snow" (ll. 191–93).
"Locksley Hall" shows a way out of irony, a very amusing one. By
raising grim problems in such a trivial way and for such primitive

reasons, the poem implies that these problems are not much as problems go, certainly no challenge at all for the childish but unshakable comic ego.

With these 1842 volumes Tennyson had developed his irony very fully, perhaps to the point where he could foresee little interesting progress. In any event, he turned to comedy and to various highly elaborate mixtures of comedy and irony. He, remarkably, moved away from a form he had mastered and sought to find in comedy a more satisfying, and certainly a more challenging, genre. We can see something of this movement in the poems of 1842, and it is apparent, too, in the very slight atmosphere of deliberate exercise that hangs about *The Princess*.

4

The Princess

> But cease to move so near the Heavens, and cease
> To glide a sunbeam by the blasted Pine,
> To sit a star upon the sparkling spire;
> And come, for Love is of the valley, come,
> For Love is of the valley, come thou down
> And find him; by the happy threshold, he

[sect. 7, ll. 180–85]

"Ask me no more: thy fate and mine are sealed: / I strove against the stream and all in vain: / Let the great river take me to the main." These lines occur in the last of those intercalary songs which Tennyson called "the best interpreters" [1] of *The Princess*. One would expect these climactic lines, then, to interpret the solution that is about to come. Insofar as they do, however, they expose how the comedy, *The Princess*, nearly turns into an irony, *The Defeat of Ida*. Overcome by the powerful forces against her, the heroic Ida sadly accepts her fate and abandons all resistance.

The obvious plan of the poem seems to make such a response perverse. Ida is not defeated but finds her way into a triumphant union. Such a union will allow her both to fulfill her distinctive femininity and to fight more effectively for her ideals. She is not sacrificing her heroic identity, it is supposed, but making it communal and thereby strengthening and guaranteeing her self-hood. Read in this way, the poem steers a course between the futuristic and abstract goals of the female university and the conservative, brutally concrete and instinctive views of the men. Lady Blanche and the prince's father represent extremes of these alternatives.

On one side is the primitive male conception that sees human

---

1. *Memoir*, 1:254. I am not, by the way, speaking of the blank verse lyrics, like "Tears, Idle Tears," which are part of the main body of the poem, but of the six intercalary songs added in 1850.

relations in terms of hunting, mastering, killing: "Man is the hunter; woman is his game: / The sleek and shining creatures of the chase, / We hunt them for the beauty of their skins; / They love us for it, and we ride them down" (5, ll. 147–50). These lines expose, with remarkable bluntness and precision, the secrets of the male position. The argument is not unique to the stupid old king, however; we can see it reflected in Cyril's aggressively obscene song, and especially in such unconsciously patronizing actions as Walter's patting Lilia's head. "We ride them down" is not a peculiar but a universal masculine attitude, one that the poem vigorously rejects.

On the other side, so the plan implies, is the equally dangerous counter-reaction: Lilia's primitive anger and its projected symbol, the university. This university represents a response on the same impossible grounds of battle and conquest; the women isolate themselves in protective hatred and strike out in wild, impotent fury. Thus, each party is, in the old sense, "humor-ridden," dominated by basic male or female humors. The action, as in all humor comedies, breaks the rigidity of these humors by ridiculing them and proposing a new being that is flexible and humane.

But this balancing action is not unopposed, and the poem is not so simple. Princess Ida is much closer to genuine heroism than to humorous Amazonism; her position demands a respect never given to the male argument. As her world begins to crumble from within and the external pressures mount against her, she begins to appear more a symbol of defiant and heroic will than a mere spoiled, petulant girl. Beneath the overt pattern, then, runs a counter-theme which embodies, in the battle between Ida and the world, a profound conflict between two forms of comedy. *The Princess* represents an attempt to forge a new genre by putting in opposition heroic and domestic comedy,[2] the aloof princess and the voice of "Come down, O maid," the visions of "Ulysses" and "The Miller's Daughter."

Tennyson is again dealing with the dilemma that dominated the

---

2. Gerhard Joseph's chapter on *The Princess*, in his *Tennysonian Love*, pp. 75–101, also provides a reading in terms of "a contest of genres, exploring the range of comedy in two directions" (p. 81). Joseph's two types of comedy, however, are quite different from the ones discussed here. He describes Tennyson's exploration of "the spirit" of two poles of Shakespearean comedy, "the late dark comedies and the earlier romantic ones" (p. 79). *The Princess*, he maintains, does "begin in a festive spirit of *Love's Labour's Lost* . . . and gradually darkens toward the mood of near tragedy, as in *The Winter's Tale*" (p. 81). The chapter is a suggestive one and forms a good alternative to the argument presented here.

1842 poems: the inability to merge the fully matured and complete human ego with the communal values demanded by comedy. Like "The Two Voices," "A Vision of Sin," and "The Palace of Art" before it, *The Princess* attempts to bridge this gap. It is no longer enough, however, just to dissolve this irony. Here Tennyson attempts to solve the problem by re-forming and redefining the central comic symbol: marriage. The poem tries to make the heroic vision yield to the domestic without sacrificing the heroic emphasis on personality. Marriage becomes a literal growth toward a oneness which does not obliterate difference. But it is very difficult, for us and for the poem, to grasp this unique argument very firmly or for very long. *The Princess* fails to sustain the purity of comedy and finally becomes another mixture of comedy and irony. The domestic vision is as fully embodied here as in any poem in the language, but by being directly juxtaposed to the heroic, its defects are strangely highlighted. The poem insists on being true to both sets of values and thus cannot escape giving a curious sense that its solution is both a victory and a defeat. Ida gains a great deal, but the poem is unwilling to ignore what she must leave behind: the lofty, appallingly cold but magnificent height of the undefeated personality.

Criticism of the poem[3] has certainly not ignored evidence of basic conflict or disunity, but it has generally located that conflict only in the poem's tonal diversity and has almost without exception seen that diversity as a weakness. In many ways the definitive criticism on this point is given within the poem, when the narrator comments in the Conclusion that he had, in order to please both "the mockers and the realists" (l. 24), arranged the narrative "as in a strange diagonal, / And maybe neither pleased myself nor them" (ll. 27–28). Though the poet later argues that excesses in action and, by implication, in tone, point toward eventual harmony, this positive verdict has had little support, either outside the poem or within. Most critics agree, instead, with the "Tory member's eldest son," [4]

3. Much commentary on the poem is concerned either with its topicality or with such isolated details as the prince's weird seizures. John Killham's *Tennyson and "The Princess,"* the only full-length study of the poem, demonstrates how fully it relates to topical subjects, notably the feminist controversy.

4. The most influential treatment of the poem, by J. H. Buckley, *Tennyson: The Growth of a Poet* (pp. 94–106), develops this line fully. Early critics seized on this point as well; see, for

who, though a fool whose general views are specifically repudiated, provides a most influential comment on the poem's tone: "Too comic for the solemn things they are, / Too solemn for the comic touches in them" (ll. 67–68).

The point is worth belaboring simply because the tone is so intimately related to theme. *The Princess*'s attempt to reconcile warring social, psychological, and generic elements is symbolized by the effort to bring together alternate demands as to the poem's tone. The "maiden aunt" first pompously asks for a tale which is "Heroic . . . / Grave, solemn!" (Prologue, ll. 207–08), a notion that invokes the instant ridicule of the young. Later, the contest becomes one between the mocking men and the serious women, whose silent influence "had ever seemed to wrestle with burlesque" (Conclusion, l. 16). The traditional war between old and young and between men and women becomes, thus, a challenge to poetic tact. Insofar as the tone can harmonize such contraries, the extremes of youth and age, the future and the past can blend into a mature present; more radically, the differences between men and women can be resolved into "the single pure and perfect animal" (7, l. 288). By suggesting that the resulting poetry "maybe" pleased neither faction, then, the poet is suspending the entire movement of the poem and confirming the tentative quality of its solution. The problem of tone is here a problem of total vision; it is, in this sense, the only problem of the poem, and it can be solved only by examining the thematic and generic issues it is made to include.

But one preliminary point needs to be made: the usual argument that the poem begins as "mock-heroic" and then changes abruptly to the serious distorts both the nature of the burlesque and the nature of the tonal change. In the first place, the mockery is not of the heroic. Only the excesses of false heroism are mocked, and that

---

example, the review by J. Westland Marston in the *Athenaeum* (Jan. 1, 1848), pp. 6–8. He complains of the incongruous mixture of "genial satire" and "tragic emotion" (p. 7). I acknowledge that Tennyson himself sometimes echoed this view. Frederick Locker—Lampson (*Memoir*, 2:70–71) says, "He talked of *The Princess* with something of regret, of its fine blank verse and the many good things in it: 'but,' said he, 'though truly original, it is, after all, only a medley.'" Not everyone shared this view; the poet's friend Gladstone expressed surprise that a term so inappropriate as "medley" should be used for a poem so remarkably unified: "Tennyson's Poems," *QR* 106 (1859): 456. Gladstone's opinion is supported by an unfortunately little-known but brilliant note, F. E. L. Priestley's "Control of Tone in Tennyson's *The Princess*," pp. 314–15. Priestley's brief statement on tone supports my own argument, and I am pleased to acknowledge my debt to it.

is done only to ensure the protection of the legitimate form of heroism. The banter protects and moves us closer to Ida, the figure of genuine heroism, by reducing her detractors. The two old kings, for instance, attack her so bluntly and stupidly that potential criticisms are invalidated. The prince's father puts the antifeminist position in the crudest possible terms, arguing that women are inferior but useful animals to be hunted and tamed, subdued, if all else fails, by the misery of child-bearing and child-rearing: "A lusty brace / Of twins may weed her of her folly. Boy, / The bearing and the training of a child / Is woman's wisdom" (5, ll. 453–56). His obscene diction threatens to give the game away; he puts the common male position so bluntly it cannot be accepted, and such instinctive objections to Ida are thus dismissed.

Similarly, the sting is removed from her own father's criticism. It is cast in the form of anti-intellectualism that is so feeble it is simply silly: her "awful odes," he says, are called "masterpieces: / They mastered *me*" (1, ll. 144–45). Any force the parody of Ida's odes might carry and any objections based on a more pervasive anti-intellectualism are blunted by repudiating their source. Finally, even her brother's mild criticism of her, "She flies too high" (5, l. 271), is balanced against his admission that he may be too crude to understand her and also against his rough but fine sense both of her stature and of the basic justice of her cause: "She asked but space and fairplay for her scheme" (5, l. 272). Throughout, then, Tennyson exercises various rhetorical means to promote our regard for heroism and for its advocate, Princess Ida. Even such direct burlesques of the school as those connected with the "daughters of the plough" are deliberately separated and kept distant from Ida, and thus they suggest only aberrations, not basic faults, in the heroic scheme.

The usual interpretation of tone denies even the linear development implied in "diagonal" and argues for an abrupt change from one mood to another. While the threats to comic fulfillment, which demand a solemn tone, are somewhat more strongly emphasized and also more protracted in this comedy than in most, the tone in all romantic comedies develops away from the banter that is necessary for the preliminary attack on the humorous, blocking characters toward the calm acceptance that comes with the victory of resilience. The movement from attack to acceptance is most marked in those comedies we are likely to think of as warm and optimistic, *A Midsummer Night's Dream*, for instance. "Jest and earnest working side by side" (4, l. 541) is the traditional slogan of integration, not dislocation.

The attempt to find the point of this presumed alteration in the poem, then, seems to be self-defeating. Edgar F. Shannon, Jr., for instance, points to the interlude between sections 4 and 5 as a "transparent" means by which Tennyson "sharply marked the shift from levity to sobriety." [5] But section 5, far from being sober, seems easily the most humorous of all, opening in "unmeasured mirth" (l. 17) at the sight of the men disguised as women, and moving to the most extensive funny attack on the two old fathers and such slapstick episodes as that between the unfortunate male herald and the eight daughters of the plow. The tone moderates, but it does not change abruptly; neither does it become "dark." It moves toward serenity, the mood that combines joy and earnestness. Whether it quite achieves this union is questionable, but that is a matter which must be settled by considering more than just tone.

The major problem remains: the conflict of the two impulses of comedy and the effort to harmonize them. Though the poem finally attempts to solve the dilemma by leaning heavily on the concept of the natural, it also maintains the image of the heroic princess, whose heroism is defined largely as her ability to resist for so long the lure of the natural. It is a comedy of normality, but in its secret heart it seems to lament the failure of the grandly abnormal. As a result of this disjunction, almost everything in *The Princess* carries with it contrary signals: positive acts are negative; victories are also defeats.

This complex dualism is apparent throughout the poem in its images and themes, perhaps most obviously in its action. Even the most ludicrous action of all, Ida's plunge into the river, cuts in two directions. On one hand, it functions as well-deserved ridicule of her pretensions, her slightly absurd readiness for tragic death: "We were as prompt to spring against the pikes, / Or down the fiery gulf as talk of it, / To compass our dear sisters' liberties" (3, ll. 269–71). The stage is set for the comic catastrophe, the comeuppance. She is brought low, significantly, by a trivial event, Cyril's ribald song; she

5. *Tennyson and the Reviewers: A Study of His Literary Reputation and the Influence of the Critics upon His Poetry, 1827–1851* (Cambridge, Mass.: Harvard University Press, 1952), p. 128.

does not spring against the pikes but clumsily misses the plank and *rolls* into the river. Instead of finding glorious martyrdom, she must suffer an inglorious rescue by a man she hates.

On the other hand, the ridicule is so extreme that it suggests not so much corrective action as a brutal assault. Why, for instance, does Cyril do such a gross and stupid thing? It is one of the issues the poem ponders—and ponders very awkwardly (4, ll. 230–38)—but cannot resolve. The obscene song seems merely a meaningless assertion of male supremacy, a primitive attack on femininity itself. From this point of view, Ida is not only ridiculed but trapped, not for any particular purpose, but simply by some basic malignity. Heroism is completely denied by the episode but to no real educational purpose, and the result can as easily be to increase our sympathy for Ida as to ridicule her. The action is as absurdly meaningless as it is comically justifiable.

This same mixture also attends the central symbol: the pursuit of knowledge. Ida's university is legitimate, as is her dedication to learning; but her scheme invokes not only the support of heroic comedy but the ridicule of domestic comedy and its insistence on the physical and intuitive as opposed to the cerebral and rational. The university, then, is its most fundamental enemy; the union of learning and implied asexuality in the female college is simply a variation of the usual anti-intellectual equation of pedantry and sterility. Turning the pedant into a woman simply reinforces the primitive appeal by invoking the atmosphere of locker-room masculinity. It makes our own response all the more tense and ambiguous.

Further, Ida's search for knowledge involves the creation of a new society, a world that is specifically utopian, bringing with it a divided response to utopias. She is, however, made specifically heroic by her loneliness and by the suggestion that she is bringing order where there was chaos, taming the beast. The parallels between Ida and the quite unambiguous King Arthur of the *Idylls* are clear. But Ida's new society, heroic as it is, liberates only in order to impose new restrictions. We hear a great deal about discipline and duty, virtues that are perhaps necessary but that are invoked almost always in comedies as enemies of the free and flexible human spirit.

The prince begins the action of the poem by disobeying his father and following the "voice" of nature (1, ll. 96–99), thus outlining the whole course of the action of domestic comedy, the rejection of the artificial, the planned, and the rigid for the values of nature and spontaneity. It is the wily and dishonest Lady Blanche who is constantly mouthing the principles of obedience—"And she replied, her duty was to speak, / And duty duty, clear of consequences" (3, ll, 135–36)—but it is the undutiful and disobedient Lady Psyche whom we are asked to approve of. Rules must always be broken in the spirit of anarchic comedy, and duty wars with love. The prince accuses Ida of barring "Your heart with system out from mine" (4, l. 443).[6] It is Ida's devotion to system that creates the heroic world and also the enemy of that world.

At the center of this difficult mixture of irony and comedy is Ida herself, the most fully developed and yet the most problematic character in the poem. For, despite the apparent ridiculousness of her plan, she is not portrayed as ridiculous. Even her plan, in the end, is seen as absurd only in the sense that irony renders all the best hopes pointless. The princess is conceived of as remarkably calm and rational, considering how deeply she perceives injustice and how firmly she believes in her cause. She almost never rants, and her speeches exactly invert the rhetorical pattern common to fervent crusaders. Instead of building to more and more excited flourishes, even Ida's official speeches of indoctrination begin with rhetorical excess and move to greater simplicity, clarity, and moderation. Since her lieutenants, Lady Blanche and Lady Psyche, both employ the more traditional strategy of gradually increasing the voltage, Ida's comparative calm is made even more noticeable. The rhetorical pattern of her speeches suggests the development beyond the mere excrescences of formal radicalism to a genuine heroic simplicity. She always ends with a position that is so moderate it is made to appear emphatically sensible.

Even the purpose of the university is not what we would surely expect in a burlesque, that is, the reversal of tyrannies and the creation of a new race of Amazons; rather, Ida wants to do away with tyranny, or at least to minimize it. Her university does not seek to combat marriage but to make it just a little less like slavery. She is not preparing celibates or man-haters but those who "may with

6. Alan Danzig, "Tennyson's *The Princess*," *VP* 4 (1966): p. 86, claims Ida can find femininity only when she "abandons system and acts intuitively." It is true that system and intuition are opposed, but I think her acceptance of intuitive action is neither so clear-cut nor such an obvious good as Danzig makes out.

those self-styled our lords ally / [Their] fortunes, justlier balanced, scale with scale" (2, ll. 51–52). This goal seems almost pathetically limited, but it brings down on her in full force the world of men. Whatever she herself may be, her institution is hardly antisocial; she seeks only a readjustment in society, a movement toward balance. Ida herself never speaks of dominance. She offers merely a chance to "lose / Convention" (2, ll. 71–72), that is, to revive and free society. But it is precisely the moribund convention that men live by, and her very reasonableness thus incurs their most instinctual wrath. If she were more radical, she would be less of a threat; *The Princess* would be a more straightforward comedy but a much less interesting poem.

Ida's refusal to be satisfied with ranting marks her deep seriousness. It guarantees the validity of the promise she holds out: "O lift your natures up: / Embrace our aims: work out your freedom" (2, ll. 74–75). The "freedom" here is very much like the inner freedom Ulysses finds in the face of the external inhibitions of old age and death. She really means to make a new world, not by re-creating society but by providing to others the secret of rebirth she herself has found: "We touch on our dead self, nor shun to do it, / Being other—since we learnt our meaning here, / To lift the woman's fallen divinity" (3, ll, 205–07). She hopes to give back to women the individual Edens they have lost.

Tennyson is very careful to give Ida no motive other than simple heroism. The other possibilities, her being spoiled by her weak father or perverted by the teachings of the sexually frustrated Lady Blanche, are entertained only to be dismissed as trivial. Her offer to her students is precisely that of Ulysses to his mariners, and she has Ulysses's insight into the necessity for absolute devotion to the unfettered, noble self: "Better not be at all / Than not be noble" (2, ll. 79–80). The human will is made triumphant by assertion, and women, Ida promises, who are now "laughing stocks of Time" (4, l. 496), may be conquerors of time and death. Heroic comedy allows a destruction of the ultimate trap.

The question is, then, why the plan is so easily upset. Ida resists courageously, but the rest of the university topples with absurd readiness. One answer, given before, is that the university is too rigid, too schematically conceived, a sure sign in all comedy of vulnerability to the forces of nature. Ida holds things together, as Lady Psyche says, with her "iron will" (2, l. 185); it is clear that her system gains coherence only from laws and rules. And comedy hates all rules. Still, there is more to this "iron will" than simply a violation of comic precepts. We sense that Ida's will is hardened because there is little genuine response to her heroism. Her enemies are not only the men without but all that is selfish, cowardly, and indolent within. In one revealing scene, the narrator discusses the flow of students after lectures and very quietly provides the proper diagnosis of the university's illness.

The picture begins with "One walk[ing] reciting by herself" (2, l. 430), then one who "In this hand held a volume as to read, / And smoothed a petted peacock down with that" (ll. 431–32). Then, however, the view shifts from the single figures to large groups of students, who are clearly not interested even in faking seriousness: some run to row on the water or merely to sit in the shade under the bridge, or in the thickets, or on the lawns. The more energetic toss a ball back and forth. The climactic picture in this gallery of presumed spiritual revolutionaries shows how ridiculously impossible the task is: the "older sort" "murmured that their May / Was passing: what was learning unto them? / They wished to marry; they could rule a house; / Men hated learned women" (ll. 439–42). The new world is ruined not by Ida's excesses, clearly, but by a sad mistake she has made in trying to share and make communal her own heroism. She has never had a chance, and all the flurry of the wars is the result of a ludicrous hysteria on the part of men who really have no cause for fear. Nothing can throw off the dead hand of convention.

The chief enemy, therefore, is time, most specifically the past. Ida wants to pull free from this bondage, but she is defeated by its attractions. She cannot combat the psychic force of time, the power and passion engendered by the most important of the lyric songs in the poem, "Tears, Idle Tears." The poem, as Ida recognizes, offers a kind of melancholy luxuriance that is regressive and imprisoning. The past sings with "so sweet a voice and vague, fatal to men" (4, l. 46). In her view, the poem has power, but of an inferior and dangerous kind. It is a sentimental poem, masking as ironic honesty an appeal to self-indulgent introspection and maudlin self-pity. It is, she says, "a death's-head at the wine" (4, l. 69), a trembling poetry that is contemptible. "Let the past be past; let be / Their cancelled Babels" (4, ll. 58–59), she proclaims, but no one hears her. Even the prince, who might have understood a little, carries with him in his invasion certificates of the imprisoning past, the absurd contract made long ago by the two fathers.

The past controls in the most outrageous forms, and eventually the prince—or his father—or time—wins. There is, from this point of view, no possibility of change. Ida fails not because she has been rigid, but because she strove to free us from the days that are no more. Her insistence that women are "Not vassals to be beat, nor pretty babes / To be dandled, no, but living wills, and sphered / Whole in ourselves and owed to none" (4, ll. 128–30) is both self-evident and ridiculous. By asserting so clearly the importance of the human will, she has demonstrated its impotence against tyranny, convention, instinct, and, most generally, the past. Since she cannot shut out the forces of the past, then, all she can do in her desire to liberate is to build a new prison.

This invasion of the past that turns her comic world into an ironic one comes, in its most insidious form, as a "voice"—not only the passionate voice of "Tears, Idle Tears" but the tired one of all conventional language. One of her most perceptive and most impossible wars is a linguistic one. When the disguised men are first presented to her, Cyril takes the opportunity to remind her of the old kings' contract, saying that the prince is "The climax of his age! as though there were / One rose in all the world, your Highness that, / He worships your ideal" (2, ll. 36–38). Ida is indignant, not about the prince but about the language, the frozen clichés that come from equally frozen attitudes:

> We scarcely thought in our own hall to hear
> This barren verbiage, current among men,
> Light coin, the tinsel clink of compliment.
> Your flight from out your bookless wilds would seem
> As arguing love of knowledge and of power;
> Your language proves you still the child.
>
> [2, ll. 39–44]

Ida sees that the language of men is just like, indeed is, the imprisoning voice of the past. Love songs, she says, "mind us of the time / When we made bricks in Egypt" (4, ll. 109–10). The platitudes of love have within them the deceptive lures of slavery. They "lute and flute fantastic tenderness, / And dress the victim to the offering up, / And paint the gates of Hell with Paradise, / And play the slave to gain the tyranny" (4, ll. 111–14). She tries to counter this conventional language with a new one, forging Valkyrean hymns or songs of prophecy, urging that "song / Is duer unto freedom, force and growth / Of spirit" (4, ll. 122–24). The academy is primarily a school of new poetry, hoping above all to remold the language: "And everywhere the broad and bounteous Earth / Should bear a double growth of those rare souls, / Poets, whose thoughts enrich the blood of the world" (2, ll. 162–64). But it is the old unpoetic language that tears apart the university. Ida is defeated by voices, by words.

So that we do not miss the force of this theme of imprisonment in language, Ida's own downfall is foreshadowed by an exactly parallel defeat of Lady Psyche. When she discovers the identity of the three men and resolves to tell the princess, the men turn on her with their world of words. They deliberately combat her new self with stereotyped images of a generalized female. The prince begins the assault with, "Are you that Lady Psyche?" and proceeds to cite a fixed image, a portrait that hangs in his father's hall, an idealized version of womanhood (2, ll. 219–27). This tactic is so obviously the right one for their purposes that each speaker uses it in turn, picking up with a repeated "Are you that Lady Psyche?" when his predecessor has run out of breath. She is thus recalled to an imaginary, womanized, selfhood, quite at odds with the independent woman she has, with Ida's help, presumably become. She is pushed toward an unreal past, toward sentimental images of marriage, nurturing care, and passivity. The men finally entrap her so firmly in the assumptions contained in this world of conventional language that she paces about "like some wild creature newly-caged" (2, l. 281) and at last yields to their absurd conception of what she is, thus betraying Ida. She had broken away with her princess into a new freedom and a new tongue, but here she is "newly-caged" in the old clichés of sentimental tyranny.

In a similar fashion, then, Ida herself is beaten down by words, by the relentless assault (6, ll. 147–248) of the most instinctive of men: her brother and the two kings. She is threatened, flattered, denounced, but the one image before her always is that of "woman": tender and submissive. "O if, I say, you keep / One pulse that beats true woman, if you loved / The breast that fed or arm that dandled you" (6, ll. 163–65), Cyril begins, and the others chime in with similar appeals, climaxed by Gama's sentimental evocation of Ida's mother on her deathbed gasping out, with her last breath, "Our Ida has a heart" (6, l. 218). She is simply dragged down: "But Ida stood nor spoke, drained of her force / By many a varying influence and so long. / Down through her limbs a drooping languor wept: / Her head a little bent" (6, ll. 249–52). Having forgiven Lady Blanche, the princess is then vulnerable to the same tactics, a point the prince is not slow to grasp. He realizes the efficacy of repetition and pressure: "Nor did her father cease to press my claim, / Nor did mine own, now reconciled; nor yet / Did those twin-brothers, risen again and whole; / Nor Arac, satiate with victory" (7, ll. 72–75). Nowhere is the ironic image of the lonely hero ingloriously assaulted more firmly set than in this theme of language and its culmination in Ida's fall.

But the ironic defeat is also a comic victory, depending on our angle of vision and whether we respond more fully to the collapse of the heroic or to the fulfillment of the domestic comedy. This ambiguity is apparent even in the figure of the child, a symbol Tennyson used quite deliberately, strengthening it through the various revisions, presumably to clarify the meaning of the poem. "The child is the link thro' the parts," he said,[7] and indeed that is true. It is the most important and complex symbol in the poem and thus the most important key to interpretation. From the point of view of domestic comedy, the child is an essential and nearly perfect symbol. It can be used both statically, as a symbol of innocence, or dynamically, as a symbol of growth and development. The actual child, Aglaïa, is a static image used to evoke responses of tenderness and maternal warmth in Ida, but the symbol has much broader applications in the poem that suggest process and an acceptance of change.

Disturbances, then, can be almost automatically set aside as youthful excesses, not only excusable but valuable as educational preludes to growth. This is the exact argument used by the narrator at the very end to explain the poem's relevance: "This fine old world of ours is but a child / Yet in the go-cart. Patience! Give it time / To learn its limbs: there is a hand that guides" (Conclusion, ll. 77–79). Ida's utopian radicalism is thus reduced from a threat to a mistake, and not a serious mistake at that. All of comedy's charity and generosity (even if, as here, it is an evasive, patronizing generosity) are thus implied by the child symbol, which clearly gives very useful support to one side in the comic battle.

7. *Memoir*, 1:254.

The support to domestic comedy is not only useful; it is continuous. The child is central to most of the songs that link the sections and anticipate so sharply some of the issues about to be raised. Tennyson's comment that the importance of the child was "shown in the songs which are the best interpreters of the poem" [8] may, however, be misleading; for while the appropriateness of the songs is usually clear enough, they often seem far more simple than the action they are presumably interpreting so well. They distort things a great deal, though they are still noteworthy for the half-light they throw.

The first, "As through the land at eve we went," presents the major and reiterated use of the child symbol in the songs. Here the couple who have fallen out "kiss again with tears" (l. 9) when they see the grave of their child. The child acts as a force for unification and reconciliation. It is also, here and in the main action of the poem, a natural and physical symbol, inciting the kisses in this song and Ida's reawakened sexuality. Apart from this, the child also suggests that unity is even stronger after the experience of disunity: "And blessings on the falling out / That all the more endears" (ll. 6–7). This notion supports the argument of domestic comedy to the effect that Ida's experiment is valuable when abandoned because, though abnormal and therefore to be rejected, it acts to expand the boundaries of life, to extend what we think of as normal. Ida, of course, might very well call this song sentimental and evasive; and she would, no doubt, be right.

But she is allowed no direct comment, and the next linking song, "Sweet and low," is much more subtle in its evocation of the child as a binding force between man and wife. The father is drawn back from the "dying moon" to home and new life, apparently not by the wife in the first stanza, but by the child in the second. "Father will come to his babe in the nest" (l. 13), even if he resists the call of his mate. There is the mildly subversive suggestion that the only genuine male response is to a child, since men themselves are children; but the principal linking is of the child with love and unity.

The third song, "The splendour falls on castle walls," does not specifically mention a child, but it does deal directly with the associations developed around that symbol. The song expressly

8. *Memoir*, 1:254.

denies the power of fame to combat time (that is, it denies Princess Ida's argument), as well as the sustaining power of heroism. The terms associated with the heroic vision here—splendor, castle, wild cataract, cliff, sea—evoke echoes that diminish as time passes. Against this decay is the personal, introverted domestic love whose power grows as time goes on and thus is served by time, not defeated: "Our echoes roll from soul to soul, / And grow for ever and for ever" (ll. 15-16).

In the next two songs, which belong among the least effective lyrics Tennyson ever wrote, the child symbol is reinforced without much development. In "Thy voice is heard through rolling drums," the warrior gathers courage and strength from imagining "his brood" (l. 6) and then goes out and hacks his enemy to pieces. There is in this song, as in the narrative itself, a curious connection between children, men, and barbarism, but it is not developed. The last song to deal with a child, "Home they brought her warrior dead," simply reaffirms the child's ability to minister to life, love, and personality. Rather than committing suicide, the newly widowed woman looks at her child on her knees and weeps sustaining, life-saving tears. It is easy, as I said, to see that poems like this have some bearing on the problems Princess Ida faces, but it is not easy to see how they are the "best interpreters" of these problems. They seem, rather, to give support, less and less effectively as the poem goes on, to those aspects of the child symbol that serve the argument for domestic comedy.

But there is another side and another argument. From the standpoint of heroic comedy, the child is associated with regression, defeat, and deadly traps. Against the arguments of domestic comedy for the natural and ordinary in marital affairs, heroic comedy insists that the present relation between men and women is grotesquely perverted and unnatural: "they had but been, she thought, / As children; they must lose the child, assume / The woman" (1, ll. 135-37). Time and again the child image is brought up not in reference to sweetness and tenderness but in reference to ugly containment. Ida's chief aim, one might say, is to invert the values that collect around this symbol and to rob it of its enormous sentimental force.

In order to mature, to "lose the child," women must abandon, not children of course, but the tradition of falsifying sentimentality associated with that image. And that tradition is located exactly with domestic comedy. Again like Ulysses, Ida's stern realism refuses to ignore the fact that heroic life is a life of exclusions; the comforts and values of domesticity are among those things excluded. The child, as the emotional center of domestic life, is the central trap, and Ida uses the symbol in reference to all her enemies. Even in attacking the barren language of love she refers to this symbol: "Your language proves you still the child" (2, l. 44). The child which can, in one way or another, promise eternal life for domestic comedy is seen by Ida as the very prototype of the time-bound. In her most impassioned speech she admits the force of the symbol, arguing that it is because the suggestions that surround children are so powerful that their appeal must be resisted: "Yet will we say for children, would they grew / Like field-flowers everywhere! we like them well: / But children die; and let me tell you, girl, / Howe'er you babble, great deeds cannot die" (3, ll. 234–37).

"But children die" is the difficult admission at the heart of her heroism. She rejects the sentimental illusion of permanency which, to her, is all normality can offer, and she sets out really to destroy time, not evade it. When men use children as weapons—"Children —that men may pluck them from our hearts, / Kill us with pity, break us with ourselves" (3, ll. 240–41)—they are instinctively denying not only heroism but genuine life to women. They are pulling them back into the shadowy world of ignorant childhood, where there are only hints and counters of basic being. The famous advice of the prince's father—"Man for the field and woman for the hearth: / Man for the sword and for the needle she: / Man with the head and woman with the heart" (5, ll. 437–39)—explains just why Ida must pursue life away from men. They are out to kill her.

Finally she collapses: "Her iron will was broken in her mind; / Her noble heart was molten in her breast" (6, ll. 102–03). But this climactic fall, strangely enough, bears no overt relation to the child. The removal of Aglaïa softens her up, but her will cracks only when she sees the prince and imagines him to be dead. The capitulation of Ida and her followers is symbolized by their all becoming nurses, not directly of children but of men. The princess, it seems, has lost one child, Aglaïa, only to have her replaced by another, the prince, her future husband. The basic relationship imaged here is clearly not that between man and woman but between mother and child. Men expose their childlike natures to trap women and perhaps form them into children too. Ida is defeated not by the bloody war, the image of man's might, but by his prostration and weakness. Wanting so much to lose the child, Ida is attacked by one, and she loses her heroism: "azure pillars of the hearth / Arise to thee; the children call" (7, ll. 201–02).

At the end, when the prince argues for the wonderful new state they can achieve together, one cannot help wondering how exactly to take his many references to children. It is one thing to urge women not to lose their "distinctive womanhood" (7, l. 258), but he defines that distinguishing quality as the ability not to fail "in childward care, / Nor [to] lose the childlike in the larger mind" (7, ll. 267–68). Beneath all the fine words is a deeply regressive tendency. Perhaps we are traveling right back to where we began.

We cannot really know, I think, since the form of the poem is finally as ambiguous as its central symbol; but there are some possible answers given in the crucial seventh section. At the beginning of this last section, Ida's new Eden is shown transformed into a wasteland: "So blackened all her world in secret, blank / And waste it seemed and vain" (ll. 27–28). Her isolation now is arid and she succumbs to the lure of the valley. The conclusion presents a brilliant case for domestic comedy, but it does not allow the arguments to remain unopposed even there.

The most effective arguments for domestic comedy are not really "arguments" at all but the two seduction songs in this seventh section, "Now sleeps the crimson petal" and "Come down, O maid." These mark both the occasion and the cause of the princess's final yielding. The first song is, most obviously, a celebration of sexual release and fulfillment,[9] appropriate since, as the force of domestic comedy becomes more and more dominant toward the end, Ida is seen less as an idealist and more as a virgin.[10] But the song also operates to urge an openness to all experience, not just sexual experience. Ida's isolation now appears to be fearful withdrawal. As a counter to this assumed fear, the poem offers very

9. There are two readings of the poem which emphasize this level of the action, though each suggests different implications for the sexuality: see R. B. Smith, "Sexual Ambivalence in Tennyson," *The College English Association Critic* 27, no. 9 (1965): 8–9; and T. J. Assad, "Tennyson's Use of the Tripartite View of Man in Three Songs from *The Princess*," *TSE* 15 (1967): 52–58.

10. This point is made in relation to "Come down, O maid" by Valerie Pitt, *Tennyson Laureate*, p. 143. James Kissane provides an interesting reading of the issue of sexuality in the entire poem; see *Alfred Tennyson*, pp. 94–99.

elementary reassurance, soothing her and promising that comic existence is both beautiful and, more important, secure: "So fold thyself, my dearest, thou, and slip / Into my bosom and be lost in me" (ll. 173–74). It offers both excitement and protection. The poem's emphasis on *now,* the word that begins each of the four stanzas, creates a tone of sweet urgency to the reassurances and defines the movement of the new comedy away from the bondage of the past and futuristic abstractions alike. The present, both in its intensity and comfort, its combined images of waking and sleeping, and its unification of the remote and the transient ("the silent meteor," l. 169) with the immediate and permanent ("be lost in me," l. 174), is the basis of the new solution.

This solution is reemphasized and completed in "Come down, O maid," which directly follows "Now sleeps the crimson petal." The poem presents most clearly the opposition between the two kinds of comedy: the heroic world of the cold and splendid mountain, and the domestic, pastoral world of the valley. It is also a fine and subtle rhetorical work, of course, which seeks to demolish the world of heroic comedy; its "splendour" (l. 179) is granted, but it is a splendor that is alien to man and to nature—finally to life. Heroic comedy, it suggests, may move "near the Heavens" (l. 180) and elevate man to the company of the stars, but it is not pleasant: "What pleasure lives in height (the shepherd sang) / In height and cold" (ll. 178–79). The simplicity of the appeal is deliberate. Against the grandeur of isolation is placed mere comfortable joy.

Death, ice, and blasted pines, wild eagles, and especially the image of great waterfalls that break up a mighty stream into diffusive foam "that like a broken purpose waste[s] in air" (l. 199) make up the pointless, lonely world of irony. Domestic comedy offers fulfillment, sexuality, and, most of all, an integral place in teeming life. All nature awaits the maid's coming and participates in her welcome. The final promise is contained in the merging of the sweetness of her own voice with the sweetness and abundance about her. The poem embodies the unified harmonies it discusses and thus revivifies pastoral clichés. The new comedy, in fact, works by asking that clichés be deliberately accepted as such, just as Ida accepts the cliché of feminine tenderness, the child, and the prince accepts the cliché of masculinity, "the blind wildbeast of force" (5, l. 256). The clichés are not confirmed but made over, so that childhood and age merge into maturity, the past and future into the eternal present.

The best part of the new solution, certainly, is that Ida does not completely abandon her dream: "She still were loth to yield herself to one / That wholly scorned to help their equal rights / Against the sons of men, and barbarous laws" (7, ll. 217–19). Tennyson wants still to keep alive the hope of heroic comedy. Both the poem's greatness and its major difficulties are due to this insistence. The fullest argument for the reconciliation of the two comic principles is found in the prince's long closing speech, but even that does not make such an impeccable case as one could hope for. He maintains, as one would suppose, that they should forget the past and all wasteful opposition between the sexes. "The woman's cause is man's," he says; "they rise or sink / Together, dwarfed or god-like, bond or free" (7, ll. 243–44). But the prince goes further: this unification is to be accomplished by a preservation of important differences.

Man and woman should each protect his "distinctive" unique-ness (thus the child and the war) in order to form a more perfect bond: "Not like to like, but like in difference" (7, l. 262). By doing so, they will quite undeliberately become more like each other, rising toward the ultimate goal: "The single pure and perfect animal, / The two-celled heart beating, with one full stroke, / Life" (7, ll. 288–90). Opposites are reconciled not by superficial, overt compromise but by a crystallizing act of the creative imagination. Their universality is ensured by their being most fully realized in their finite particularity; the poet attains to full creative participa-tion in the universe not by denying but by fulfilling his personality. The prince's paradoxical solution may baffle us, but it would have made good sense to Shelley and Keats.

The prince ends this climactic argument with a benedictory "May these things be!" (7, l. 280). One would suppose that all that remained would be an "Amen" and a wedding. But there is neither. The harmony is disrupted by the most startling and important lines in the poem: the princess responds to the prince's hope that all these things will be accomplished with a sighing "I fear / They will not" (7, ll. 280–81). The prince argues some more, but the princess again sighs and calls it "a dream" (l. 290). He then becomes less abstract, citing his mother as the type of perfection that can be realized in Ida and completed in marriage. Still, she resists: "It seems you love to cheat yourself with words: / This mother is your model" (ll. 314–15). The old theme of language reappears at the end to reassert the ambiguity of the situation and to hint at the final irreconcilability of the two comic modes. Ida suggests that the rhetoric is wearing a little thin, that the deceptive language can create a trap for them both. Ida cannot easily be mother or child to this child-man. She does not deny him, of course, and the fact that all her objections are put "tremulously" (l. 313) at the end does suggest that she is about to yield.

But her questions are never answered, and her doubts remain unresolved. The prince simply reasserts the vison of glorious comic existentialism—"all the past / Melts mist-like into this bright hour" (ll. 333–34)—and stops arguing. The final line of the narrative proper reinforces only the ambiguity: "Lay thy sweet hands in mine and trust to me" (l. 345). This is not what we would expect as the inauguration of "the single pure and perfect animal." We never hear Ida's answer. The poem thus ends on a question mark, with this image of the prince's condescension taking us back to the very source of all the trouble, indeed of the poem itself: " 'Where,' / Asked Walter, patting Lilia's head (she lay / Beside him) 'lives there such a woman [as the feudal warrior] now?' " (Prologue, ll. 124–26).

The poem that arises from an act of condescension may, then, close with one, hinting at an ironic circularity that mocks the ostensible educational progress of the poem's narrative. Perhaps no one learns anything. These questions concerning the poem's efficacy, as well as its cause and relevance, are, surprisingly, points dealt with by the poem itself. *The Princess*'s frame, the elaborate modern idyl, not only surrounds the story of Ida[11] but also explains it. By maintaining an extensive series of parallels to characters and themes in the narrative, the frame acts as a commentary on that narrative and as a confirmation of its final ambiguity.

The prologue, the first half of the frame, provides a strong impetus to the argument for domestic comedy. It presents an image of discontinuity contained within and yielding to a larger continuity, the union of diverse elements in a single unit. The poem opens on a scene of harmony: the broad, sunny lawns of Sir Walter Vivian

---

11. The importance of the frame is also kept before us by Lilia's interruptions midway through the poem, between sections 4 and 5.

are given over to his tenants. The house itself is a unified medley of
styles, of places and times. It provides a sense of continuity and
control, of complete mastery: fossils become ornaments; lava is
made into "toys" (l. 18). The images of nature's awesome destruc-
tive power are thus made safe and manageable in the domestic
atmosphere. Though the tenants are there partly to learn, the
comic pedantry later to be associated with Ida's scheme is carefully
removed from these lessons. There are references to teachers and
"facts," but the real purpose is enjoyment. The "patient leaders of
their Institute" (l. 58) collect all manner of scientific equipment,
but it is used for quite unscientific purposes. The telescopes show
beautiful views, the electrical demonstration unites a group of girls
in a dancelike ring, and so forth. Sport and science are joined (ll.
79–80), with sport, clearly, out in front. There is thus a good deal of
light cast forward, anticipating the power of the domestic comedy
later to be fulfilled.

But against this background of harmony is the disharmony
among the young people, who forecast the tension and disunity of
the tale of Princess Ida. The argument among them is caused by
their response to a legend of female heroism, a story of a lady
fighting to preserve her will: "O noble heart who, being strait-
besieged / By this wild king to force her to his wish, / Nor bent, nor
broke" (ll. 36–38). Objectified by history, such a person becomes a
pleasant joke to the men, but she is a serious figure indeed to the
women. The resistance of the historical lady to the wild king's desire
to "force her to his wish" is subtly echoed in Lilia's contempt for
Walter's pat on her head. As in the main body of the poem, women
struggle against the smothering assumptions of male dominance.
Male courtesy is equated with brutal power, war with love songs.
The central conflict between heroism and gentle submission is thus
begun. The group becomes an image of ironic tension yearning for
resolution, divided against each other and against themselves.

The plan for the medley is a brilliant idea, for it promises to
provide an end to the quarrel and a new unity of time: "Why not a
summer's as a winter's tale?" The seven men are to speak as one,
with the women's voices separate and distinct but harmonious,
foreshadowing the unity of the prince's final argument. There is
also, in the very spontaneity of the poem's composition, a strong
echo of domestic comedy's insistence on natural development,
natural values. Finally, the light-hearted sense of game or interlock-

ing dance is also suggested, providing a context that is implicitly critical of solemnity, isolation, and rebellion.

But the ancient tale itself does not so single-mindedly support the values of domestic comedy. The historical lady, forced against her will, is the type both for the lonely figure of the princess, hammered at by men and held to a contract she considers "invalid, since my will / Sealed not the bond" (5, ll. 388–89), and also for little Lilia, who alone resists the aggression of the seven men. The ambiguity of the young people's position is made apparent immediately on the ending of the narrative in the Conclusion, where, after a moment of quiet, Walter, the male supremacist who had begun the conflict, is stirred to a deep and startlingly compassionate insight: "I wish she had not yielded!" (l. 5). All the prince's rhetoric has not been enough to erase from his mind the image of heroism dragged down. That Walter, of all people, should be the one to represent this response shows how deep the generic split has become and how impossible has been the task of merging heroic and domestic comedy.

The Conclusion proceeds, then, to the feud over tone and the decision to remold the work so as to find a unifying attitude toward its subject. Interestingly, Lilia, the frame's parallel to Ida, takes no part in the dispute but sits musing, plucking the grass, and wondering. Her sudden question to the aunt, "You—tell us what we are" (l. 34), is left unanswered, both because the workmen are now noisily taking their leave and because no answer would help. The lovely vision of harmony and satisfaction, then—"The happy valleys, half in light, and half / Far-shadowing from the west, a land of peace" (ll. 41–42)—is mocked by the unsettled dispute, the inadequate solutions, and the unresolved questions.

The poem focuses on Lilia for its close: "Last little Lilia, rising quietly, / Disrobed the glimmering statue of Sir Ralph / From those rich silks, and home well-pleased we went" (ll. 116–18). The feminine silks are removed from the noble Sir Ralph. The heroic and the domestic, male and female, thus safely disjoined, we could perhaps be "well-pleased," were it not for the fact that the poem has illustrated the price we pay for the easy pleasure of domestic comfort. Like Walter, we are haunted by Ida's fall and by the poem's refusal to evade the consequences of that fall: the sacrifice of the heroic will.

5

In Memoriam

But there is more than I can see,
And what I see I leave unsaid,
Nor speak it, knowing Death has made
His darkness beautiful with thee.

[sect. 74, ll. 9–12]

"Its faith is a poor thing, but its doubt is a very intense experience." [1] T. S. Eliot's famous judgment has a nagging persistence about it. Everyone quarrels with it, but no one lays it to rest. Of course the terms are useful: "faith" and "doubt" invoke issues both larger and more basic than religious faith or ponderings about the existence of God. The poem is, as Basil Willey says, concerned with questions that antedate Christianity, those which confront "the natural man." [2] The real problem is not the connection between God and man but the nature of connection itself; Tennyson searches not so much for religious continuity as for *any* continuity. *In Memorium* goes behind religion to the comic myth that informs and contains religion. But Eliot's comment suggests that the poem fails to locate that comedy effectively, that somehow the poem remains badly divided, unable satisfactorily to complete the two-part form it had set for itself.

Tennyson seeks to extend here the solution presented in *The Princess*. Both poems combine the traditions of the pastoral and of domestic comedy, and both are concerned with the isolation of the hero and his subsequent return to social acceptance. In each poem the central problem is the preservation of personality. But the enemies are very different. These differences—between the social enemies of convention, bigotry, and primitivism stressed in *The Princess*, and the cosmic ones of space, time, and death in *In*

1. "In Memoriam," *Essays Ancient and Modern*, pp. 200–01.
2. "Tennyson," *More Nineteenth Century Studies*, p. 81.

Memoriam—indicate to what extent the latter poem radically modifies the very convention it is, at the same time, accepting.

For one thing, the comedy of *In Memoriam* is much more venerable than that of *The Princess*. In place of the modern tradition of the comedy of manners, Tennyson looks to the firm order and values of medieval comedy. *In Memoriam* "was meant to be a kind of *Divina Commedia*," [3] he said. On the surface, *In Memoriam* is at the opposite pole from Dante's rational and ordered world: the occasion for Tennyson's poem appears to be the collapse of the very coherence that had sustained the earlier poem. Dante shows how the Inferno is itself a manifestation of God, is, in fact, contained in Him. The careful ordering and control of sinners and punishments gives continual evidence of the exercise of reason and justice. Paradise is implied by Inferno; it is its logical and certain complement. Since it is just this harmonious superstructure of accepted cosmological certainty that Tennyson lacks, he must find a new way to order the vision of his new and modern hell. He does so by creating a comparable argument that shows solution in the midst of dissolution—more specifically, that faith lives in and is assured by doubt, that death leads to life. The affirmations do not transcend the negations but grow through them. All of life is a single and coherent unity.

The point is stated most argumentatively and directly in section 96, added very late, even after the trial edition of March 1850. Here the poet summarizes and explains the basis for the climactic vision recorded in the previous lyric and for the positive resolution of the poem: "And Power was with him in the night, / Which makes the darkness and the light, / And dwells not in the light alone, / But in the darkness and the cloud" (ll. 18–21). It is necessary to the poem's solution that the unity should come not merely from a happy ending that shows "light" triumphant but from a coalition of the two opposites. The predominant darkness must yield to the light, but the light must be shown to proceed directly from the darkness. The despair of the first half of the poem must contain within it the hope of the conclusion. It is customary to cite as somehow cogent Henry Sidgwick's comment, recorded in the *Memoir*, that "the

3. *Memoir*, 1:304. Gordon D. Hirsch, "Tennyson's *Commedia*," *VP* 8 (1970): 93–106, gives a detailed comparison of the two works, arguing that *In Memoriam* is "an embodiment of the Dantean theories of Arthur Hallam" (p. 98).

whole truth is that assurance and doubt must alternate." [4] But *In Memoriam* is an attempt to go beyond alternations or the suspended, doubtful comedy of poems like "The Two Voices," into complete assurance. The two alternatives must be made one, and this unity must be implied from the first dark lyric. This, then, is *In Memoriam*'s debt to *The Divine Comedy*: Tennyson is attempting to rebuild a world of meaning by rebuilding medieval comedy.

He substitutes for the implied structural logic of this medieval form a new and profound generic argument, whereby the absence of order is made a necessary antecedent to order. The causelessness mirrored in the first half of the poem and its parody of tragic values are made part of a larger system of confirmed and settled values, a system that does not escape but includes its own rejection. By treating Hallam's death not as a tragedy but as a grotesque mockery of life itself, the early sections of the poem establish a viewpoint that is explicitly ironic. The irony is defined, however, as always, in reference to a competing order. Here the arguments of life and happiness, the symbols of rebirth in nature, the lures of friendship and communion—in short, all the components of comedy—are used in the first half of the poem to show how futile and pointless the narrator's griefs and hopes are. That is, the comic images create by their concurrent power and remoteness the narrator's ironic bondage.

Tennyson is careful always to present the positive values with some measure of validity; they themselves are never mocked. What *is* mocked is the human tendency to live by a system of promises that is now rendered irrelevant. The momentum of comedy continues long after its true substance has been lost and appears to make a dupe of hopeful man. The irony thus holds comedy in suspension; it makes it one half of its argument. The early lyrics derive their power from an evocation of the distance between the narrator and a very real and promising order. From the very first lyric we are made aware of the solution.[5] These inescapable

4. *Memoir*, 1:304.

5. A similar perception is applied somewhat differently but with some of the same results by Michael Y. Mason, "*In Memoriam*," *VP* 10 (1972): 161–77, in reference to the psychology of the poem; by Ward Hellstrom, *On the Poems of Tennyson*, pp. 54–64, in reference to the poem's imagery; and most notably by Francis P. Devlin, "Dramatic Irony in the Early Sections of Tennyson's *In Memoriam*," *PLL* 8 (1972): 172–83. Professor Devlin's argument that the narrator early "expresses his obsession with death and separation through imagery connoting rebirth and renewal" (p. 173) is parallel to mine. I do not think that the narrator

connections between comedy and irony often proved very trouble-some for Tennyson, shadowing and disrupting his attempted affirmations, but here he attempts to use these same connections to assure the validity of those affirmations.

It is more proper, then, to speak of the poem's organization than its structure. *In Memoriam* mirrors the absence of a structured world in its deliberate discontinuities, its utterances that refuse to connect easily or logically. The poem explores how man can live in a world that is denied easily perceived structure, one where human experience can no longer be explained by analogy with linear mathematics. Attempts to divide the poem into integral parts, whether based on the Christmas sections, the anniversary poems, or Tennyson's own nine-part scheme, depend upon notions of linearity and regularity that the poem regards as no longer valid.[6]

The poem is determined, I believe, by the dynamics of the opposition between comedy and irony, a counterplay that is progressive but irregular. Though the irony gradually moves toward comedy, the movement is not fully continuous—there are lapses, pauses, even doublings-back—nor is it completed. Nonethe-less, there is a pivotal section where, at the climax of the nihilistic fury, the narrator suddenly stops and effects by the power of his will[7] a change in mood and attitude. Irony does not gradually diminish and then melt into comedy; it increases, becomes more and more powerful, until, just at its height, it seems for a time to disappear. Though irony later reappears, one can see the poem trying to move decisively away from the Inferno.

Just after the climactic statement of cosmic trickery in section 56,

"ignores or slights" these connotations (p. 170), though, or that there is a separation at this point between narrator and poet that would lead to "dramatic irony." W. David Shaw's "*In Memoriam* and the Rhetoric of Confession," *ELH* 38 (1971): 80–103 provides excellent generic criticism from another direction. He relates the poem and many of its structural details to the tradition of confessional literature. He also argues, as I do, that the poem's final resolution is given very early. Since his own evidence (see pp. 82, 92–97) for the poem's "circular form" is different from my own, I take it that our studies are complementary.

6. That the poem's structure is not architectural but developmental is supported by Alan Sinfeld's brilliant work, *The Language of Tennyson's "In Memoriam."* See also Mason, "*In Memoriam,*" and John D. Boyd, "*In Memoriam* and the 'Logic of Feeling,' " *VP* 10 (1972): 95–110.

7. The importance of the will in the strategy of the entire elegy is discussed by William Brashear, who claims that the real victory is in "the triumph of the 'living will' " (*The Living Will*, p. 105; see pp. 92–114), and by K. W. Gransden, who says, "Much of *In Memoriam* is . . . a search for a formula of endurance" (*Tennyson: In Memoriam*, p. 25).

where man, "who seemed so fair," becomes "a monster," "a dream, / A discord" (ll. 21–22), Tennyson attempts to mark a division and to begin developing the new hope that comes from the darkness:

> Peace; come away: the song of woe
>   Is after all an earthly song:
>   Peace; come away: we do him wrong
> To sing so wildly: let us go.
>
> Come; let us go: your cheeks are pale;
>   But half my life I leave behind:
>   Methinks my friend is richly shrined;
> But I shall pass; my work will fail.
>
> Yet in these ears, till hearing dies,
>   One set slow bell will seem to toll
>   The passing of the sweetest soul
> That ever looked with human eyes.
>
> I hear it now, and o'er and o'er,
>   Eternal greetings to the dead;
>   And 'Ave, Ave, Ave,' said,
> 'Adieu, adieu' for evermore.
>
>   [sect. 57]

The "Peace" with which the section opens forecasts the "All is well" that closes the entire poem. The peace is apparently uncaused, a relaxation from the previous strain into a great simplicity. The horrible dilemmas that had occupied the poet up to this point are, "after all," only "earthly," a dismissal which seems to work precisely because it refuses detailed explanations. He has somehow evolved or willed a new perspective, one that is not yet clearly defined, except that it depends upon something other than the "earthly."

The section's sad tone, of course, includes the earlier despair; it really does not dismiss it. But this section also faces death more directly and personally than any lyric so far. The simplicity of "The passing of the sweetest soul / That ever looked with human eyes" (ll. 11–12) implies a new, unexaggerated acceptance. The fact of death is now confirmed as it had not been before, almost suggesting a mastering of that fact. Even the control of diction and phrasing implies a newly gained mastery. The second stanza does express concern about himself and his poetry, but such matters are quickly cast aside. The language of poetry is no longer, as it was, a shield against the terror of death but a means of controlling and understanding it. Death could earlier be admitted only as a force distinct from personality. If love could survive, the poet had argued, it must survive in a preservation of personality.

As long as death is seen as annihilation, then, it could never be allowed to have touched the essential person. Death and personality are joined now for the first time, and the potential solution is thus foreshadowed. Those "terribly pathetic lines" [8] from Catullus—*ave atque vale*—which end the lyric evoke a sad continuity through time, a union of all who have been left desolate by death and who could yet summon will and energy to continue. His benediction summarizes the poem to this point by concluding the meditation on death; it also points the way forward by evoking a new power of controlled articulation that is bound to find a new form in which to express itself. With section 57 we are at the planned center of the poem. The negative issues have presumably been resolved, and the rest of the poem should image the rehabilitation of the narrator and give form to the comic values already there by implication.

While it is true that the irony is never quite contained by the comedy, one can see the dualistic pattern at least in the process of developing, both in theme and technique. The general tension between assured technique and highly tentative statement[9] in the first half of the poem is generally dissolved in the second half. The tentativeness is still sometimes there, but it is no longer covered or submerged; where there is shifting or hesitancy it is on the surface and more often expresses not doubt but a search for the most honest and precise expression. Ideas are not tested and rejected in the second half, but refined; certainties are not discarded, but rephrased.

The same principle of reversal between the first and second halves applies as well to most of the key themes of the poem. Nature, for instance, whose evidences of waste and purposeless slaughter provide such an apt and inescapable analogy to his despair, develops in the second half into an image of peace and

8. This is Tennyson's own description of these lines; see Ricks, p. 913.

9. Gransden, *Tennyson*, p. 44, demonstrates this point admirably, though he treats as valid for the whole poem what seems to me true only for the first half.

hope. It becomes, as James Benziger says, an "imaginative counter-part" to the logical argument from design;[10] so that, though rejecting the argument, the poet can accept the intuition. Also, as he himself comes to life, he brings nature back to life with him. The traditional pastoral element in the poem, then, though muted, is not at all incidental. It is used in the first half to indicate what is missing from the poet's condition and from his world,[11] so that in the second half the pastoral values may be affirmed. The continu-ous presence of nature's hope for restoration and rebirth, even in parody, foreshadows the narrator's planned restoration.

The plan, then, is that the solution be embedded in the presentation of the problem. The problem is occasioned by death and exacerbated by science but it is not centered in either of these; rather, the poem accepts a less pretentious and more difficult subject: "I long to prove / No lapse of moons can canker Love, / Whatever fickle tongues may say" (sect. 26, ll. 2–4). *Proving*, of course, involves the question of the nature of knowledge and the conflict between empirical and imaginative ways of knowing. Once he finds out *how* to prove, the answers are much easier to find. The other important components of the poem—love, time, self ("*I* long to prove")—are all suggested here. He is out to demonstrate the validity of his own self and the human personality generally by establishing that its primary value—love—has permanence. Love guarantees the authenticity of the self in time, and the rediscovered self proves the supremacy of love: the terms of the problems move toward mutual solution. Time, the "lapse of moons," suggests all motion and change, not just death, and becomes the active agent in the equation, the catalyst of the poem. It first separates the self and love and thus renders them both suspect; it later brings them together in a new and more permanent harmony.[12]

One final important element of the problem is also suggested in the line "Whatever fickle tongues may say." These fickle tongues suggest the denials voiced by irony, faithless to him and to

10. "Tennyson" in *Images of Eternity*, p. 147.

11. This point is also emphasized by Buckley, *Tennyson*, p. 115, though he does not make the necessary allowance for the poem's duality and therefore talks of what happens in half the poem as though it occurred throughout.

12. There is an excellent discussion of the role time plays in the poem by J. C. C. Mays, "*In Memoriam*: An Aspect of Form," *UTQ* 35 (1965): 30–31. He argues that it is time which resolves opposites and solves the problems in the poem.

themselves, refusing to provide even the constancy of negation. But they also represent outside voices, an external society that first alienates and then welcomes the narrator. He must try to find a solution that first brings into accord the self and its essential principle of love and then moves this unified self out of its privacy and into social being. To do this he must come to terms with time (including death), the natures of self and of love, and the connection between his private and public selves.

These are not, of course, four problems, but one, and the solution likewise is a single one. It is provided by the *experience* of love, but love of a special sort. It is not a self-denying, ascetic, or exalted love, but a love based on a vivid realization of common life and a full participation in it. Valerie Pitt calls this love simply "friendship," [13] which describes it very well. Tennyson is drawn away from philosophical and theological argument, even from the ecstatic spiritual love that is celebrated in his model, *The Divine Comedy*. As in *The Princess*, the "azure pillars of the hearth" are sweeter and more real than heroic isolation. The guarantee of love's perpetuation is its existence in *him*, not in Hallam; in life, not in or beyond death. *In Memoriam* leaves its ostensible subject further behind than the most disengaged elegy. It is highly personal, of course, but in the end it sacrifices the unique personality of Hallam for that of the narrator. The values of domestic comedy, of friendship and unremarkable love, are substantiated and win out over the arguments of philosophy, science, personal grief, and the ironic perspective.

Almost, that is. If, as I have argued, the solution is contained in the form of the problem, if the irony is really forced to give way to comedy, then the power of the affirmation ought to be in direct proportion to the power of its negations. If the doubt is indeed "a very intense experience," as Eliot says, how can the faith be "a poor thing"? The fact is that comedy's move to dominate the poem is blocked by several very large problems: the nature of the narrator's particular demands; the dangerous movement toward vague abstraction in the solution; and, most important, a clear breakdown in the comic machinery, a disturbance of the solution at section 100 which continues, more or less, until the end of the poem. The existence of these problems means that the pattern of the poem is

13. *Tennyson Laureate*, p. 115.

never quite completed; the counterplay between comedy and irony is never entirely resolved.

Perhaps the most obtrusive of these problems is the early insistence that any sort of rehabilitation would mean the death of love. He ties himself so closely to the figure of Hallam that a clear dilemma occurs; insofar as he remembers that half his life is left behind with Hallam, he has little chance to develop, to master, or even to understand his grief; insofar as he does grow, he is disproving what he set out to prove, that "no lapse of moons can canker Love." There are ways out of this problem, but Tennyson seems uncomfortable with any one of them; so he gives several. As a result, none seems very convincing: many seem too general (the evolutionary argument, for instance) or too flippant.

The most persuasive argument is based on the experience of transitory but very intense imaginative or mystical visions. During these visions, love is made permanent and the poet understands and affirms his own real self. Though the visions themselves do not last, their authenticity is secured by memory, so that the child, even though crying, senses that help and security are nearby, in his father. But this argument from memory is not quite enough to override the loss of the enthusiasm which is present only during the fleeting moments of visionary experience. Full certainty, therefore, is withheld.

Also, as Tennyson moves away from Hallam—and the solution of the poem demands that he must do so—the love that he talks about tends to become more and more generalized and abstract. *In Memoriam* really needs a Beatrice, and we can see Tennyson searching for substitutes among his relatives. The poem becomes a romantic comedy with no romance. "Friendship" does seem to provide the implied solution, but where is that friendship bodied forth?

This lack of concreteness is made doubly important by the poet's refusal, early in the poem, to accept any form of the continuation of life other than the highly concrete preservation of the individual personality. In a powerful and almost primitive way that explains much of the poem's appeal and authority, he insisted that only the survival of the unique ego had meaning. The concept that the fragmented soul is reunited in death with the great "general Soul" he bluntly called "vague," grandly asserting that in the afterlife "Eternal form shall still divide / The eternal soul from all beside"

(47, ll. 6–7). The fact that at the end of the poem the poet sees
Hallam as a "diffusive power" (130, l. 7) does not necessarily imply
a contradiction: it may simply be the result of his new development.
But the development, in that case, is from the concrete to the
abstract—an unusual and difficult direction for comedy to take.
Eliot's feeling that the abstraction was "a poor thing" may be due
in part to private aesthetic preferences to which we may refuse to
grant any authority, but it is almost certain that he felt, as well, the
violation of the comic tradition in which Tennyson was writing.

These qualifications would not, perhaps, amount to much if it
were not for the sudden buckling of the comic solution with section
100 and beyond. Tennyson turned all his art—even the power of his
ironic vision—to the defeat of irony. But it could not be done.

The first half of *In Memoriam*, up to lyric 56, presents the poem's
affirmations by inversion. The vision in this part mocks comedy so
continuously that the solutions are held in suspension; they are so
nearly fully developed that they should only need to be released in
the second half of the poem. The poem begins in the first lyric by
explicitly rejecting one form of what it will later accept: the
rejuvenation of self and the rebuilding of something out of nothing,
the doctrine "That men may rise on stepping-stones / Of their dead
selves to higher things" (ll. 3–4). Such a consolation now seems
callously abstract, a superficial matter of "loss" and "gain," mere
monetary "interest" (ll. 6, 8) that cannot touch the depth of the
narrator's grief. All assurances, even the most profound ones, are
irrelevant. They point to the future, and the future, though it will
later hold all promise, now presents the greatest threat. "Let Love
clasp Grief" (l. 9), he cries, voicing what is now only an emotional
need but forecasting the uniting of affirmative love and negative
grief, of faith and doubt.

The first lyric evokes a fear not of pain but of the absence of
feeling, of a detachment that will finally be a necessary prelude to
restoration. The early poems are not so much unwilling displays of
emotion as deliberate proofs of it. The narrator begins by struggling
against the solution that is there before him. He does all he can to
solidify his negative, dead love, to nurse his self-absorbed and static
being, and to resist the pull of expansive, outgoing love and a
growth into new being. The strength with which the comic
generalizations are rejected anticipates their later acceptance.

The second lyric, "Old Yew, which graspest at the stones," similarly presents to us a negative image of hope and beauty by inverting the values of the pastoral. The Romantic dream of imaginative identification with nature is accomplished—and turned into a nightmare. Time, whose cycles bring life to nature— "The seasons bring the flower again, / And bring the firstling to the flock" (ll. 5–6)—also operates linearly, bringing only destruction to man: "And in the dusk of thee, the clock / Beats out the little lives of men" (ll. 7–8). The cycles of nature are cruel deceptions,[14] mocking the narrator and forcing on him a consciousness of his own eventual annihilation. So he turns to the yew, whose "fibres net the dreamless head" (l. 3), as a symbol of stasis, a form that is so incorporated with death that it "changest not in any gale" (l. 10). The one stable image is of grief; the one natural symbol that remains constant does so only because it is fed by death, in turn the only immutable fact of existence. At the climax of the lyric the poet achieves a union with the plant, grimly burlesquing the true imaginative act. He finds not liberation but ironic paralysis: "I seem to fail from out my blood" (l. 15).

Lyric 39 returns to the image of the yew to cap this irony. The narrator recognizes that the plant does, after all, partake of nature's cycles, flowering and sending forth its "fruitful cloud and living smoke" (l. 3). It is part of spring's renewal: "To thee too comes the golden hour / When flower is feeling after flower" (ll. 6–7). But the voice of Sorrow disrupts the idyllic reflection with the dark suggestion that the flowering of the yew involves no real change but a simple succession of gloom and death, paralleling the poet's change, which is no change: "Thy gloom is kindled at the tips, / And passes into gloom again" (ll. 11–12).

Though it has earlier been established (3, l. 4) that Sorrow lies, Sorrow is the informing voice of the poem at this point. The ambiguous lying does allow us to perceive that the fruitfulness of nature and its power to create life out of death are never questioned. In fact, they are presented vividly and feelingly precisely because they are so real and so distant from man. Furthermore, even in lyric 39, where the tone becomes particularly

14. The parody of comic rebirth is reinforced by the fine section 7, "Dark house, by which once more I stand," where the "noise of life" breaks on his terrible solitude, not to bring a return to normal human bustle and activity, but only the "ghastly rain" and an image of nothingness: "On the bald street breaks the blank day."

sardonic and where the narrator is caught between the alternate traps of everlasting change and everlasting death, the eventual answer is given: a stability that contains all variability. He had identified (in 3) with what he had assumed was the constant yew but now finds himself caught up in a process of growth. He is now tempted to see that growth as sheer chaos, but out of these ironic perceptions can come comic ones. By associating with paralytic grief, he can find rehabilitation. Out of death, then, comes life, just as the yew itself symbolizes a great vital constancy that pervades and controls all seeming change.

In the first phase of the poem similar images of nature are always kept before us. Nature's power is seen as deceptive; it can restore, but man appears somehow to be excluded from the restoration. Though it is evoked with great bitterness, this constant acknowledgment of nature's potency is a way of building a solution as well as solidifying the irony. Even in the most ironic of these lyrics, nature mocks man only with its manifestly authentic powers. In 11, "Calm is the morn without a sound," for instance, nature is allowed the ability to create a unity of all divine elements—"Calm and still light on yon great plain / That sweeps with all its autumn bowers, / And crowded farms and lessening towers, / To mingle with the bounding main" (ll. 9–12). It is just this unity, reinforced by the repetition of *calm,* that makes for the shock that comes at the end:[15] "Calm on the seas, and silver sleep, / And waves that sway themselves in rest, / And dead calm in that noble breast / Which heaves but with the heaving deep" (ll. 17–20). The mellifluous flow is halted abruptly in the next-to-last line, only to return again in the ending line, with a new and startling force.

Even more subtle is the combined attack on and support of nature in the famous "The Danube to the Severn gave," section 19. It begins with nearly the same bitter tone that had marked the close of 11: "The Danube to the Severn gave / The darkened heart that beat no more; / They laid him by the pleasant shore, / And in the hearing of the wave." There are clear specific ironies in *pleasant* and

15. Ben W. Fuson, "Tennyson's 'In Memoriam,' XI," *Explicator* 4 (1946): 34, gives this same argument: "with sudden shock the reader senses the hitherto half-obscured chasm between the vibrant peace of Nature and the ultimate immobility of death." For a counterargument, see R. A. Foakes, *The Romantic Assertion,* p. 125: "the imagery counterbalances the overt statement of mood, and the effect of the lyric is one of hope rather than despair."

in the presumed life-giving quality of the waves, conveniently within "hearing," if only the corpse could hear. The salt water that hushes the Wye (ll. 5–8) kills off the babbling joy of the river and parallels the unfruitful condition of the narrator's deepest grief. The tide does go out, of course, but it releases only grief, a song of pain. The movements of nature thus seem elaborately and completely parodied. But the facts that the poet's state does change—"My deeper anguish also falls" (l. 15)—and that he gets even a "little" relief (l. 16) suggest that these cycles are not exactly pointless and that perhaps nature can effect more permanent and lasting changes as well. For all the varieties of irony Tennyson uses in this first section, he almost always shuns the conclusive final ironies of, say, Clough, preferring a more tentative and ambiguous form that is generically less stable but more profound.

The refusal to rest with definite conclusions is itself an ironic tendency, but it is a slippery characteristic which, however powerful in its support of irony, can be used against irony itself. It can, as Tennyson had displayed in the 1842 *Poems*, work against ironic conclusions as well as any other, and when tentative skepticism is established as a firm principle, it really points the way out of irony. This is especially true when it is used in conjunction with the further ambiguous symbol of nature. In section 23, "Now, some- times in my sorrow shut," the narrator imagines a time in the past when he and Hallam were in full accord with each other and with all of natural life: "And all the secret of the Spring / Moved in the chambers of the blood" (ll. 19–20). The past is presented as a fully realized pastoral in order to emphasize the completeness of his present desolation. The following section, then, by questioning the accuracy of this vision of the past—"and was the day of my delight / As pure and perfect as I say?" (24, ll. 1–2)—both increases and decreases the pain. If even memory lies, then the dead one is yet further removed; but if the past were not Edenic the present is in some sense less horrible and perhaps more endurable. Though it is terrible to doubt that past, the perception that "The very source and fount of Day / Is dashed with wandering isles of night" (24, ll. 3–4) is central to his recovery. At the heart of day is night, just as despair lies at the beginnings of hope.

Occasionally, even in the early sections of *In Memoriam*, the comedy does not lie hidden within the irony but exists side by side with it. Most of the utterances on the function of poetry, for instance, are overtly ambiguous: "For words, like Nature, half reveal / And half conceal the Soul within" (5, ll. 3–4). Language, which is here used consciously as a protection—"In words, like weeds, I'll wrap me o'er, / Like coarsest clothes against the cold" (5, ll. 9–10)—also acts, by its very nature, to *reveal*, to formulate and clarify. In the process of evading the unknown, then, he is discovering it; by seeking to bury himself in the past, he is unconsciously penetrating into the future, creating a new self while hiding in the old one.

A good many of the early poems really constitute direct statements on this use of irony both to contain and to release. *In Memoriam* openly manifests a concern with its own form. The controlling tones of Sorrow, the commanding voice of the first part of the poem, are explicitly the tones of irony: " 'The stars,' she whispers, 'blindly run; / A web is woven across the sky; / From out waste places comes a cry, / And murmurs from the dying sun' " (3, ll. 5–8). The narrator's response to this voice is, characteristically, uncertain. Sorrow offers "fellowship" (l. 1), but it is a "cruel fellowship"; her voice is "sweet and bitter in a breath" (l. 3). These oxymorons lead the poet to a frozen attitude: "And shall I take a thing so blind, / Embrace her as my natural good; / Or crush her, like a vice of blood, / Upon the threshold of the mind?" (ll. 13–16). The narrator is caught by the ironic voice, suspended between impossibilities, and unable to accept or reject it.

But there are wheels within wheels in irony, and the strategy of caving in foundations can operate endlessly. Since Sorrow's voice might be withstood by employing detachment, Sorrow is made subject to mutability. A constant predictable urge could never operate in a relativistic world; therefore, Sorrow itself changes: can "sorrow such a changeling be?" (16, l. 4). Even her changefulness is not certain; perhaps she only "seem[s] to take / The touch of change" (ll. 5–6) and actually has the deep constancy of "some dead lake" (l. 8). Thus, Sorrow is not so easily defeated, and the narrator is left, as he says, like a ship that "staggers blindly ere she sink" (l. 14). Sorrow's wiliness has "stunned me from my power to think / And all my knowledge of myself" (ll. 15–16). At the center of the poem is this destruction of self and a consequent rebuilding, a process identical with the growth out of irony. As of now, he is held fast, and he is without any certainty at all, "delirious" (l. 17), one who "mingles all without a plan" (l. 20).

"I do but sing because I must / And pipe but as the linnets sing" (21, ll. 23-24) suggests that the language follows its only possible form, the fragmented form of the early sections. The use of nature as a model also suggests, however, a movement away from disconnection and toward natural harmony. He sings of the fundamental facts of existence, those that now appear to be beneath the superficialities of public language, the assured and solid language of external purpose urged on him by the social world (21, ll. 5-20). But it is this natural, presumably private language that leads him to inevitable growth and participation in public life. Words not only conceal; they half reveal. This clarifying function allows for the development out of the sporadic, unjoined utterances of irony into the lucid, transparent diction of comedy.

For beneath all the change and destruction on the surface of nature lies the fundamental constancy of life, a solidity he senses even far below his deep despair. The Christmas bells and the hope they represent recall him from thoughts of suicide, overriding his anguish and mastering his spirit completely, "For they controlled me when a boy" (28, l. 18). The clear instincts of childhood capture the adult and hold him away from negative solutions. "They bring me sorrow touched with joy" (l. 19), he says, an uncomfortable mixture, certainly, but one that maintains present life and gives some hope for the future.

The entire first section of *In Memoriam*, despite its full awareness of pain, is filled with a concurrent recognition that in this pain lies hope for a solution. Section 27 and its famous conclusion—" 'Tis better to have loved and lost / Than never to have loved at all" (ll. 15-16)—is a welcoming of duality. Pain comes from the consciousness of loss, but that consciousness would never be present without love. Only one who has "tasted love with half his mind" (90, l. 1)—one, that is, who has never known the full power of contradiction—can rest in comfortable negatives. The force of duality is finally the force of love, a love that is established only by loss. Section 27 specifically rejects releases from tension through either unconsciousness or an avoidance of feeling. He will shun neither the experience of love nor the prison that experience may build. It is this deliberate and heroic acceptance of irony that, in the end, neutralizes its destructive power.

All this is even more overtly stated in section 34:

My own dim life should teach me this,
   That life shall live for evermore,
   Else earth is darkness at the core,
And dust and ashes all that is;

This round of green, this orb of flame,
   Fantastic beauty; such as lurks
   In some wild Poet, when he works
Without a conscience or an aim.

What then were God to such as I?
   'Twere hardly worth my while to choose
   Of things all mortal, or to use
A little patience ere I die;

'Twere best at once to sink to peace,
   Like birds the charming serpent draws,
   To drop head-foremost in the jaws
Of vacant darkness and to cease.

The argument is very straightforward: the ironic perspective, when seen clearly, provides sufficient cause for rejecting it. Though the negative force of the images is great indeed, at least the form of the argument is insistently positive.[16] It is purely a poetic argument, but nonetheless appealing for that. It is based on a sense of proportion, on tact or perhaps even taste, suggesting that life itself ("My own dim life") contains nothing that can justify the monstrously incongruous notion of extinction. If death means extinction, questions about the existence of God become absurd. Life itself would be pointless, and the poet would, in a term that parodies Keats's vision of sweet death, "cease." But it is *Life* that gives the evidence against its own cessation and against irony.

The next section, "Yet if some voice that man could trust" (35), carries on the discussion of irony's form and limitations and, beneath that, a battle against its dominance. The poet considers what he could do if he heard from a reliable voice beyond the grave

16. W. David Shaw interestingly argues that the poem's affirmations are carried by its images and metaphors and that its skepticism is put argumentatively ("Transcendentalist Problem," *PQ* 46 [1967]: 89). It is a good perception of what happens in *some* of the *early* poems, of which this section (34) is only one exception. In the last half of the poem imagery and argument are generally conjoined.

argument is clearly developing toward its turning point: love has *some* validity or there would be no perception of irony. The fact of pain, then, is cause for hope.

This complex duality informs not only those poems which directly address the subject of form but also more indirect ones, even, or especially, those whose focus seems far removed from aesthetics, the domestic poems. No single metaphor is more pervasive in *In Memoriam* than that of the family and its attendant images: marriages, dinner parties, Christmas celebrations, visits, handshakes.[17] The principal charge against death is that he "broke our fair companionship" (22, l. 13), thus putting the case in the simple and familiar terms in which it must also be solved. The narrator views external disruptions—in science, theology, and the state—only as analogues to his private chaos. The single real problem is the disruption of the family, the breaking of companionship. All the world falls apart as a result. But, by the same equation, as the narrator rebuilds the coherence of his private life and re-forms the family, he re-creates the world. The domestic values provide a concrete symbolic center for the poem.

The images of the family also help to assert a world of calm, settled values that is, at first, thrown off balance. The implied solidity of this world suggests, at the same time, that it is bound to right itself in the natural course of things. Further, the loss is made as common and as immediate as possible by deliberately putting it in the most recognizable language—the language of sentiment, nearly the language of platitudes. Tennyson manages to appeal to the broadest range of experience in these poems and, at the same time, to avoid superficiality by enclosing the sentiment within irony. Domestic values, potentially soft as they are, are given authority by the toughness surrounding them. The most striking domestic reference in the poem is the analogy of the narrator's state to that of a widow or widower, used partly to reinforce the intensity of the anguish by giving it a physical or sexual component, but also to evoke by far the most common experience of intense loss we know personally.

The language in these domestic sections strives for just this

17. See Gransden, *Tennyson*, pp. 15–17 and Foakes, *Romantic Assertion*, pp. 133–34. Both stress the importance of the family metaphor in *In Memoriam*. The domestic imagery is also discussed by Alan Sinfeld, *Language of "In Memoriam,"* pp. 112–15, and by Joanne P. Zuckerman, "Tennyson's *In Memoriam* as Love Poetry," *Dalhousie Review* 51 (1971): 202–17.

evoke by far the most common experience of intense loss we know personally.

The language in these domestic sections strives for just this quality of shared expression. Fluent verbal expression, as lyric 20 argues, is distrusted as a sign of artificial, surface grief. The servants of a house whose master is dead may "speak their feeling as it is, / And weep the fulness from the mind: / 'It will be hard,' they say, 'to find / Another service such as this' " (ll. 5–8). The degree of fluency in these biting lines is made directly proportionate to the absence of real feeling. The children can express grief only to themselves and only in the starkest and simplest terms: " 'How good! how kind! and he is gone' " (l. 20). It is often said that death proves the hopeless inadequacy of language, forcing us into the formulated meaninglessness of clichés, but here death acts to confirm the value of clichés and of the domestic simplicity supporting them.

But domesticity must initially be parodied. In the first half of *In Memoriam* it provides some of the most important subjects for irony, as in section 6: "O mother, praying God will save / Thy sailor,— while thy head is bowed, / His heavy-shotted hammock-shroud / Drops in his vast and wandering grave" (ll. 13–16). The malign trickery of nature and nature's God is given extra force here by being made to operate in a domestic framework that ordinarily excludes the absurd. Often the fact of death is made more immediate by understating it in this domestic context, comparing it not to the waste of continents but to simple loneliness, to deserted houses, parties ended, a lover "who 'lights and rings the gateway bell, / And learns her gone and far from home" (8, ll. 3–4).

In Memoriam comes close at times to "Enoch Arden." Even section 10, "I hear the noise about thy keel," moves for a moment out of the genre of pastoral elegy altogether and into the realm of melodrama or genre painting. It suggests, in feeling and form, something like Ford Madox Brown's *The Last of England*: "Thou bring'st the sailor to his wife, / And travelled men from foreign lands; / And letters unto trembling hands" (ll. 5–7). The lyric is especially interesting, though, in its clear demonstration of how such a vision can be contained and given power. The opening lines exhibit an excited sense of assurance: "I hear the noise about thy keel; / I hear the bell struck in the night: / I see the cabin-window bright; / I see the sailor at the wheel" (ll. 1–4). The reunion of man and wife, the reestablishing of all bonds is prefaced by an assertion of life and, particularly, the power of self—I hear, I see.

But all this life and joy yields completely to the fact of death, the "dark freight" (l. 8) that the ship also carries. The poet can, at the end, find "comfort" only in the fact that Hallam is not in the "roaring wells" (l. 17), where "hands so often clasped in mine, / Should toss with tangle and with shells" (ll. 19–20). This is a minimal comfort, but it is not parodied, nor is the lyric sentimental. The concreteness at both ends of the poem and the controlling ironic vision allow for the near-sentimentality at the center, the assertion of domestic values. Even the final dark image constitutes one half of the alternate domestic symbols: the empty and the joined hands. The alternatives of touch and emptiness are both maintained by the domestic focus; the empty hand demands a completion in such images as that of the family at Christmas "In a circle hand-in-hand" (30, l. 11).

The submerged force of domestic comedy is so strong that finally, in section 40, the poet makes a premature attempt to incorporate Hallam's death into the framework of domestic values. Hallam is compared to a bride on her wedding day, his death to her leaving for a new life. The analogy quickly breaks down, though—"Ay me, the difference I discern! / How often shall her old fireside / Be cheered with tidings of the bride" (ll. 21–23)—and the original cause for rejoicing becomes cause for additional pain. He sees his own life in very different terms: "My paths are in the fields I know, / And thine in undiscovered lands" (ll. 31–32). His problem is to extend the familiarity of the world of domestic comedy into the "undiscovered lands."

These lyrics preceding section 40 are almost totally dominated by irony. The poem begins at such a low point that it cannot really become tonally darker, but the problems do tend to complicate themselves and make the immediate dilemma seem worse and worse. In the lyrics from 40 to 49, however, there is a curious lightening of the tone, a series of musings on much happier suggestions: death may be only a sleep; the dead may remember their friends; personality may be continued after death. Section 46 even hints that death may only be an opening onto the past, so that the five years of love, while in one sense encapsulated, are, in another sense, open and eternal: "O Love, thy province were not large, / A bounded field, nor stretching far; / Look also, Love, a brooding star, / A rosy warmth from marge to marge" (ll. 13–16). But these hopeful lyrics (40 to 49) represent a false and unsustained movement upward. There is no real support, and all the early confidence is here expended, wasted on an abortive and premature attempt to escape. The failure leads directly, in 50 to 56, to the most extreme bondage and despair, formed in Tennyson's most unrelieved and inclusive irony.

Section 50, "Be near me when my light is low," immediately evokes paralysis. The slow cadence of the verse supports the image of stagnation and the argument that change is no change: "Be near me when my faith is dry, / And men the flies of latter spring, / That lay their eggs, and sting and sing / And weave their petty cells and die" (ll. 9–12). Even here, though there is no real hope, the desire for hope, at least, is kept alive. The form of address—"Be near me"—suggests a litany and implies that comfort is possible; more important, the reiterated *when* quietly implies that this is not the only state or the only perception.

When, in 53, the narrator attempts again to give a statement of the solution, even the light domestic form cannot be supported, and the affirmation collapses. He suggests that since many good and sober men have grown from noisy and wild youths, perhaps, "had the wild oat not been sown, / The soil, left barren, scarce had grown / The grain by which a man may live" (ll. 6–8). This is a hesitant and mild form of the argument that finally controls the poem: that God dwells in darkness and light and that doubt is contained within faith. But here, because the conjunction between faith and doubt cannot be made, he has no defense.

Sections 54–56, the famous "evolution" lyrics, do all irony can to drive a wedge between the unities that man has created: between intellect and emotion, motive and act, God and nature, man and God. Lyric 54 puts all its powerful negative imagery in a positive frame, this to parody the weak, multiple-qualified formal assertions —"Oh yet we trust that somehow good / Will be the final goal of ill" (ll. 1–2). Though the affirmation tries to stagger on, it cannot stand long against the force of the images: "That not a worm is cloven in vain; / That not a moth with vain desire / Is shrivelled in a fruitless fire, / Or but subserves another's gain" (ll. 9–12). The beginning hope dwindles by the end of the poem to the helpless cry of an abandoned and benighted child.

The next section, 55, summons conclusive irony to question the

basis of intuition—that is, the basis of religion and of self. All the
poet can receive finally is a faint trust, since nature not only gives
factual evidence against the doctrine of controlling love but also
"lends such evil dreams" (l. 6). It is not just the empirical judgment
that is corrupted but the imagination as well. Nature gives
intuitions too, it seems, and the dark power of these sections comes
not from any split between intellect and emotion but from a more
horrible division between a reality supported by reason *and*
intuition, and a hope that seems totally unsupported. Section 56
presents the nadir of the experience of *In Memoriam,* a vision of
hopelessness and waste. At the ironic center, the only coherent
ruling power is that of "discord" (l. 22). The one cosmic principle is
deception.

   Then suddenly, with the vision of futility at its most climactic, the
word *peace* is uttered and a change begins. The world and the poet
have been destroyed by an act of the imagination and must
similarly be built anew. The construction of a new self and a new
cosmos is the business of the second half of the poem. Or rather, of
about half of the second half of the poem; for the developing
solution progresses unsteadily and nearly collapses at about section
100. Before that, however, the comedy which had been held within
the irony is released, and the faith that lives in doubt and grows
from it begins to assert itself.
   In its catharsis of grief and mastering of the fact of death, the
transitional section 57 suggests an end to the entire poem. But what
has been achieved is only a negative triumph; the fuller comedy
begins to develop in section 58, in the announced decision to
continue the poem and to work toward genuine affirmation. More
important, even, the poet must develop a clear articulation of the
triumph he has in part already won. The struggle to put into words
the nature of his faith is partly a struggle to solidify that faith and
define his new self; but it is also partly a response to a newly felt
need to make his affirmations available to all. In order to realize his
new self he must move out of himself and thereby release the social
values implicit in domestic comedy. He decides not to conclude the
poem because his earlier exclamations of despair may have
disturbed others and "broke[n] the peace / Of hearts that beat from
day to day" (58, ll. 5–6).
   It is this "day to day" life to which he must now respond, the new

call of his "brethren" (l. 10) that not only brings him social responsibility but allows him the social definition of being. The domestic focus is, therefore, reasserted at once: "My spirit loved and loves him yet, / Like some poor girl whose heart is set / On one whose rank exceeds her own" (60, ll. 2–4). The imagery of these later domestic poems seems similar to that in the ironic poems, but there is a new tone and a new detachment. The poet seems able, in the poems from 60 to 70, to deal with Hallam much more personally and actually to experiment quite freely with domestic situations and images. There is a strong sense of liberation in this switch from hesitancy to creative freedom. Subjects and techniques shift rapidly, not necessarily because any one is unsatisfactory but because they are all satisfactory and give pleasure in the varieties of appropriateness they provide.

The poet first attempts the simple and undefensive "Love's too precious to be lost" (65, l. 3). The phrase has so much power that he sings it "Till out of painful phases wrought / There flutters up a happy thought, / Self-balanced on a lightsome wing" (ll. 6–8). A delicate happiness is found in the midst of pain, and the image of the reemerging butterfly provides the type for his rehabilitation. He goes on, in 66, to state that his loss, which, in one sense, has turned all to fruitlessness and waste, making "a desert in my mind" (l. 6), has, at the same time, increased his fellow feeling. Robbing him of one life, it has caused him to be more alive, "kindly with my kind" (l. 7). He compares himself to a man whose physical sight is lost but whose imaginative powers are thereby strengthened: "His inner day can never die, / His night of loss is always there" (ll. 15–16). The final symbol in 67, of Hallam's memorial tablet that "glimmers to the dawn" (l. 16) similarly uses a negative image to suggest positive effects, the sense of gain that comes from loss.

In one of the periodic summary sections, 69, "I dreamed there would be Spring no more," the poet stops to review his progress to this point. The dream charts his development away from the depths of irony, the vision of a dead nature. Isolated by his grief from all men and their "noisy town" (l. 5), he takes from nature a crown of thorns, symbolic of the ugliest negations of beauty and rebirth. Wearing this (that is, enunciating in poetry the negative vision of irony), he thereby turns it into "a civic crown" (l. 8), a badge of the great public service he is rendering through his vocal anguish. By entering the world of nature's deceptions, he will be able to clarify the meaning of life, rejuvenate nature herself, and bring life back to the world and to man. He sees himself as the suffering god who offers salvation. His purpose is misunderstood by men, who scorn him, but he is blessed by "an angel of the night" (l. 14), the divinity in Tennyson's hell, who brings the thorns "into leaf" (l. 18) and transforms death into life.

Though the words spoken by the angel "were hard to understand" (l. 20), and though the narrator is not yet able to explain exactly how it is that despair contains joy, the fact at least seems to be verified by the strongest experience. The thorns do come to life; the divine voice "was not the voice of grief" (l. 19). Though he must now try to interpret, for himself and the people for whom he suffered, the divine voice, the experience temporarily confirms the pattern whereby irony leads to comedy.

He now has such inward assurance that he can even raise with impunity the old specters of time and destruction: his verses will eventually be reduced by time to book bindings, box linings, curl papers. "But what of that?" (77, l. 13), he says. The ironic perspective can be grandly brushed aside. As in 57's "Peace, come away," the darkness is simply dismissed in the face of a "something else" (l. 11), which is again hard to understand but is certainly sweeter and truer. The sophistications of irony are opposed by the most unadorned simplicity.

Through these lyrics, Tennyson seems consistently to argue that his unhappiness is a matter of perspective, not a response to a unified, objective hopelessness. The anniversary of Hallam's death (section 72) again brings irony back, and with it a vision of the death of nature, but now there is at least a consciousness that nature only appears to be dead, or at least is dead only to him. Though the day is, in fact, stormy, he admits it might have "played / A chequer-work of beam and shade / Along the hills, yet looked the same" (ll. 14–16). This admission of relativism is crucial, since, even in this bleak poem, it allows that nature's restorative powers are still there.

He soon manages a partial reconciliation with death, at least in the abstract. By imagining Hallam's reaction to his own death, he sees that his wise friend would have turned "his burthen into gain" (80, l. 12). With this imaginative distance now achieved, the narrator suddenly grasps liberation: "His credit thus shall set me free" (l. 13). Death becomes an agent of love, saying, "My sudden frost was sudden gain, / And gave all ripeness to the grain, / It might have drawn from after-heat" (81, ll. 10–12). Death does not destroy love; it perfects it. Because of this general, if vague, assurance of gain, the narrator can reconcile himself to "Eternal process moving on" (82, l. 5) and to the fact that death does not mean waste or even destruction (82, ll. 9–12). But the comic momentum is suddenly checked: "For this alone on Death I wreak / The wrath that garners in my heart: / He put our lives so far apart / We cannot hear each other speak" (82, ll. 13–16). All the reassurances, it seems, are still too abstract. The inescapable insistence on personality keeps intruding, even here in the center of renewal. The deliberate honesty of *In Memoriam* holds it back from solutions that seem even the slightest bit facile.

As always in this second half of the poem, when the comedy falters and irony threatens to reappear, Tennyson turns to images in nature to renew confidence and reform the energies of the poem. In 83, "Dip down upon the northern shore," and especially in 86, "Sweet after showers, ambrosial air," nature's deep rhythms catch him up and he feels the elemental breath of life that provides a "peace" that is alive and vibrant, contrasting with the dead and awful "calm" of 11. Nature lends not only helpful analogies for his situation but life itself. The "Wild bird, whose warble, liquid sweet, / Rings Eden through the budded quicks" (88, ll. 1–2) is an evocation of a Hopkins-like symbol of compressed energy and life. But Tennyson's bird is more than just a symbol of Eden; it suggests the mixing of senses and the meeting of all passions (ll. 3–4), the ability to find "in the midmost heart of grief" (l. 7) instincts or energies that clasp "a secret joy" (l. 8). The bird sings of a new and modern Eden, a Paradise that is won out of the agony of loss and a self new-built. Having willed his own endurance, the narrator now sacrifices that will to the deep "glory of the sum of things" (l. 11) that now controls his vision even when he intends a song of woe.

Because of this unlooked-for new joy, he finds himself unable to rest only in the past, not because he forgets Hallam, but because their friendship is one that "had mastered Time" before and which now "masters Time indeed" (85, ll. 64, 65). He is not paralyzed by his love for Hallam but led outward to realize "The mighty hopes that make us men" (l. 60). Precisely because he never slackens in his love for his friend, he finds in his dedication a growth rather than a contraction of his affection. Even from the tomb, a voice speaks to him, "Arise, and get thee forth and seek / A friendship for the years to come" (ll. 79–80). He is unwilling yet to respond fully to this command, but he does realize that his heart "seeks to beat in time with one / That warms another human breast" (ll. 115–16).

The solutions are by now present, but the narrator is reluctant to accept them: they never seem fully adequate for very long. It is not, then, surprising that the progress is discontinuous, nor that he seems to welcome the frequent relapses. The early poems of the nineties (90 to 94) return again to the concrete absence of Hallam and the awful sense of physical separation the poet can never overcome. He almost implies that, if the personality is immortal (and it must be if immortality is to have meaning) and love depends on personality, then love can defeat death only by retaining contact with the actual person. He never really ceases to want kinetic proof.

But he can, at times, forget this impossible, self-defeating demand, particularly in the important 95, "By night we lingered on the lawn." This lyric climaxes the comic movement with a vision of absolute assurance, a full realization of a new self, and a concurrent realization of the unity of all creation in love. By tracing dark "Suggestion to her inmost cell" (l. 32), he finds not the expected darkness but hope. "The living soul was flashed on mine" (l. 36), and he feels "The deep pulsations of the world" (l. 40). Although he cannot explain his new state, he is transformed: "that which I became" (l. 48) is something essentially new and different. And though the mystical vision[18] is by its nature transitory and is itself "stricken through with doubt" (l. 44), the doubt is itself even more transitory. The lyric ends with a symbol of transcendence of this intellectual uncertainty: a breeze, "sucked from out the distant gloom" (l. 53), just as his hope has sprung from the blackness, comes up and spreads sweetness and beauty everywhere. The "doubtful dusk" (l. 49) yields the breeze's voice, "The dawn, the dawn" (l. 61). Death mingles with and becomes life: "And East and West, without a breath, / Mixt their dim lights, like life and death, / To broaden into boundless day" (ll. 62–64). Irony's tenuous mixture becomes comedy's pure and triumphant assertion of continuity.

He now does seem able to give some more direct explanation of

18. For an extended and convincing treatment of this section and of the importance of the mystical vision in *In Memoriam*, see Stephen Allen Grant, "The Mystical Implications of *In Memoriam*," *SEL* 2 (1962): 481–95; also Carlisle Moore, "Faith, Doubt, and Mystical Experience in *In Memoriam*," *VS* 7 (1963): 155–69.

his transformation, and he proceeds to do so in section 96, which justifies doubt by relating it to a God that lives in darkness as well as light. On the second anniversary of Hallam's death (99), then, he celebrates a kinship both with nature and with man. The impulses of autumn are those both of life and death; the "dim dawn" (l. 1) brings the voices of birds whose consolations are no longer mocked. Though he feels sorrow, it is no longer an isolated sorrow but a feeling of kinship with all mourners everywhere: "Today they count as kindred souls; / They know me not, but mourn with me" (ll. 19–20). Developing the suggestion first stated in the pivotal section 57, this lyric provides a proof of human connection and a social binding force. Death is not seen as insignificant, but the grief engendered by death can now be contained within greater comic forces.

But suddenly the assurances lose power and images of profound irony intrude. Partly because the issue of concrete personality and loss cannot be settled and partly because the solutions have been too abstract, all the hard-won sense of unity suddenly dissolves, and the narrator is nearly back where he began. "I think once more he seems to die" is the terrible reflection that ends lyric 100. The removal from Somersby, described in 100–05, seems to break all the connections he had established and to reintroduce the images of transience and annihilation. Section 101, in its grim force, is a poem that might have been found at the very beginning of *In Memoriam.* This lyric combines images of the impermanence of nature and its dislocation from man: "Unwatched, the garden bough shall sway, / The tender blossom flutter down, / Unloved, the beech will gather brown, / The maple burn itself away" (ll. 1–4).

The barely disguised sentimentality here, the heavy use of the pathetic fallacy, is used to set us up for the final irony, the impermanence and triviality of man: "As year by year the labourer tills / His wonted glebe, or lops the glades; / And year by year our memory fades / From all the circle of the hills" (ll. 21–24). There is no real connection between man and nature, certainly not the sentimental one with which the poem opened. The fact that the narrator cannot escape the remembrance that "There in due time the woodbine blows, / The violet comes, but we are gone" (105, ll. 7–8) means more than that he cannot forget Hallam. The general movements of life again alienate him; all solutions seem impersonal

and remote. Nature is able to create life out of death more fully
than man because nature cares little for memory or for concrete
personality. The power and supremacy of life are not denied, but
the narrator can acknowledge them only formally. The conclusive
affirmations never come.

Instead, the poem offers a wide range of solutions, a clear signal
that no one of them is adequate. "Ring out, wild bells" (106) offers
glib abstractions. The next section (107) tries for a highly unlikely
simple accommodation to a dark but uncomfortable world. It
begins by acknowledging the bitterness of Hallam's death, pauses,
and then abruptly switches its ground:

> . . . But fetch the wine,
> Arrange the board and brim the glass;
>
> Bring in great logs and let them lie,
>   To make a solid core of heat;
>   Be cheerful-minded, talk and treat
> Of all things even as he were by;
>
> We keep the day. With festal cheer,
>   With books and music, surely we
>   Will drink to him, whate'er he be
>
> [ll. 15–23]

The note of cheerfulness is in a different key entirely from
everything around it. The "whate'er he be," instead of affecting us
as a mature and hearty acceptance of death, seems, in context,
callous and insincere.

Still another inappropriate solution is given in the next lyric, 108,
"I will not shut me from my kind." The determination to "take
what fruit may be / Of sorrow under human skies" (ll. 13–14) is
precisely what we would have expected earlier, but here it is oddly
jumbled in as just one of many solutions. It is, further, made a
matter of steely determination rather than a consequence of natural
forces and natural development. Even the tone is petulant. Such
statements as "What profit lies in barren faith" (l. 5) strike us as
loudly evasive, jarring especially with the odd, sneering "profit."
Instead of welcoming human companionship, the narrator seems to
turn on his old sorrow, even on Hallam, with an almost childish
anger: "I will not eat my heart alone" (l. 3); " 'Tis held that sorrow
makes us wise, / Whatever wisdom sleeps with thee" (ll. 15–16).

There is a kind of coarseness about these last two sections, a quality that touches the poem so clearly as to allow Tennyson to introduce his most unconsidered and angry political views in the lines on "The blind hysterics of the Celt" (109, ll. 13–16). The poet is somehow relaxing here, writing away at a conclusion that has lost connection with the vital part of the poem to which it was attached. The moving and highly indirect eulogy of Hallam becomes a generalized and sometimes trite echo of early Trollope: "And thus he bore without abuse / The grand old name of gentleman" (111, ll. 21–22). For a short time, he can think of nothing better than this, or the almost ludicrous particularity of the vision of Hallam's future as "A life in civic action warm / A soul on highest mission sent, / A potent voice in Parliament" (113, ll. 9–11). One wonders that he did not specify the borough!

Again nature is used to attempt a refurbishing of the comic solution. The poet finds in the unity of Hesper and Phosphor (section 121) a coalition of past and present, life and death, a benign sameness that flows through all things. In 115 and 116, he affirms that the renewals of spring, of "life re-orient out of dust" (116, l. 6), "Cry through the sense to hearten trust / In that which made the world so fair" (116, ll. 7–8). The movements of nature, then, are not entirely foreign to him; they touch him deeply. But not deeply enough. He can only say that "less of sorrow lives in me" (l. 13), that he feels "Less yearning for the friendship fled, / Than some strong bond which is to be" (ll. 15–16). In sum, he says, he finds "Not all regret" (l. 9). But "not all regret" is not enough for comedy, and the poem nearly slips back once again into conclusive irony.

Even the fine 119 ("Doors, where my heart was used to beat"), which forms such a clear and important contrast to the gloom of 7 ("Dark house, by which once more I stand"), does not allow unqualified joy. It does celebrate the power of the newly found self—"I come," "I smell," "I hear," "I see," "I take"—and the participation of nature's calm in the love that conquers death. There is, however, a subtle sense, much like that in Wordsworth's "Composed on Westminster Bridge," that all this serenity is transitory, a moment of perceived unity that is wonderful precisely because it is so unusual. "I come once more; the city sleeps; / I smell the meadow in the street" (ll. 3–4). It is this "meadow in the street," the infusion of nature into the haunts of men, that allows for the assurance that all life—and death—is a continuum ruled by love: "I take the pressure of thine hand" (l. 12). But now "the city sleeps."

If the crucial union of man and nature is possible only in these suspended and rare moments, then the solution will, at best, entirely lack the solidity generally associated with comedy. The transient, even evasive nature of the solution is evidenced over and over; he asks that Hallam be with him and "enter in at breast and brow" (122, l. 11) so that his blood may "Be quickened with a livelier breath, / And like an inconsiderate boy, / As in the former flash of joy, / I slip the thoughts of life and death; / And all the breeze of Fancy blows, / And every dew-drop paints a bow, / The wizard lightnings deeply glow, / And every thought breaks out a rose" (ll. 13–20). The passage is alive, but it is alive with change, with a perception of vivid transience: joy is expressed in images of dewdrops and lightning; the verbs are evanescent—*quickened, slip, blows, glow;* the stressed nouns are those of things that pass—*breath, flash, breeze, rainbow.*

Other problems are created by Tennyson's old tendency to search for consolations that are impossibly remote: "Move upward, working out the beast, / And let the ape and tiger die" (118, ll. 26–27) offers hope to generations a few million years from now, but very little to us. Even his famous intuitive answer to doubt, "I have felt" (124, l. 16), is qualified very deeply by the tone. It does affirm the primary self and the primary reality: "And what I am beheld again / What is" (ll. 21–22). These points have been won precisely because, as he says in the next section (125), they have been implicit in the early irony. The real power of the ending is in the beginning—not, unfortunately, in the final articulation of the solution, but of the problem.

What he finally comes to say about love and being are true enough, but they imply, in the "All is well" (127) benediction, a greater permanence and finality than the poem supports. And even here, Tennyson's impressive honesty enters in to insist that there really is no final resolution: "I see in part / That all, as in some piece of art, / Is toil coöperant to an end" (128, ll. 22–24). Genuine comedy has nothing to do with this "in part."

There is, then, a solution to the problem, but it is not sustained. He has won a new self and some perception of the interrelationship of death and love, despair and hope. But he can neither trust nor fully understand this unified knowledge; it never dominates his being as it should. The irony that returns to the poem at section 100 is never fully overcome. The narrator senses that his solution lacks the firmness of comic structure, but he is unwilling to face that fact—or perhaps faces it too squarely. In any event, though the last part of the poem returns to the valid emotional assurances won earlier, it is unable to weld them to the permanent forms of comedy. Instead of a genuine conclusion, we are given a series of skillful but inadequate substitutes.

The Epilogue is one of the most skillful of these, nearly accomplishing a miraculous repair. It is written in a different voice entirely, no longer at all tentative, but straightforward and fully controlled. It is the best evidence of the narrator's emotional rehabilitation and the consequent validity of *In Memoriam*'s arguments. The graceful public poetry here evokes better than any direct statement what it means to find new dedication and a new life. The "evolutionary ending" is not meant as any kind of "solution" to the problems presented in the poem; it has little connection with them. It is simply a tactful compliment to the marriage, connecting the child-to-be of Cecilia and Edmund Lushington to the divine subject of the poem and pointing all men to a unified and coherent future: "One God, one law, one element, / And one far-off divine event, / To which the whole creation moves" (ll. 141–43). All this is evidence of a new mood and a new mastery; it is a fitting close.

But it is much like having a joyous dance at the end of *The Winter's Tale*: no matter how well executed, it cannot counterbalance the darkness and irresolution that remain suspended in the play. Tennyson's Epilogue is a brilliant attempt, but it is essentially disconnected from his magnificent but deeply troubled poem. Its doubt is, just as Eliot said, a very intense experience; if we find the faith a poor thing, it is only because the poem never reaches the level of assurance that our participation in its negations had demanded. *In Memoriam* presents itself to be judged as the finest comic poem of the nineteenth century. It also illustrates how terribly difficult, if not impossible, the comic form was to sustain.

6

Maud

"Sooner or later I too may passively take the print
Of the golden age—why not?"

[pt. 1, ll. 29–30]

Maud, the last of Tennyson's major comedies, is by far the darkest.
Like *The Princess* and *In Memoriam* before it, *Maud* keeps at its center
the symbol of the reconstruction of the human personality; it traces
a similar movement from isolation to social acceptance. But here
what has hitherto been the symbolic annihilation of the old self
becomes almost literal, and the society into which the hero is reborn
is neither very loving nor very promising. Tennyson's three
comedies are progressively more complicated and more extreme.
They form a continuum, each beginning with a rejection of the
solutions arrived at previously. *The Princess* defeats a humor-domi-
nated world and unsociable heroism by reformulating the clichés of
domestic sociability. But the power of these clichés derives from an
assumption of a unified, harmonious creation, and this assumption
is canceled by the images of fragmentation and meaninglessness
which dominate the first part of Tennyson's next comedy, *In
Memoriam*. The answers of *The Princess* must be cast aside so that the
rehabilitating force of love may operate.

Maud, however, sees love, especially romantic love, as a problem
not a solution, and must move beyond it. All three poems ask
essentially the same question: how is it possible for an individual to
live in a world that makes unjust or unreal demands on him? [1] In
The Princess love does not so much remake Ida as correct her and
allow her to move back into a world which, if seen properly, has
always been sane and loving; in *In Memoriam*, love clearly must

1. A. S. Byatt, "The Lyric Structure of Tennyson's *Maud*," in Isobel Armstrong, ed., *The
Major Victorian Poets*, pp. 69–92, gives a somewhat similar statement of the dramatic question
in *Maud*: "what it means to have sufficient identity to be capable of consistent and
meaningful action" (p. 69). His reading of the poem's concern with identity is a good one.

transform both the narrator and his world. But in *Maud*, love does not release the narrator from self but imprisons him in it. The perception that ironic dilemmas, even though they may not be solved, can be rendered trivial by love provides the narrator of *In Memoriam* with the key to new being and new life. When the same perception appears in *Maud*, it comes not at the conclusion and as an answer but midway, in the midst of the hero's conflict, bringing him only loss and anguish. Behind both *In Memoriam* and *Maud* lies the pattern of death and resurrection, a pattern whose personal focus increased just as its general historical and mythical power (at least in religion) declined: it is not a God but an individual ego that is crucified and reborn. *Maud* accepts this personally focused myth, but very hesitantly. That it accepts it at all makes the poem, despite everything, comic; its extreme reluctance to do so, however, leads us to a very dark side of comedy.

Along with other great comic poets, Tennyson moved away from a pastoral or Edenic vision toward one which, while darker, is also more tolerant and accepting. The narrator of *Maud*, like the hero of *In Memoriam*, experiences nothingness, but that experience allows him merely to live in the world, not to transform it. *Maud* gives the sense of being either more cynical or wiser than *In Memoriam*. It is, in any case, an answer to the earlier poem, suggesting that its demands are too absolute, too pure, too egocentric.

Just as *In Memoriam* shows the natural relationship of irony and comedy, so does *Maud*. But in the former, domestic or romantic comedy, by growing *out* of irony, provides an answer to that irony; here it merely continues and confirms it. *Maud* shows the development of protective, simple irony into romantic comedy, then into chaos, a nightmare of complex irony that no longer protects but assaults, and finally into a liberal but undemanding comedy of accommodation. The ending shows comedy at its most ironic, just as the early love lyrics in the poem had shown comedy at its most romantic.[2] What is missing is the common middle ground, an area that Tennyson has obviously lost faith in entirely. *Maud* is an exploration of comic extremes. It is, like the two major poems preceding it, modeled on a generic battle; but instead of the mild conflict in *The Princess* between two different forms of comedy or *In*

2. See Frye, *Anatomy of Criticism*, pp. 177–86, for a discussion of the relationship of comedy to irony and to romance.

Memoriam's contest between irony and comedy, *Maud* presents a doubled movement: irony → comedy; irony → comedy. The first development from irony to comedy is only apparent growth; the second is real.

All this can be made somewhat less opaque by restating it in reference to the hero and the plot. While it is not very fruitful to begin by trying to *explain* the hero by means of the psychic shock caused by his father's death,[3] it is clear that his problems have a sexual component or even a sexual basis. He connects all images of male power with deadly aggression, animalism, and corruption. A male-dominated commercial system is, thus, not only corrupt but murderous. Women—his own mother, Maud's mother, Maud herself—are made to carry all the opposite associations: calmness, purity, and civility. He creates in fantasy a complete and quite simple division in the world and its concerns: there are those (the men) who are corrupt and those (women) who are not. He, of course, is one of the pure. That he is a man and the son of his father makes for an awful contradiction and an impossible dilemma. He is, as he says, "At war with myself and a wretched race, / Sick, sick to the heart of life, am I" (1, ll. 364–65). His war with himself, it turns out, is quite different from and infinitely more important than his mock battle with the "wretched race" of man. He must accept his own manhood, his own wretchedness, and this involves an inner struggle that almost destroys him.

His first impulse is to make peace with himself by loudly proclaiming his separation not only from manhood but from all men. He does this by becoming an ironist, a *simple* ironist. That is, he uses specific irony as a tool, thus protecting himself from irony's real force. He can attack with biting and indiscriminate irony all that is connected with manhood and even with mankind in order to assure himself of his separateness. He deliberately emphasizes and builds his own inhumanity in order to protect himself from the corruption that he sees around him and that he fears to see in himself. He thus occupies himself in constructing a psychic model of the real world, a model that simplifies and purifies in order to protect. The other side of this attack on the masculine is an equally unreal idealization of the female. The irony called into service to bolster and, at the same time, to camouflage identity creates its

3. For an example, see S. Ronald Weiner, "The Chord of Self," *L&P* 16 (1966): 175–83.

comic component. This, then, is the end of the first development from simple irony to romantic comedy.

By accepting love with Maud, the narrator is not really changing his fantasies, but he does attempt to force these once private fantasies onto the external world. By seeking to confirm his world in this way, he exposes himself; and by seeking to draw Maud away from her complex self and into the world of his own false Paradise, he violently destroys both her and his fantasies. Instead of romantic fulfillment, he discovers genuine and complex irony.

He can find his way out of this general irony only by creating a new being. He must accept his own corruption in order to join the fallen world. The terms that define his restoration are those of the unity of male and female, energy and stasis, death and life, purity and corruption, honor and dishonor.[4] The easy contraries of *The Princess* (male and female) or even the more difficult ones of *In Memoriam* (death and life, energy and stasis) no longer exist; we now find a nearly cynical balancing of the opposites that control the world *as it is,* untransformed and untransformable. The poem thus duplicates the early movement from irony to comedy, but this time it is an unprotective, complex irony and an unromantic, mature comedy. Now, Maud, who had seemed so separate and unique, is one with her brother, and they divide their parents' traits equally: Maud's brother is both animalistic and tender; Maud is a gentle singer of war songs. The lovely shell found by the narrator suggests beauty and endurance but also death and waste. War, the last and most difficult symbol, is both honorable and dishonorable, restorative and deadly. This frightening, disunified world, the poem insists, is all there is. It cannot be transcended by fleeing into mystic states of purity, but must be accepted. The real enemy and the real dangers, *Maud* claims, are not from evil or complexity but from the rigid and simple expectation of good.

Insofar as the poem is an investigation of the active limits of moral purity, it is, incidentally, a fable for our time—a conservative fable, certainly, but an apt one. It shows how dangerous are both the self-serving cynicism of irony and the self-exalting absolutism of romance. It proposes in their place a tough maturity, able to endure

---

4. E. D. H. Johnson, in a deservedly well-known article, "The Lily and the Rose: Symbolic Meaning in Tennyson's *Maud*," *PMLA* 64 (1949): 1222–27, shows how the symbols of lily and rose, once opposites, coalesce to form a new balance. James Walton ("Tennyson's Patrimony," pp. 754–55, 758) emphasizes the importance of Maud's brother in this regard.

an uncomfortable status quo. It is a poem about the pathos and terror embedded in the self-delusions of purists, revolutionary or otherwise. The extremely sophisticated conclusion finds its source in a rugged humanistic tradition that runs from Chaucer to Camus.

It might be objected that if such universality does attend the poem it would have been more widely recognized and appreciated. One barrier to acceptance by modern critics was erected, I think, by Tennyson's extremely unfortunate remark, "This poem is a little *Hamlet*." [5] G. Wilson Knight's deliberately perverse, "corrective" reading of *Hamlet*[6] happens to fit *Maud* very well, which goes to show how little correspondence between the two works there really is. The crucial and obvious difference is that *Hamlet* is a tragedy and *Maud* a comedy.[7] Tennyson thus invites all manner of unsound and spurious comparisons.

But a chance comment of Tennyson's, no matter how unfortunate, could hardly account for the violence of the reactions of Tennyson's contemporaries and of ours. Leslie Stephen called the hero "not only morbid, but silly," [8] and even Tennyson's friend Gladstone could not hide his initial repulsion: "the effort required to dispel the darkness of the general scheme is not repaid when we discover what it hides." [9] The twentieth-century version of this distaste is given voice by T. S. Eliot, who provides a whole list of pronouncements on the poem's emotional unreality, its "feeble violence." [10] The poem has had its defenders, then and now, but the ferocity of some responses is not easy to understand.

Tennyson may have been writing a poem that was more psychologically topical than he knew, portraying the moral and psychic fantasies of a puristic culture with more accuracy than was healthy for sustained popularity. "Sir, I used to worship you, but now I hate you. I loathe and detest you. You beast!": [11] thus began a letter from an apostate admirer of Tennyson's. It might have been written by the narrator of *Maud* himself in his early days, when he

5. *Memoir*, 1:396.

6. G. Wilson Knight, "The Embassy of Death: An Essay on *Hamlet*," in his *The Wheel of Fire: Interpretations of Shakespearian Tragedy* (New York: Barnes and Noble, 1965), pp. 17–46.

7. For a reading of *Maud* as an imitation of tragic action, see Gerhard Joseph, *Tennysonian Love*, pp. 104–16.

8. "Life of Tennyson," in *Studies of a Biographer*, 2:237.

9. "Tennyson's Poems," p. 460.

10. "In Memoriam," in *Essays Ancient and Modern*, pp. 193–94.

11. Quoted in *Memoir*, 1:400.

too believed in a world of purity and impurity, a world that allowed only extreme responses like the worship or hatred mentioned here. He might also have signed himself, as did the erstwhile fan, "Yours in aversion."

There are, of course, other reasons for the poem's unpopularity. One of these is not, however, that it is shrill or frenzied. These and similar catchwords crop up in all attacks and in many of the defenses. What is granted as a fine coalition of form and substance in *In Memoriam* is for some reason denied here, though it seems clear that Tennyson achieves throughout the poem a sense of great passion which is at the same time ordered and controlled, a tension between extreme, even chaotic diction and artful, intricate metrical and stanzaic patterns. The control provided in *In Memoriam* by the repetition of the same stanza is accomplished here by drawing our attention to elaborate, often even ostentatious, rhythms. The one exception to this ordered tension is the deliberate rhythmic disorder of the mad scene. "Frenzy" seems to me a very weak charge to bring against the poem and a very woolly substantiation of a critical view.

The most crucial problem surely lies with the ending, not just with the curious use of the Crimean War but with the more general treatment of the hero's rehabilitation. The poem so mistrusts absolutism that it is bound to mistrust absolute and ultimate cures. The war is therapy, not a final solution; it suggests the most extreme demand society can make on a person's tolerance and ego. It asks not so much for self-sacrifice as for the expansion of egoistic morality even to the point of allowing that honor may come from slaughter. War also represents a public and social version of the cathartic horror the narrator has experienced. The ending suggests that society as a whole should undergo the same process of reduction and annihilation so that it may live with itself and its corruption. But these are only suggestions; the ending only points toward a solution: it does in no sense embody one. Again, Tennyson is somewhat distrustful of his own answers. The tone is very bleak; war is an uncertain symbol; even the cynical comic solutions remain unfulfilled. The poem is not only dark but generically frustrating. No wonder it is unpopular.

Tennyson's final division of *Maud* into three parts is reasonable and obviously sound. The first part[12] presents the complication; the second, the crisis; the third, the resolution. In the terms outlined earlier, the first part presents the original and false movement from irony to comedy, the hero's attempts to maintain his fantasies of purity; the second moves him into the genuine irony of madness; and the third presents the final comedy. The discussion that follows will preserve this order, with one slight change: I wish to divide the first part in half, treating the ironic and comic movements separately and assuming a division between the two at section 11, "O let the solid ground," where the narrator gives in to the romantic impulse he has thus far resisted. Such an extra division should obscure neither the fact that the narrator fluctuates between cynicism and romantic love more or less throughout the first section nor the more important fact that the irony and comedy reflect there a single frame of mind and no real development.

The poem opens with the narrator luxuriating in the perverse comfort of cynicism, particularly in the escape from coarse life that cynicism provides him. As in *In Memoriam*, the fact of death is physically present, but here death is made terribly concrete, almost in the vaguely sensual way common in Poe or bad horror movies. The narrator may be terrified by the death of his father, but he is also drawn to it and feels a strange comfort in dwelling on its details: "Mangled, and flattened, and crushed, and dinted into the ground" (1, l. 7). He has been shocked into a morbid and perilous self-sufficiency, yet he has no real self. His father's death has violently brought to him a perception of fundamental awfulness in the world, and he has no ability either to accept or to escape that perception. What he tries to do is to dodge it: "Villainy somewhere! whose? One says, we are villains all. / Not he: his honest fame should at least by me be maintained: / But that old man, now lord of the broad estate and the Hall" (1, ll. 17–19).

Since there is clearly villainy abroad, he feels compelled to locate it, but not because he is Hamlet, searching out causes to correct. There is "villainy somewhere," but not in his father or in *him;* that is nearly all that counts now. The voice that says, "We are villains all" offers one of the most basic truths the poem contains. The interlinking of evil and good is a principle the narrator must later

---

12. I will use Tennyson's term "part" for the three main divisions of the poem; the lyric divisions within each part will be called "sections" and given Tennyson's numbers.

accept, but now it is an unthinkable suggestion. He must protect his weak and undefined self, and he does so by creating various simplicities, namely, a world in which the pure and the impure are separated by a wide gulf—the gulf of irony. By making himself into a simple ironist, the narrator can assure himself that however black things are in general, he himself is undefiled. In fact, the strength of his purity is in direct proportion to the darkness he can find—or invent—outside him.

His favorite exercise—and therapy—therefore, is ranting. Whenever troublesome ideas like "we are villains all" come up, he turns to the world at large, projecting his own fear of corruption on all externals. The carefully arranged witticisms, the heavy alliterations, the conscious excesses, the sacrifice of accuracy to neat parallelisms and superficial rhetoric, all suggest the self-flattering tinniness of a political speech, a kind of neurotic showing off: "While another is cheating the sick of a few last gasps, as he sits / To pestle a poisoned poison behind his crimson lights. / When a Mammonite mother kills her babe for a burial fee, / And Timour-Mammon grins on a pile of children's bones" (1, ll. 43–46).

These and other such denunciations are sometimes taken very seriously by critics; Valerie Pitt argues that *Maud* is really Tennyson's "central political poem" and that the hero's illness is caused by social corruption.[13] The vision of social corruption seems to me not to be part of the disease, except insofar as it is a dangerous medicine. The hero uses these outbursts time and again to reinforce his pathetically inadequate identity and to avoid looking for genuine problems. He is not angry but smug: "Sooner or later I too may passively take the print / Of the golden age—why not?" (1, ll. 29–30). He is not the spasmodic but the dandy, suggesting with jocular insincerity that the world's evil may, in the end, be powerful enough to include even him. And in the end the world does include him, though now, being unsuited for it, he can in his loneliness and confusion only shout at it.

These dramatic ironies, which really forecast eventual resolution, are reinforced by several references to war and peace, the social conditions that will finally determine and symbolize the hero's restoration. Again he articulates the solution without realizing it. War is evoked as a grim and obviously undesirable image—"the

13. *Tennyson Laureate*, p. 179.

heart of the citizen hissing in war on his own hearthstone" (1, l. 24)—in order to attack the present commercial peace. In his fury, he can think of nothing worse to say about society than that its spirit of competition is really viler than actual war. There is no rational reason for saying so, one might suppose, but to the narrator anything that is cloudy, mixed, or complicated is an enemy. Peace that partakes of war is too difficult a complexity to comprehend.

He must have clear, well-marked villains; the current condition is "underhand, not openly bearing the sword" (1, l. 28). This clarifies at least one reason why war is attractive here and, sadly, even a little so at the end: it is direct, primitive, uncomplicated. Also, he argues that war would ennoble even the tradesman, that if England were—happily—invaded, "the smooth-faced snubnosed rogue would leap from his counter and till, / And strike, if he could, were it but with his cheating yardwand, home" (1, ll. 51–52). In such a case, unity of a kind would be provided, a unity of all the world with him and his purity. He is, as it turns out in the poem, right in viewing war as an extreme but effective unifying force, but he has the terms backwards. He wants to bring the world into unity with his own ego; he must, in fact, renounce his own ego in order to regain it and bring it into harmony with the world. All this may seem like the process at the heart of most Romantic dream-vision poems, but here the world remains untransformed; the central vision is one of hell, not of emperors and clowns.

The ironies at the beginning of *Maud*, then, emphasize the distance that separates the narrator from true identity. He is lonely and hesitant; so he uses the loud, glib cynicism of specific irony to evoke a strong being he does not have. That he is a man without a vital center, without will or control, is made apparent when, after more than fifty lines of ranting, he tells us he has made a law that he will be above such things: from now on, no more brooding on his father's corpse, on "a wretched swindler's lie" (1, l. 56), or on social evils. He can make laws for himself, but he has no power to enforce them. Behind the ironist we see a larger irony, of which he is unaware. His shouts of liberation are entirely defensive, coming as they do from within a prison. His decision at the end of the first section, to "bury myself in myself" (l. 75), indicates the necessity he feels to entomb his secret wishes as deeply and securely as possible.

The narrator is so defensive that he fears, even before he sees her, that Maud "may bring me a curse" (1, l. 73). She does, in a sense, but only because he makes her a part of his protective fantasy of incorruptibility. He instinctively fears the menace of comedy. It offers him the necessary final solution but it also threatens him with exposure. It demands that he sacrifice the paralyzing neurotic life he is leading, but he is not sure he can. The battle that follows is between Maud and the narrator's fantasies. They both lose in the end, as he tries for an impossible conjunction between love and fantasy.

The hero's first impulse, though, is to resist her and her immediate assault on his neurotic sanctity. He finds himself able to reach absurdly final conclusions after a single glance at her: "Faultily faultless, icily regular, splendidly null, / Dead perfection, no more; nothing more" (1, ll. 82–83). Contrary evidence, which he cannot help sensing, must be blocked, for it would upset his egoistic view of things. So he tries to fit Maud into a melodramatic formula: the beautiful but heartless aristocratic lady. But she simply is not Lady Clara Vere de Vere. The impulse she stirs cannot be contained within any single image; her presence threatens to change the world and, more important, to change the narrator. Section 4 begins with a vision of loveliness and bounty in nature so powerful that it begins to arouse the hero to wish himself a part of it. This movement toward comic union and humility is so frightening to him, though, that he desperately retreats back to the therapy of simple irony.

For the next fifty odd lines he vigorously tries to erase the danger of the gentle attraction of love and to protect his old identity. He turns to the first thing in the scene that catches his eye, the village, and hysterically exaggerates its inhabitants' actual frailties—a love of "gossip, scandal, and spite" (l. 109)—into gross and total malignity: "And Jack on his ale-house bench has as many lies as the Czar" (l. 110). Here, surely, the neurotic base of his absolutism is clearly exposed. He makes no distinctions at all; a lie is a lie. Lies are especially dangerous to him since they again stand in the way of his reductive "let's find out" (i.e. "let's not really look") attitude. He is a truth-teller, he thinks, and a rigorous moralist, operating under the confused but prevalent theory that by ignoring obvious distinctions moral values can be somehow clarified. If one has the acuity and uncommon penetration to perceive murderous evil in Jack's lazy and presumably harmless lies, it will hardly do to question the morality of the moralist. The psychology of moral absolutism is thus exposed, not in anger but in pathos. The narrator really has no choice at all.

He can respond only with more ironic platitudes: "For nature is one with rapine, a harm no preacher can heal; / The Mayfly is torn by the swallow, the sparrow speared by the shrike, / And the whole little wood where I sit is a world of plunder and prey" (1, ll. 123–25). He strikes out angrily at the nature which has tempted him away from himself. And though there is a superficial resemblance between these attacks and the cosmic ironies in *In Memoriam*, here the tone is not one of fear but of almost greedy relish. Nature is attacked; it does not attack him. It is easy to say "We are puppets" (l. 126) when the tone so clearly indicates that *we* really means *they*. The dilemmas created by scientific discoveries and by the implications of the scientific method are genuine problems in *In Memoriam*, but here they merely present the narrator with a chance to fulminate and thereby to prove his superiority to the scientist: "The man of science himself is fonder of glory, and vain, / An eye well-practised in nature, a spirit bounded and poor" (1, ll. 138–39). The general ironies on time, nature, and man, in other words, simply have no personal force. The narrator thinks it would be best to be what he most certainly is not, a calm stoic or epicure teaching himself "not to desire or admire" (1, l. 142). He protects his ego by allowing it no direct experience whatsoever; the ironies are merely sarcasms. He must attack all experience, not only that which suggests evil. In fact, "most of all would I flee from the cruel madness of love" (1, l. 156). Love and Maud are the greatest dangers because they demand the most involvement.

Maud's battle-song, in section 5, is her most important utterance, even though it is not, as the narrator repeatedly says, so much Maud that he hears, as a "voice." It is a voice "singing an air that is known to me" (1, l. 164)—really a song that is within him, arising from the deep and unconscious sense that only in full acceptance of all life can he live. It is the voice of comedy, which is here vitally connected to Maud herself. She announces the fully realized self and calls the narrator, not just to masculinity—though, as in *The Princess*, this may be a small part of it—but to participation in a world of unified contraries. She sings "in the happy morning of life and of May" (1, l. 168) of men who march gaily, "with banner and bugle and fife" (1, l. 171) but who march "to the death" (l. 172). "Her exquisite face" (l. 173) is combined with her "wild voice" (l.

174), and she sings "of Death, and of Honour" (l. 177) "in the light of her youth and her grace" (l. 176). All opposites unite here in this realization of liberal and accepting comedy. Because this unity is such a threat to the narrator, he must now deliberately silence it (l. 180) lest it open him to the world. But at the same time he instinctively realizes that this completeness in Maud is what he needs, and he later recalls her specifically in reference to this martial song: "I wish I could hear again / The chivalrous battle-song" (1, ll. 382–83). Though he must finally sacrifice Maud to gain the hope she symbolizes, he does gain it.

But before the hero can rebuild himself and join the mixed, impure world, he must complete the puristic logic of separation. He is stirred by Maud's song, but he wants comic rewards without the comic sacrifice of ego. He is willing for the world to be wholly fair as well as wholly gross, so long as his neurotic absolutism is not affected. Maud's song exposes him to the limitations of such easy optimism, to nature's attacks on purism:

> Morning arises stormy and pale,
> No sun, but a wannish glare
> In fold upon fold of hueless cloud,
> And the budded peaks of the wood are bowed
> Caught and cuffed by the gale:
> I had fancied it would be fair.
>
> [1, ll. 190–95]

"The wannish glare" and the "hueless cloud" are the blank denials of meaning and feeling found in all genuine irony, just as his poor "fancy" suggests irony's element of foiled comic expectations. Love thus threatens him with annihilation of self and with authentic prisons, not the fake ones he had been building.

His "fancy" for fair weather, however, shows that he will not long resist a simplified romanticism, that he will, if all else fails, rearrange or reinvent the elements. Though he tries again to assert the pose of the cynic, imagining that Maud is merely trying to lure him out of hiding in order to torture him, the brighter vision is beginning to win. In order to protect himself and still accept the promise of love, however, the narrator manages to ignore Maud's battle-hymn, the symbol of sacrifice and comic realism, and to substitute in its place a soft romantic comedy that is substantiated by nothing but his fantasies: "If Maud were all that she seemed, / And her smile were all that I dreamed, / Then the world were not so bitter / But a smile could make it sweet" (1, ll. 225–28).

The notion that the world, which is "bitter," can be so simply made "sweet" is a terribly attractive one, and it gradually captures his imagination completely, so that "sweetness" and Maud are inextricably linked, joined in an incantatory, romantic union. The magic phrase transforming the world is picked up again later; in fact, from this point on, the adjective *sweet* nearly always appears when Maud does. It is the same sweetness that had typified and controlled the domestic comedy in *The Princess*: "sweet is every sound, / Sweeter thy voice, but every sound is sweet" (7, ll. 203–04). Yet pure love simply will not transform the world envisioned in this poem.

The attempt to separate Maud from her battle-song is the disastrous attempt to wrench her from her own natural world and transplant her in the alien ground of the narrator's mind. This dislocation is symbolized most fully in the relationship between Maud and her brother. When the hero first saw the two together, he found it necessary to effect some separation: "I met her today with her brother, but not to her brother I bowed" (1, l. 115). In order to worship Maud, the narrator must utterly detest her brother, "her brother, from whom I keep aloof" (1, l. 235).

Aloof is exactly the right word; he cannot admit that this "Assyrian Bull" (l. 233) has any relation to him or to any other human. Maud's brother represents everything vile: energy, sexual power, male animalism. His presence allows (or forces) the narrator to purify Maud by draining all negative human characteristics onto him. The brother, he suggests, has been the result of some genetic magic whereby he has inherited only from his father, who has "heaped the whole inherited sin / Of the huge scapegoat of the race, / All, all upon the brother" (1, ll. 484–86). Maud, by the same token, is "only the child of her mother" (1, l. 483). What he cannot face is their kinship, the plain fact that they combine the traits of both their parents: the power and sexuality of the wolfish father, the tenderness and sweetness of their mother.

Even the hero's hope for Maud's love is based on a contract made long ago by their fathers, so that in approaching Maud, he is, in effect, approaching her father. To shield himself from this troubling complexity, he keeps at his side a raven who croaks, "Keep watch and ward, keep watch and ward, / Or thou wilt prove their tool"

(1, ll. 247–48). He still feels the need to defend himself with simple irony, particularly when, as here, he admits the possibility that Maud and her brother are connected. He almost never speaks of them together, and the use of the plural *their* suggests why he very much needs the raven at his side. It allows him convenient and necessary retreats into petty attack: he invents a jealousy of a "new-made lord" (section 10) whom he only supposes he saw riding with Maud.

Again, the sheer irrelevance of the spite and the self-consciously witty language alert us to the real motive here, which is not social criticism but protection from society and its concerns: "Seeing his gewgaw castle shine, / New as his title, built last year, / There amid perky larches and pine, / And over the sullen-purple moor / (Look at it) pricking a cockney ear" (1, ll. 347–51). The narrator settles quickly into the regressive comfort of sarcasm and returns again, significantly, to his favorite theme, "the bad times." His extremism and absolutism lead him again to the crucial symbol of war and the attack on the peace-monger, "This broad-brimmed hawker of holy things" (1, l. 370). Whether or not this is a reference to John Bright,[14] it does represent the psychic processes of the narrator very well. This peace advocate is stained, naturally, by contact with the world, with money and manufacturing.

Using a wild generic fallacy, then, the narrator proceeds to argue that the advocate's stains discredit peace itself. War, he says, is the honest symbol of this society and its natural passions—"so don't tell me about peace!" Everyone has been in arguments where he has heard (and used) such unanswerable non-logic. The narrator is not making a statement about war and peace at all; the only real subject is himself. If society were perpetually engaged in war, he could at least understand that, since war seems to him the inevitable sign of the world's profound corruption. Peace is a more highly advanced state, one that is far too complex for him to grasp. He demands simplicity at any price:

> Ah God, for a man with heart, head, hand,
> Like some of the simple great ones gone
> For ever and ever by,
> One still strong man in a blatant land,

14. As a matter of fact, it surely is not; see Ricks edition, p. 1059.

> Whatever they call him, what care I,
> Aristocrat, democrat, autocrat—one
> Who can rule and dare not lie.
>
>   [1, ll. 389–95]

Autocracy is the same as democracy, so long as there is pure power without deception or complexity.

As it turns out, this hysteria is the last strong upsurge of his therapeutic sarcasm. From now on, it will appear more and more rarely and never with much strength. The hero has moved beyond simple irony into the beginnings of romantic comedy. But with disastrous ingenuity he will file down comedy itself and fit it into his simplistic mental frame. With section 11, this narrow comedy takes over and begins to dominate. Even the wild section 10 had ended on a calm note, with hope for rebirth: "And ah for a man to arise in me, / That the man I am may cease to be!" (ll. 396–97). This hope will be accomplished in the end, but only by the murder of "the man I am." The romantic comedy he now proposes offers no real change and no hope at all.

But it seems to. The hero does appear to be moving out of himself into a recognition of community. He vows to experience "what some have found so sweet" (1, l. 401), the love that is assured, not by private experience but by social bonds. The world, he again believes, can be re-created with all its bitterness removed by the sweetness of love. Love can bring him into unity with the world in which he lives, thereby assuring both the power of love and the firm reality of the narrator's personality: "O let the solid ground / Not fail beneath my feet" (1, ll. 398–99). Love will provide a reality that, presumably, can contain the hero and make him "solid" too. In the first flush of this grand hope, the narrator recognizes at once the vital and beautiful connections between man and nature: "For her feet have touched the meadows / And left the daisies rosy" (1, ll. 434–35). If passionate purity and warmth connect all things, he can realize his own being by opening himself to this harmony: "if *I* be dear to some one else, / Then I should be to myself more dear" (1, ll. 531–32). The romantic imagination is seen as the central agency both of redemption and of creation.

The problem, finally, is that the imaginative powers remain fixed on the self; they operate, in Keats's terms, entirely in the

Wordsworthian and never in the Shakespearean sense. The narrator is the "egotistical sublime," seeking to make all the world over in the image of himself. He lacks entirely the power of "negative capability," the facility of rendering himself nothing in order to enter other states and other beings. Despite appearances, then, he is not moving out into the world; he is swallowing the world whole. Even Maud, or that part of her he can accept, will become a part of him: their fathers, he says, "On the day when Maud was born; / Sealed her mine from her first sweet breath. / Mine, mine by a right, from birth till death. / Mine, mine—our fathers have sworn" (1, ll. 723-26).

The world, thus artificially sweetened, seems fit for consumption. That things are not, in fact, so universally sweet or so simple to accept is made clear by the reappearance of Maud's brother. Do what he can, the narrator is unable to ward off this powerful specter. He wildly asserts that "Maud to him is nothing akin" (1, l. 481), but he can never dislodge her from a connection with this brother. The narrator continuously links Maud with gardens, addressing the cedar tree as the descendant of the trees that grew in "the thornless garden" (1, l. 625), "Shadowing the snow-limbed Eve from whom she came" (l. 626). Eden, finally, is the only world in which he can live. The attempt to bring Paradise back by recreating another Eve lies at the mythic heart of much romantic comedy, particularly that of the nineteenth century. But here Eden is beyond recall; if there are any Paradises now to be found, they are beyond death—or in the private world of insanity.

The narrator, however, is a great artist, and his egoistic imagination has great powers. He not only insists that Maud is Eve but tries to make her so. Her brother is allowed all energy and motion, since they are associated with the corrupting influences of power and sex; Maud is made static, in her "own little oak-room" (1, l. 497), "like a precious stone / Set in the heart of the carven gloom" (ll. 498-99). The past in which the narrator is trying to live, the powerful and dangerous image of perfection, must lead to death. The desire to fix firmly and protect an absolute beauty and an absolute innocence must, in the world envisioned in this poem, logically lead to murder. The narrator fulfills symbolically the action which Porphyria's lover performs directly. Both the narrator of *Maud* and Porphyria's lover give overt expression to what we all secretly know—what every amateur photographer, for instance, knows in his heart: the desire to preserve life shares lodgings with the desire to freeze it.

The most ecstatic utterance of the narrator's love, "Go not, happy day," section 17, is an expression of this static unity, contained entirely within his puristic fantasies. The day is to be preserved so that it can partake of one grand unity—the rosy warmth of a blush. Despite the wonderful incantatory language, we see that the world is fully imaged, as the last line says, in her "mouth" (l. 598); it is the old, simple notion of the world being made sweet by a smile all over again. The principle of unification, the blush, seems reductive, not so much because it is coy as because it is so static and pervasive. There is no consummation here, no real hint of motion or of life. The ecstasy is created not by the thought of her eventual yielding but by the image of a perpetual and universal shyness. The world is fixed in a delightful "attitude" only. All the narrator wants is the smile that will make the world sweet, a confirmation of purity that sanctifies not the world but himself.

It is interesting that, as Christopher Ricks points out,[15] this lyric was originally intended for *The Princess*. Ricks suggests that this accounts for the fact that the poem, with its odd, "nursery-rhyming" style, seems out of place in *Maud*. Tennyson seems to me, rather, to have made a totally appropriate rearrangement. The values of domestic comedy implicit in *The Princess* and in this song are precisely those which the narrator now needs to express. The simple nursery-rhyme scheme supports the sense of release (false though it is), the childlike joy, and the irrational nature of the emotion we sense as important at this point in the poem and in the general movement of *Maud*.

The answers of *The Princess* fill him with such confidence that the narrator can now raise ironic ghosts for sport. The serious images that he had once used to insulate himself from a corrupt society become toys he can play with, only to discard. He turns melodramatically to the stars and the perceptions of "sad astrology": "the boundless plan / That makes you tyrants in your iron skies, / Innumerable, pitiless, passionless eyes, / Cold fires, yet with power to burn and brand / His nothingness into man" (1, ll. 634-38). We sense, as before, a secret relish in these lines, but the pleasure now comes from tossing the hissing, searing ironies off as unimportant.

15. "Tennyson's Method of Composition," *Proceedings of the British Academy* 52 (1966): 216.

They may, as they did not before, include him in their force, but
their force, after all, is nothing at all: "But now shine on, and what
care I" (1, l. 639). "What care I" may seem a remarkably balanced
attitude, but its assertion here is premature. The pose of benign
solidity recalls the similar pleasant sarcasm in *In Memoriam*: "What
matters Science unto men, / At least to me?" (120, ll. 7–8).

The parallels to *In Memoriam* are, at this point in the poem,
deliberate and startling. Irony is now defeated by comedy, not
disproved but made unimportant by the force of love, which, "in
this stormy gulf" (1, l. 640) provides man with "the countercharm
of space and hollow sky" (l. 641). Exactly as in *In Memoriam*, love
defines the meaning and value of life and, more importantly, of
death. He vows that he would die for his love—"for sullen-seeming
Death may give / More life to Love than is or ever was / In our low
world" (1, ll. 644–46; compare *In Memoriam*, 81)—and imagines
Maud saying, "The dusky strand of Death inwoven here / With
dear Love's tie, makes Love himself more dear" (1, ll. 658–59). *In
Memoriam*'s benedictory "All is well" is picked up here too: "Let all
be well, be well," (1, l. 683). *In Memoriam*'s answers and consolations
appear, then, only to reinforce the deadly promise of romantic
comedy. They are part of the problem, not a solution. Even *Maud*'s
"Let all be well, be well" is no longer the calm, reassuring voice of
God but the narrator's own frightened attempt to disguise "some
dark undercurrent woe" (1, l. 681). And instead of the benediction
acting to dismiss the problem and close the poem, it is interrupted
by a flat statement that rudely burlesques all assurances: "Her
brother is coming back tonight, / Breaking up my dream of
delight" (1, ll. 684–85).

The narrator's only alternative to the complexity represented by
this brother is to create a fantasy love by which Maud is separated
from her brother, which means separating her from her own true
self. He denies Maud's full humanity because he denies his own,
and egoistic romantic love leads directly to destruction. At the
climax of their love, Maud vainly urges him to accept her brother:
"And [she] wishes me to approve him, / And tells me, when she
lay / Sick once, with a fear of worse, / That he left his wine and
horses and play, / Sat with her, read to her, night and day, / And
tended her like a nurse" (1, ll. 754–59). The brother is "rough but
kind" (l. 753), not so much Maud's complement as a total human
being like herself, male and female, pure and impure, "nurse" and

"bull." The hero does try to bury his hatred but cannot. Even his
self-confident vows of liberation lead directly to imprisonment:

> So now I have sworn to bury
> All this dead body of hate,
> I feel so free and so clear
> By the loss of that dead weight,
> That I should grow light-headed, I fear,
> Fantastically merry;
> But that her brother comes, like a blight
> On my fresh hope, to the Hall tonight
>
> [1, ll. 779–86]

The finale of this acceptance of romantic love, "Come into the
garden, Maud," section 22, represents the definitive act of separa-
tion. The narrator, "here at the gate alone" (l. 853), urges Maud to
leave social life and, clearly, genuine comedy: "She is weary of
dance and play" (l. 871). But the narrator offers, in the place of the
life of comedy, dance, and play, only egoistic absorption. He taunts
the "young lord-lover" (l. 878) for sighing after one who is not his,
"But mine, but mine . . . / For ever and ever, mine" (ll. 880–81).
The hero imagines an Eden that is gone; he calls Maud into a dead
world to play a dead Eve. His romantic ecstasy rises steadily until,
in a final, unconsciously prophetic metaphor, he asserts the power
of his love for Maud to triumph even over the grave: "My heart
would hear her and beat, / Were it earth in an earthy bed" (ll.
918–19). Though he does not know it, he must undergo the death of
the heart in order to live again, not with Maud but with the real
world and with himself.

"O dawn of Eden bright over earth and sky, / The fires of Hell
brake out of thy rising sun" (2, ll. 8–9). Hell rises *out of* Eden; it is
the natural consequence of the narrator's mad insistence on purity.
Part 2 of *Maud* portrays the necessary counter-reaction to protective
irony and delusory romantic comedy. The duel that has taken place
between part 1 and part 2 is the inevitable result of the narrator's
neurotic logic. Unnatural attempts to decontaminate life bring all
natural forces of life against him. The assault of Maud's brother is
the action of an outraged Nature rejecting the narrator's perverse
demands. The first words of part 2 exonerate the brother, proving
his nobility and expansive being. Even in death he is generous,

claiming, "The fault was mine." By insisting on perfection and order, the narrator opens himself up to the darkness and chaos within. He ironically duplicates the action of Maud's wolfish father and finds in himself the animalism he had been so vigorously denying. He is taught that full humanity requires an acceptance, not a dangerous repression, of corruption. The fact that Maud must die to further his education makes the poem move close to tragedy. The focus is not, however, on Maud but on the narrator; so rehabilitation, not sacrifice, is the main theme.

But the hero must first lose himself in order to find that rehabilitation. He struggles, early in part 2, to retain a grasp on his earlier fantasies, his earlier weak self, but he can no longer do so. He tries the cynicism that had once worked so well—"Strike dead the whole weak race of venemous worms, / That sting each other here in the dust; / We are not worthy to live" (ll. 46–48)—but it now lacks all efficacy. He finds an image for what he must accept and what he must become in the lovely but empty shell, the deliberately planted symbol for his destruction and renewal. Tennyson himself claimed that "the shell undestroyed amid the storm perhaps symbolizes to him his own first and highest nature preserved amid the storms of passion." [16]

One must allow that as one possibility, but there are many others, some of which seem a good deal more consonant with the poem. The shell also suggests remarkable beauty, now wasted and lifeless, an image of lovely desolation that mocks picturesque views of life (such as the one in which the world is one large blush). It is also a rebuke to his earlier self in other ways: this "miracle of design," so "exquisitely minute" (ll. 56, 55), attacks his crude simplifications; the fact that its beauty simply exists, in defiance of any mere *name* (ll. 57–60), mocks his earlier need to classify and catalogue all experience. Most important, the shell unites beauty, delicacy, and strength, the components that combine to form all successful human life. The acknowledgment of this strange coalition leads him to think directly of Maud's brother and the lock of his mother's hair that the brother had kept in a ring.

Maud, her brother, and the shell all combine opposites and directly refute simple Edenic notions. The shell is a fine, ambiguous symbol, which acts as a lesson to the narrator on his past mistakes

16. *Memoir,* 1:404.

and as a promising sign, a vision of his wasted past and his future
hope, a direct image of himself and a sarcastic image of what he is
not. The fact that the shell is empty, a tomb, "forlorn / Void of the
little living will / That made it stir on the shore" (ll. 61–63),
provides a symbolic connection to himself that he cannot now
accept. He insists that as long as Maud lives and loves him, he will
preserve, "however weary, a spark of will / Not to be trampled out"
(ll. 104–05). Maud's death is necessary, then, to complete the
analogy to the shell, the final destruction of the human will so that
a new will and a new self can be born. He passes through that
which is more than death (l. 140) in order to emerge on the other
side—not cleansed, but at least prepared to live.

Before this experience the hero takes one last look at comedy.
Section 4, "O that 'twere possible," is the compositional germ of the
entire poem and contains, in many ways, its central emotion: the
sense of useless loss. He recalls again the sweetness that had once
seemed to permeate all life: "We stood tranced in long embraces /
Mixt with kisses sweeter sweeter / Than anything on earth" (ll.
148–50). And he dreams of the early delight he had found with
Maud: "Do I hear her sing as of old, / My bird with the shining
head, / My own dove with the tender eye?" (ll. 184–86). But these
dreams are shattered as Maud's song becomes, in the next line, a
scream: "But there rings on a sudden a passionate cry" (l. 187). She
is not just a tame and passive "dove," but, as her battle-song should
have told him, a complete being.

The narrator's inability to accept that fact cuts off the song and
brings him to a new desolation: "The day comes, a dull red
ball / Wrapt in drifts of lurid smoke / On the misty river-tide" (ll.
205–07). There is no longer any comfort in irony, and certainly no
protection. Instead of separating him from mankind by reinforcing
his sense of superior purity, irony now isolates him by insisting on
his extreme and unique guilt: "Through the hubub of the
market / I steal, a wasted frame . . . / And on my heavy eye-
lids / My anguish hangs like shame" (ll. 208–09, 213–14).

At the center of this episode he loses his reason and his old self. In
section 5, he buries himself in himself, in his own corruption. He is
now as much beneath the world as he previously was above it; even
the horses' hooves are on his head. He is being punished by that
which he most offended: the fallen world. It is the vital connection
between evil and good, purity and impurity, between Maud and

her brother, that still tortures him most. He has visions of his very mind being violated by this impurity, of all his secrets being "shouted at once from the top of the house" (l. 288). He now feels that he has no separate self, that social forces invade his most private being: "Everything came to be known. / Who told *him* we were there?" (ll. 289–90).

The inability to separate himself from society—"Everything came to be known"—is exactly his final inability to separate Maud from her brother, the *him* who somehow knew where Maud was and went with her. By entering the real world the narrator unconsciously and inadvertently has entered the world of Maud's brother and has left his isolated self behind. He must now return to that self to see how much damage has been done. The more the better; there will be no repairing, only the completion of the necessary destruction. At the end of this section, he asks for a deeper burial, a fuller immersion in this old self, so that he may, paradoxically, understand and live with the corruption within and without.

The comic solution to *Maud*, given in part 3, presents many critical problems, not the least of which is that it is so short. Comedy generally gives a brief but very firm image of its final disposition of things, but here the brevity nearly becomes negligence. There is more to this problem even than the mere number of lines; *Maud* almost strikes one as an unfinished work, as if Tennyson had died before he could tell us what effect the initiation by means of the Crimean War could have. The poem ends with the hero *about to begin* his growth. But no destination is given in *Maud*, only a vision of a world and a self in motion. It is a motion that implies a definite but unclearly defined unity. The image of Maud supporting the war "lightened my despair" (3, l. 18), he says, and the war itself will presumably complete the process, but in just what way it is difficult to see.

Another difficulty is that this symbol of war carries such an enormous weight in providing the resolution. The resolution is almost entirely symbolic, which is not a fault but may allow for more ambiguity than is usual in comedy. It is also, to the narrator, a highly personal solution. One real question is whether or not the symbol can provide the universality and the social resonance demanded of all comic endings. It is even possible to argue, as Roy P. Basler does so very well, that the hero at the end has only traded absolutisms: "He is not completely cured of psychic illness, but has merely exchanged one obsession, self-destruction, for another, self-sacrifice in a noble cause." [17] According to this reading, the form of the poem becomes ironic; the hero's presumed liberation is only another trap. Thus, for Basler, the war symbol has no generalized relevance, nor is it intended to have. It does not release but ensures the narrator's neurosis. The "official" explanation, given in the *Memoir* and in R. J. Mann's *Tennyson's 'Maud' Vindicated* is that military war is a lesser evil than commercial war.[18] But this is an answer that serenely evades any genuine questions, and the questions are very real. The hero does seem to be in some measure returning to a form of his early purism, cleaving, as he says, "to a cause that I felt to be pure and true" (l. 31).

At the same time, however, war is never presented as a symbol of his final position, but as a device by which he may be reintegrated. It is a transitional form that fits very well into the pattern of denial-acceptance in which comedy works. Having rejected the true, fallen nature of the world and its union of opposites, he must reenter that world through its most elemental and extreme coalition. He must accept the existence of honor in murder, life in death, purity in hideous slaughter. If his statements on war as a "pure and true" cause were all we had, one might indeed agree with Basler and see the hero's acceptance of war as another neurotic evasion. But the narrator also sees that "many a light shall darken, and many shall weep / For those that are crushed in the clash of jarring claims" (ll. 43–44). He does not misunderstand or "pretty up" war; he realizes that this arbitrary and meaningless suffering is a part of a "pure and true" cause.

War, thus, is the nearly absurd but legitimate demand that society makes on those who would be accommodated to it; it stands as the final rebuke to all absolutists. The narrator can finally learn to live with his own dark self when he can learn to live with the darkness of war. A kind of critical and moral absolutism of our own, then, has perhaps obscured the artistic appropriateness which this symbol can rightly claim. It is a dynamic, though transitory, symbol that will lead the narrator into a society which itself will be

17. "Tennyson the Psychologist," *SAQ* 43 (1944): 154. Reprinted in his *Sex, Symbolism, and Psychology in Literature*, pp. 73–93.

18. *Memoir*, 1:401; R. J. Mann, *Tennyson's 'Maud' Vindicated*, p. 74.

undergoing, in war, the same restoring movement through death and back into life that the narrator himself has experienced. The absence of a final resolution and a fixed symbol is confusing and tempts us to misread the symbol of war. The poem does not claim that war is better than peace. But in this bleak world one can live with peace only after he has been initiated by war.

The comic solution, then, shows a growth not only away from insanity but from the prison of the private self. The hero now can accept society's most terrible contradictions, mixing his breath with and giving life to a concept of "a loyal people" (ll. 34–35), united and one. He realizes communal life and a communal self: "I have felt with my native land, I am one with my kind, / I embrace the purpose of God, and the doom assigned" (ll. 58–59). The echo of *In Memoriam* is probably accidental, but it is highly suggestive all the same. Insofar as *In Memoriam* rests on the power of "I have felt" as a solution to despair (and to a great extent it does), it is a private poem with a private answer. *Maud* picks up the same words to rebuke *In Memoriam*'s subjectivism: now, "I have felt *with my native land*." He ends by saying that he accepts "the doom assigned." Eden has been lost and dismissed long ago; now, in the final line of the poem, individual freedom is renounced for God and the larger doom. It is hard to imagine a conclusion that would be darker yet still remain comic. *Maud*, at its very close, has already invaded the territory of irony.

7

The Late Phase

Maud pushes comedy to its ironic limit; it marks the end of Tennyson's attempt to work seriously with that form. After *Maud*, nearly all of his major poems are ironic. This is not to say that the comic vision failed Tennyson or vice versa; there was simply little more for him to do in that genre. Tennyson's moods or emotional states may or may not supplement his poetic instincts; they hardly exist on the same level. Most major nineteenth-century art was becoming ironic in form, a fact that seems far more important than anything that may have happened to Tennyson personally.

Still, there does seem to be in Tennyson a remarkable desire to resist the generic dominance of irony. His major poems after *Maud* are ironic, but there are not many of them that can be called major. *Idylls of the King* and a few dramatic monologues stand against a barrage of domestic idyls, political poems, occasional verse, and miscellaneous minor poems. "Lucretius" is counterbalanced by many poems like "De Profundis," poems which are nominally comic but which restrict the range of their appeals very narrowly, to those who can, for instance, be moved by lists of paradoxes: "Of this divisible-indivisible world / Among the numerable-innumerable / Sun, sun, and sun, through finite-infinite space / In finite-infinite Time." (ll. 43–46). "De Profundis" is a poem that might be called technically happy: "Hallowed be Thy name—Halleluiah!— / Infinite Ideality! / Immeasurable Reality! / Infinite Personality! / Hallowed be Thy name—Halleluiah!" (ll. 57–61). One can recognize a kind of dusty exuberance here, the sort of pedantic flight one associates with amateur nineteenth-century metaphysics, which, of course, is exactly what this poem and others like it consist of.

The remarkable quantity of the late comic poems is as important as their uneven quality. Tennyson did keep trying in comedy, but if not quite all the late poems that matter are ironic, the qualification is so trifling it can be ignored for now. Irony dominates the later major poems, so much so that it invades even poems which are clearly intended as positive statements. For instance, Tennyson obviously admired Sir Richard Grenville's lone fight against fifty-three Spanish ships. The poet's imagination was deeply stirred by the Hemingwayesque image of valor in defeat. But, while perceiving fully the heroic aspects of Grenville's endurance, Tennyson cannot entirely exclude from "The Revenge" [1] a glimpse of the ironic extension of that heroism. He catches, therefore, both great determination and also mania, the sense that heroism itself is fascinating but unnatural. Grenville's full-toned speeches about not giving in are played off against flat details like: "But in perilous plight were we, / Seeing forty of our poor hundred were slain, / And half of the rest of us maimed for life" (ll. 75–77).

The poem even hints at a suicidal quality in the hero, a perverse delight in self-destruction, presented in such a way as sometimes to seem slightly callous, even absurd: "Sink me the ship, Master Gunner—sink her, split her in twain! / Fall into the hands of God, not into the hands of Spain!" (ll. 89–90). The heroism contains a touch of vulgarity, a crude and narrow irrationality at odds with the expansive serenity common to the heroic tone. Sir Richard Grenville's sacrifice, further, spares no one and therefore comes to seem a trifle wild: "And a day less or more / At sea or ashore, / We die—does it matter when?" (ll. 86–88).

To any human being in his senses it matters a great deal. It matters very much, surely, to Grenville's men; they say so: "We have children, we have wives, / And the Lord hath spared our lives. / We will make the Spaniard promise, if we yield, to let us go" (ll. 92–94). Not so anxious to fall into the hands of God as their leader, the brave men leave Grenville to die if he likes—and of course he does. This odd disagreement and separation of Grenville from his men at the end of the poem upsets the directness of its

1. A brilliant and very detailed reading of this poem is given in Robert M. Estrich and Hans Sperber, *Three Keys to Language*, pp. 236–75. The authors show how Tennyson modified his sources and manipulated the language of the poem to create a precise and controlled image of heroism—a peculiarly Victorian heroism, they maintain, which is untouched by irony.

predominant motive: the celebration of devoted and single-minded patriotism.

But irony is the enemy of the single-minded, and here mixes into the heroic celebration the token images of domestic comedy—children and wives. And the two cannot easily be mixed. The poem takes as its center the celebration of what we think of as modern qualities: the acceptance of defeat and isolation. Even so, the image of defeated nobility is too complacent for irony. Sir Richard Grenville is not satirized, of course; but very strategically, just at the end of the poem, we are made to question the real desirability of his virtues.

Irony is nearly omnipresent in these late poems. The deliberately or overtly ironic poems are not really improvements over those in the 1842 volume; in many ways they are not even fundamentally different from them. What is apparent in the later poems is a more intricate and also less dramatic irony. The same themes and situations are there and the same rhetoric, but they are developed with more complexity and quietness.

Such changes are, in a general way, to be expected; what is surprising is the extent of this development. Tennyson's assurance in the form is such that he is able to extend it and establish its essential parodies less obviously. In the case of some early poems that were revised and published later, we have a good basis for examining this change. Poems like "The Captain," "The Voyage," and even "Tiresias," originally written in the mid-1830s though not published until much later,[2] are interesting ironic poems, but they are, I think, quite simple in comparison with the other late poems.

"The Captain" is not an unsubtle poem, but the source of its power is blatantly clear. A certain beleaguered crew conspires to turn the tables on a brave but stern and generally unlikeable captain. When a roaring fight comes, they fold their arms and refuse to take part, grinning at the captain and gleefully dying: "over mast and deck were scattered / Blood and brains of men" (ll. 47–48). The poem pretends to supply a moral to the effect that severity is an ineffective tactic for leaders to adopt (ll. 1–2), but such

2. According to Ricks, "The Captain" was "probably written in its original form [in] 1833-4" (p. 605); it was published in 1865. "The Voyage" was composed ca. 1836 (Ricks, p. 653) and was published in 1864. In the case of "Tiresias," "it is probable that the poem is substantially that of 1833" (Ricks, p. 568); it was revised in 1883 and published in 1885.

cautions are absurdly inadequate, failing entirely to explain the central action. The grotesque juxtaposition of such gory results with motives that are in every way childish defies any explanation. The poem emphasizes this pointlessness by picturing at its close both the ironic fellowship of the crew and captain "side by side beneath the water" (l. 67) and their final triviality: "There the sunlit ocean tosses / O'er them mouldering, / And the lonely seabird crosses / With one waft of the wing" (ll. 69–72). The poem has a dark power, but its strategies are fairly simple.

Just as direct is the ironic structure of another of these early-late poems, "The Voyage." Eleven of the poem's twelve sections present a virtually untroubled vision of the pursuit of the "Ideal," a vision and a goal that are as soft and mellow as they are vague. These sections avoid giving any concrete picture at all but simply exude an atmosphere of warm acceptance. The final section none too subtly disrupts all this with some grim actuality: "Now mate is blind and captain lame, / And half the crew are sick or dead" (ll. 91–92). The conclusion picks up lines from the first section and echoes them with a loud, sardonic jeer: "We know the merry world is round, / And we may sail for evermore" (ll. 95–96).

"The Voyage of the Maeldune," published in 1880 and written in the same year (Ricks, p. 1276), provides a good contrast to these two earlier poems. Though quite similar in its subject, the late poem demonstrates Tennyson's development toward compression and certainty of tone, largely by means of the technique of ambiguity he had mastered in the *Poems* of 1842. On one level, "The Voyage of the Maeldune" presents a very clear picture: a progress through various temptations to a highly appropriate moralistic conclusion, the holy saint's rebuke of vengeance. The men of the Maeldune presumably learn, after passing through the symbolic ordeals of the Isle of Fire, the Isle of the Double Towers, and the rest, the virtue of forgiveness.

It is characteristic of Tennyson's later ironic poems that the obvious and non-ironic statement of the poem, like the one just outlined, should be given greater and greater strength: the ironic counterstatement is put with much more reserve than in the earlier poems. Here, the vengeance-forgiveness motif is not subverted at all; rather, it is rendered inadequate to explain the poem's details. It is not, finally, vengeance that causes the men to kill one another but simply life's experience. The islands themselves have no connection to the purpose of vengeance (except for the first isle, and the wind blows them away from that one). These strange lands suggest, in their diversity, the complex of sensations and acts that make up all of life, particularly a good life. But all impulses act the same on these men, as they do on all men. Silence makes them yearn to kill each other; noise makes them actually do so. They are frustrated by the Isle of Flowers, but the fulfillment they find in the Isle of Fruits leads to something worse than frustration: "And we stayed three days, and we gorged and we maddened, till every one drew / His sword on his fellow to slay him, and ever they struck and they slew" (ll. 67–68). The Isle of Fire and the Paradise under the sea cause more deaths; even the Bounteous Isle, which encourages them to play, leads to war games and the inevitable result: "we slew and we sailed away" (l. 96).

This grim absurdity is climaxed in the episode of the Isle of the Double Towers, where, because there is *some* division, no matter how arbitrary, the men choose sides, naturally in order to kill one another: "and all took sides with the Towers, / There were some for the clean-cut stone, there were more for the carven flowers" (ll. 111–12). The saint's verdict about forgiveness at the end, then, touches only a part of the problem. The final lines are brilliantly ambiguous, supporting the moralistic warning of the saint but also suggesting that vengeance for these men is not so much wrong as superfluous after so much murder, that it is not morality but simple weariness that renders the whole quest pointless:

And we came to the Isle we were blown from, and there on the
    shore was he,
The man that had slain my father. I saw him and let him be.
O weary was I of the travel, the trouble, the strife and the sin,
When I landed again, with a tithe of my men, on the Isle of Finn.
                                                        [ll. 127–30]

The indirectness of this late irony is highlighted by comparison with one more of these early-late poems, "Tiresias." This poem is a good deal more complex than poems like "The Captain" or "The Voyage," perhaps because it was later revised more extensively; still, it does have a somewhat greater directness than is usual in poems composed later.[3] The poem is partly about sacrifice; but the

3. The poem is often read as quite unironic. Christopher Ricks, for example, comments that "*Tiresias* finds strength and consolation in deliberate self-sacrifice." He also goes on to

form, structure, and context all call into doubt the nobility, even the purposefulness, of such a sacrifice. Presumably, Menoeceus will, by killing himself, appease Ares, end the slaughter, and create for himself an enduring fame. None of this is exactly denied, but the loud voice of heroism is accompanied by ironic whispers that tell us that Menoeceus's death merely supports a senseless and bloody order and ensures the extinction of his own name at the hands of a fickle populace.

Further, Menoeceus and his free sacrifice are clearly displaced from the center of the dramatic monologue, which is occupied by Tiresias and his bondage. Tiresias has been cursed, in Tennyson's version, for presuming to search for beauty and knowledge. He wanted to see "that more than man / Which rolls the heavens, and lifts, and lays the deep" (ll. 21–22). This aesthetic and religious longing takes him to the heart of life and to the center of all wisdom, where he finds the Goddess Pallas Athene. She reveals to him the principles on which the universe operates: malignity and pettiness. Because he dared to worship, Tiresias is made the subject of a vicious joke. His religious desires are cruelly completed: his inner sight is made perfect, while his outer sight is destroyed.

What more could a transcendentalist want? Because he now has the secrets of truth, Tiresias is effectively isolated from all men; there is no need for any further curse than the ability to see what is and will be. He can "only speak the truth that no man may believe" (l. 49). The phrase is significantly ambiguous. Tiresias speaks the sort of truth men will not believe; or he speaks the truth, and therefore [so that] men will not believe him. Tiresias is given the answer to all human prayers, but what a bitter and cynical answer it is. He sees all essential truth—that is, all "famine, plague, / Shrine-shattering earthquake, fire, flood, thunderbolt, / And angers of the Gods" (ll. 59–61)—and therefore no one hears him.

Tiresias himself only partly understands that he has been cruelly tricked. He has slipped farther into the hands of the mocking gods than he realizes. He can still recall with pleasure the vision of Pallas Athene, that alien deity who denied all mankind by denying him.

---

say that "the sacrifice of God and His Son" is here "tenuously adumbrated" (p. 569). I would have said "parodied." One cannot deny that Tennyson may have had some very positive motive in writing the poem; but motives aside, "Tiresias" is ironic in form and undermines to a great extent its prescribed "strength and consolation."

There is, in other words, a dramatic irony working here that asks us to perceive Tiresias's position as even more terrible than he himself acknowledges. He fails to see, for instance, that Menoeceus's sacrifice really only allows Ares to win and thereby confirms what Ares, "whose one bliss / Is war and human sacrifice" (ll. 108–09), represents. Ares can be satisfied with Menoeceus's sacrifice only because it is, in itself, an emblem of the senseless slaughter that delights him. Ares and Pallas Athene, the two deities mentioned in the poem, form a grim unity, supporting the principles of trickery and absurdity. Yet the climax of the poem is a paean to these gods, a hopeful vision, in fact, of an eternity spent in praising these agents who have made him such a pitiable victim.

On the other hand, Tiresias does see, though he can do very little about, the ineffectiveness of truth itself. But he blames this not so much on the gods, on the very nature of things, as on the *people*. Cosmic injustice becomes, in his blindness, a matter of political ranting against the stupidity of the populace. The poem is framed by these very important complaints. He early laments that casting "wise words among the multitude / Was flinging fruit to lions" (ll. 65–66), and argues bitterly near the end of the poem that "the wise man's word / [is] Here trampled by the populace underfoot" (ll. 165–66). Yet in the center of these attacks are his pious exhortations to Menoeceus to slaughter himself for the good of these very people.

It is interesting that he rests his appeal to Menoeceus so very little on altruistic or ethical grounds; almost his entire argument is based on Menoeceus's achieving fame with the people, and thereby a kind of immortality. These people, so unable to hear truth and so feeble, are suddenly, in this argument, endowed with wisdom, courage, and stability. Tiresias is forcing Menoeceus into an even more horrible version of the fate he himself has experienced: a useless public life. The heart of truth is deception, whether it lies in Tiresias or in the gods. Tiresias's greatest curse was not to be disbelieved but, in this one instance, to be believed. He has unwittingly but surely become Pallas Athene herself.

The full achievement of the late ironic work, other than *Idylls of the King*, is represented very well by two poems, "Lucretius" and "Rizpah." Both are essentially dramatic monologues; both demonstrate Tennyson's growing ability to manipulate the two rhetorical poles of the dramatic monologue, sympathy and judgment, so as to include us more surely in the final irony.

The first thing to notice about "Lucretius" is Lucretius's wife, or more exactly, the frame of the poem in which she appears. Such frames almost always function in a dramatic monologue to add a necessary context and thus to strengthen the reader's judgmental response. These tactics are necessary in order to maintain the conflict between sympathy and judgment, to keep the poem from being rhetorically direct. When the central figure or the argument is implicitly outrageous, judgment is automatically brought into play; but when, as here, the speaker is given great intellectual power and dignity, it is necessary to do something more to call forth our judgment and ensure the proper tension. That something more, in this case, is the story of Lucilia and her passion, which surrounds, although it does not explain, Lucretius's tortured soliloquy. The incongruously flat, domestic opening of the poem—"Lucilia, wedded to Lucretius, found / Her master cold" (ll. 1–2)—acts to focus our attention on the human passions and needs Lucretius is denying. Tennyson boldly uses the stock comic figure of the sterile pedant for very serious purposes. Lucretius's denial of the passions is seen, right from the start, as a denial of all that is human. We see, too, that his unnatural excision of passion, his rage for intellectual placidity, must inevitably evoke the retribution of nature and humanity, symbolized here by Lucilia's potion. The potion acts directly to check "his power to shape" (l. 23). The ordered, rational world of this heroic and potentially tragic philosopher is destroyed by the simple jealousy of his wife. As in *In Memoriam*, then, instinctual feeling overcomes controlled, rational system, the difference being, of course, that "Lucretius" completely burlesques *In Memoriam*'s solution.

The force of this burlesque is maintained in Lucretius's soliloquy as well, though we do very much need the clearer ironies of the opening twenty-five lines of domestic actuality to alert us to the sad contradictions[4] that control his life. He is caught in the indifferent

4. Allan Danzig locates a comic dimension in the poem, arguing that Lucretius is caught by his single-minded inability to admit to contraries, his insistence on seeing negation where there is actually tension ("The Contraries," *PMLA* 77 [1962]: 579–82). The best reading of the ironic force of the poem is by W. David Shaw, "Imagination and Intellect in Tennyson's 'Lucretius,'" *MLQ* 33 (1972): 130–39. Shaw sees the poem as a study in dissociated sensibility, the problem being presented by the split of imagination and intellect. The

universe he has created—or rather perceived; for there is no indication that he is wrong about the universe or about the remoteness of the powers that control it. What mocks him, at least in this central section, is the chaos that underlies all human life and makes ridiculous the ideal of calm indifference after which he has sought. "I thought I lived securely as yourselves" (l. 210), he cries to the gods, but such glorious serenity is denied to man. It is not that Lucretius errs in imagining the world as cold and atomistic; he miscalculates only in supposing that man has an integral part in that world. He prays to "The all-generating powers and genial heat / Of Nature" (ll. 97–98), but it is just this force which creates a mixed and unsettled life. In his dream he is haunted by visions of a universe whose genial heat has become a raging fire.

The most remarkable of these visions is that of the naked breasts of Helen[5] overpowering and turning to the ground a threatening sword. Masculinity, particularly masculine control, is powerless in the face of utter sexuality, perhaps, but it is also "all that beauty" (l. 64), as he sees, which masters control and force. This is a completely ambiguous symbol. Furthermore, the power over one sort of violence—the sword—issues not in peace but in another form of violence: "and as I stared, a fire, / The fire that left a roofless Ilion, / Shot out of them, and scorched me that I woke" (ll. 64–66). For man, all beauty, desire, power, destruction, nurture, and murder are intermingled, not in real unity but in a wild, unmanageable chaos.

Lucretius is not satirized, then, nor is the heroism of his attempt to save a coherent universe denied. In trying to save humanity, however, he has abandoned it. His dying response to his anguished wife is the terrible issuance of the desire to make men gods: "Clasped, kissed him, wailed: he answered, 'Care not thou! / Thy duty? What is duty? Fare thee well!' " (ll. 279–80). This black denial of care, duty, and need is what comes of a philosophy that attempts to make sense of the universe and man's place in it. Lucretius is mistaken not because he adopted the wrong explana-

---

speaker, he says, makes "a brilliant, though unsuccessful, attempt to hold fact and values in unison" (p. 130).

5. An admirable and extensive investigation of the use of and sources for this image is conducted by James A. Freeman, "Tennyson, 'Lucretius' and the 'Breasts of Helen,' " *VP* 11 (1973): 69–75. Freeman does, however, see the pattern as more coherent than I; he argues that the image shows "that ideal beauty entails complete destruction" (p. 73).

tion of coherence but because he tried to find coherence at all. He betrays human nature, to be sure, but the human nature we see in Lucilia is that of a murderess. Sympathy and judgment work together to keep before us with equal force the grandeur of Lucretius's attempt and the trivial but disastrous nature of his failure. His betrayal is our own, and he is, in another sense, betrayed by us. All our dreams of hope and meaning, the poem finally asserts, are canceled out by our glaring insignificance.

"Rizpah" works for a similar inclusiveness in its irony, though its rhetoric operates very differently. Despite a certain false staginess, the poem achieves an effect that is very rare in Tennyson's dramatic monologues. It is absolutely direct in its appeals, rejecting almost entirely the intricate imagistic and structural movement of the early dramatic monologues in order to force us into full identification with the speaker. There is no ironic structural order, no reversals, and no tricks in this poem, simply a linear movement of intensification. The images become more and more concrete, but all to the same purpose. In one sense, "Rizpah" supports Langbaum's arguments on the dramatic monologue: it makes us into the speaker. Most kinds of judgments are rendered trivial by the sheer emotional power of the mother's language and by the carefully arranged dramatic context.

By presenting her case to a Protestant do-gooder, Rizpah shows how desperately inadequate mere benevolence is. The general level of concern and understanding, she suggests, cannot touch the primitive feelings that control human life. The charitable lady parodies genuine charity; she can only prattle on about sin, retribution, and election, abstract and meaningless catchwords when weighed against the concrete source of Rizpah's knowledge: feeling her son's bones move in her side (l. 54). The dramatic situation seems fashioned to disallow conventional responses. The visitor represents not so much the failure of Christianity (the poem goes on to demonstrate that she understands Christianity as little as she understands maternal love), as the failure of social being, our conventional selves. The charitable lady constantly makes judgments, invoking the grand symbols of religious justice. But these have no meaning to Rizpah and do not touch her experience; like her, we are forced to leave them behind. Conventional judgment is made to appear callous and, most of all, blatantly superficial.

The poem carefully connects this conventional religious and

moral judgment to the legal judgment that has sentenced Rizpah's
son. Just as the Christian lady is removed from Rizpah's elemental
reality, so is social and ethical justice remote from true justice. The
law is invoked as an instrument of decision so cruel and indifferent
to humanity that we must reject that judgment and the whole
complex of social institutions it represents—for instance, the asylum
where they beat the mother in order to cure her. This last, hideous
nonsequitur is emblematic of all our customary responses and
kindnesses. We must cast aside our social judgments and our social
beings, it appears, in order to live with the elemental love and
devotion of Rizpah.

But the rhetoric of the poem is not, I think, quite this simple.
Though we do reject a whole range of judgments, we retain others.
The tension in the dramatic monologue between sympathy and
judgment is preserved, but the judgment evoked is of a very special
kind. Unlike almost all of Tennyson's other dramatic monologues,
"Rizpah" does not evoke a judgment from outside the speaker;
there is no appeal to any of the normal responses that create the
pole of judgment in "The Lotos-Eaters" or "Ulysses." Here the
speaker herself generates both the sympathy and the judgment.
Though the poem appears to be stripping away our superficial,
social facades, it is actually just selecting a possible social frame-
work for us.

Rizpah counters the charitable lady's Calvinism not only with
the terrible, chaotic image of a grim contest for her son's bones,
which would in itself seem to repudiate all religions, but with a
different religious interpretation. Rizpah has not turned her back
on God; she has "been with God in the dark" (l. 79). She has found
the more basic and real Christianity: "Sin? O yes—we are sinners, I
know—let all that be, / And read me a Bible verse of the Lord's
good will toward men— / 'Full of compassion and mercy, the
Lord'—let me hear it again; / 'Full of compassion and mercy—
long-suffering.' Yes, O yes!. / For the lawyer is born but to
murder—the Saviour lives but to bless" (ll. 60–64). We reject
lawyers and Calvinism and asylum-keepers—that is, one *form* of
existing social being—but in its place we are given a different social
plan: one of mercy, forgiveness, rewards, and happiness. The strict
world of law is replaced by what, in its implications, is a comic
world with comic order. Rizpah provides us with a new standard for

judgment, a new context which, though given only in outline, can easily be created in full by the reader.

The ironic tension, then, is provided by the split between the actuality of experience presented and the joyous vision of the Christian frame of values that is evoked. Only one kind of judgment, the comic kind, is appropriate to human life; but, then, what does comedy have to do with such things as scratching for bones? We are forced to see the absolute validity of two quite different worlds: the world of nightmare and the world of forgiveness and mercy. Instead of raising a critical judgment, this poem disallows criticism altogether. But it does preserve a more profound conflict between the judgment, or the image, of a comic world of desire, and the sympathetic identification with the terror of the world of experience.

There are, as I have said, many late poems that are probably comic, though one would not want to so classify such works as "The Ancient Sage" with much conviction. Virtually all these poems are generically incomplete, lacking the confident vision of harmony and the ability to project solutions that are both concrete and evocative. They tend to rely instead on sonorous abstractions: again and again we are asked to accept as a climax lines like "A deep below the deep, / And a height beyond the height! / Our hearing is not hearing, / And our seeing is not sight" ("The Voice and the Peak," ll. 33–36). Such generalized assertions may be presumed to have a cheering effect; they are a kind of transcendental "Good morning." When Tennyson's late comedy does move toward specifics, it either degenerates into Polonius-like aphorisms—"Nor roll thy viands on a luscious tongue, / Nor drown thyself with flies in honied wine" ("The Ancient Sage," ll. 267–68)—or else dissolves into the anomalous "sunnier side of doubt" ("The Ancient Sage," l. 68) he often recommends. Cleaving to doubt, sunny or not, suggests a tentativeness which properly belongs to irony, not comedy. Tennyson developed the habit of adding question marks to nearly every affirmation he could bring himself to make in the late poems, for example, "A whisper from his dawn of life? a breath / From some fair dawn beyond the doors of death / Far—far—away?" ("Far—Far—Away," ll. 10–12). The best he can do now is to offer the hope that all is not quite lost—yet.

The facts of existence seem to him so overwhelmingly *un*comic that he can support comedy only by an act of faith, and a weak act at that. The happiest expression he can honestly find is a wary hope against hope:

Chaos, Cosmos! Cosmos, Chaos! who can tell how all will end?
Read the wide world's annals, you, and take their wisdom for
    your friend.
Hope the best, but hold the Present fatal daughter of the Past,
Shape your heart to front the hour, but dream not that the hour
    will last.
                ["Locksley Hall Sixty Years After," ll. 103–06]

This particular poem is a vivid illustration of the general inability of these late poems to find peace. Though Hallam reports that the poet had "endeavoured to give the moods of despondency which are caused by the decreased energy of life," Tennyson himself said that "the old man in the second 'Locksley Hall' had a stronger faith in God and in human goodness than he had had in his youth." [6]

    These explanations seem to me slippery at best. The old man who speaks in the second "Locksley Hall" tries very hard to put things in a positive light—at least some of the time—but he keeps falling back into the negations that dominate the poem. The uniquely personal comedy of the first "Locksley Hall," where progress and the dynamic movement of the age were used to call the speaker out of himself, is now repudiated: "Good, this forward, you that preach it, is it well to wish you joy? / Is it well that while we range with Science, glorying in the Time, / City children soak and blacken soul and sense in city slime?" (ll. 216–18). The general solutions have failed, interestingly, not so much because of city slums and city slime, but simply because such solutions have not helped him:

Poor old voice of eighty crying after voices that have fled!
All I loved are vanished voices, all my steps are on the dead.
All the world is ghost to me, and as the phantom disappears,
Forward far and far from hence is all the hope of eighty years.
                            [ll. 251–54]

As in the first poem, the focus is intensely personal; the speaker is

6. *Memoir*, 2:329.

not asking for a social utopia (or really even for social improve-
ment) but for some happiness. The pleasantest things he can find to
say—"Follow Light, and do the Right—for man can half-control
his doom" (l. 277)—hardly indicate the strong "faith" Tennyson
ascribed to him, nor do they provide sufficient assurance to support
a comic poem.

There are a few poems which, whether or not they are major, do
manage much more certain comedy. "Vastness," for instance, is an
interesting late attempt to repeat the comic formula of *In Memoriam*.
It puts irony on trial, allowing it to display its own climactic
insufficiency. The ironic platitudes are given more than free play;
they are presented in the harshest and most stinging way: "What is
it all but a trouble of ants in the gleam of a million million of suns?"
(l. 4). The compressed bitterness and, at the same time, the range of
allusion represent ironic technique at its most effective. Still, the
long line and the fast meter, made generally more regular and thus
quicker as the poem proceeds, suggest a mounting frenzy, as does
the increasingly frequent use of inclusive words like *all* and *every:*
"Spring and Summer and Autumn and Winter, and all those old
revolutions of earth; / All new-old revolutions of Empire—change
of the tide—what is all of it worth?" (ll. 29–30). Such lines give a
subtle hint of a loss of control that is less and less well hidden.
Instead of the expected cool detachment, the tone becomes more
heated, and after thirty-five lines of this the ironic momentum
peters out.

In one line, then, only one-half of a stanza, the calm assurance of
love is stated: "Peace, let it be! for I loved him, and love him for
ever: the dead are not dead but alive" (l. 36). Exactly as in *In
Memoriam*'s section 57, the fury is silenced by the word *peace*, which
allows a new tone and a new attitude to take over. In *In Memoriam*,
of course, more than seventy lyrics go on to support and define this
new tone; here, there is only this one line. The power of that line
and the force of the comic solution depend, in a negative sense, on
our perception of the mounting fury and weakness of the irony and,
in a positive sense, entirely on the word *love* and its ability to evoke a
whole range of experience and values contrary to those of irony.
The assertion here is necessarily bald because it cannot be
supported by logic or the emotional turmoil that accompanies
irony. Love gives "peace," as the poem says; therefore further words
are superfluous, really impossible. Tennyson is, one could argue,

more tactful here than in *In Memoriam*, allowing the cumulative force of irony to backlash and to provide by inversion a borrowed energy to the comic term "love."

This poem is, at any rate, a unique and, I think, successful comic experiment. What needs to be emphasized, however, is not the success of this sort of poem but its rarity in Tennyson's late work. Even here Tennyson had enormous difficulty persuading himself to put the last line in a positive form. Earlier versions are strongly qualified or are stated negatively. We can see, in fact, each of the four versions (the last is the published one) growing gradually but surely stronger and slightly more affirmative, as if the poet were expending a great deal of effort to work himself up to write a single comic line:

Save for a hope that we shall not be lost in the Vastness, a dream that the dead are alive?   *MS 1st reading*

Peace, for I hold that I shall not be lost in the darkness, the dead are not dead but alive.   *MS 2nd reading*

Nay, for I knew thee, O brother, and loved thee, and I hold thee as one not dead but alive.   *MS 3rd reading*

Peace, let it be! for I loved him, and love him for ever: the dead are not dead but alive.   *Published version*

[see Ricks, p. 1348]

Perhaps the almost pathetic hesitancy recorded here gives some indication of why there is so little comedy in Tennyson's late poems. "Demeter and Persephone," in fact, seems to me the only fully realized comic poem written in conventional terms (unlike the very special form of "Vastness"). It is a mellow and, surprisingly, quite simple and undisturbed comedy. There are complex implications in the myth, of course, which is not simple at all, but Tennyson's presentation of that myth, even with his much discussed frame, follows a direct comic form. The poem may, as James Kissane points out,[7] have some connections with an essay by Walter Pater, "The Myth of Demeter and Persephone." Tennyson had a copy of this essay,[8] which he marked rather carefully, noting, among other

7. "Victorian Mythology," *VS* 6 (1962): 25–28.
8. To be precise, a copy of part 2 of the two-part article, published in *Fortnightly Review*, n.s. 19 (February 1876): 260–76, is in the collection of the Tennyson Research Centre in Lincoln. The passage cited later in the sentence is on p. 275.

things, Pater's suggestion that the image of Persephone "is meant to make us in love, or at least at peace, with death."

Such an attitude, we know, is not foreign to Tennyson; it is one major effect of "The Lotos-Eaters." "Demeter and Persephone," however, does a good deal more, celebrating not death but full and harmonious life. Even in her painful search for her daughter, Demeter finds that death and life, good and evil, are interrelated, not in conflict: "The Bright one in the highest / Is brother of the Dark one in the lowest" (ll. 93–94). Out of this basic unity the myth resolves itself by making Persephone queen of both life and death. This classic belief does not, however, fully satisfy Tennyson, who augments it with a vision of the future, where "kindlier Gods" (l. 129) will bring these related opposites of death and life into an even fuller and more complete unity: "Till thy dark lord accept and love the Sun, / And all the Shadow die into the Light, / When thou shalt dwell the whole bright year with me" (ll. 135–37). The comic wholeness of the present is not denied, but it is made prefatory to the richer comedy to come.

All that remains are those short and highly evocative religious poems which are among the very last poems Tennyson wrote.[9] The series of brief lyrics written at the end of his life are very different from anything else in the corpus. They have about them a quietness and peace totally absent from the earlier poetry. Poems like "Faith," "The Dreamer," and "The Making of Man" present solutions which are still general but have a solidity that is missing from the vague abstractions he had depended on in other late poems. Especially in "God and the Universe" he achieves a suggestiveness and confidence that recall the religious comedy of George Herbert and Milton: "Spirit, nearing yon dark portal at the limit of thy human state, / Fear not thou the hidden purpose of that Power which alone is great, / Nor the myriad world, His shadow, nor the silent Opener of the Gate" (ll. 4–6). Tennyson thus continues, right up to the time of his death, to strive for comedy. But on the whole his late poetry after *Maud* really belongs to irony.

9. These very late poems and those of the decade of the 1880s are defended very ably by Francis Golffing, "Tennyson's Last Phase," *SoR*, n.s. 2 (1966): 268, who makes a case for Tennyson as a genuine seer, bridging cultural barriers with a poetry that is "frankly naturalistic, this-worldly." Also see Sir Charles Tennyson, "Tennyson: Mind and Method," *Tennyson Research Bulletin* 1 (November 1971): 127–36.

8

Idylls of the King

> . . . till the loathsome opposite
> Of all my heart had destined did obtain.
> ["Guinevere," ll. 488–89]

"The Arthurian Romance has every recommendation that should win its way to the homage of a great poet. It is national: it is Christian." [1] It is also ironic, and that, one gathers, meant a great deal more to Tennyson than the patriotic and religious possibilities Gladstone was publicly urging on him. The ostensible purpose of Gladstone's exhortation was to persuade the Laureate to continue his Arthurian work beyond the four idylls published in 1859. To that extent Tennyson followed his political friend's advice, though the finished *Idylls* is hardly the sort of pious article Gladstone seems to have had in mind.

What exactly it *is* forms the subject of a lively controversy these days. It is no longer possible to call *Idylls of the King* a neglected masterpiece. Nor can one now set about the pleasant and easy task of defending the poem from its well-meaning friends—like Bradley: "Let us take the *Idylls of the King*. They swarm with beautiful passages." [2] The best Tennyson criticism in recent years has been devoted to this poem, which has more and more come to be recognized as his major work and one of the two or three most important poems of the century.

The critical controversy over the *Idylls* bears out E. D. Hirsch's contention that "every disagreement about an interpretation is usually a disagreement about genre." [3] Arguments about the theme of the poem, about whether the prevailing ethic is absolutist, relativistic, or existential, and especially about the role and function

1. "Tennyson's Poems," *QR* 106 (1859): 468.
2. *The Reaction Against Tennyson*, p. 12.
3. E. D. Hirsch, *Validity in Interpretation* (New Haven: Yale University Press, 1967), p. 98.

of Arthur, all derive from varying assumptions about the poem's genre. Those who assume that the *Idylls* is or should be tragic are prone to see Arthur as a redeemer who fails; those who assume a comic form likely see him as a defective human being. Tennyson clearly insists that Arthur is both hero and human, ideal and real, thus suggesting the inability of either comic or tragic conceptions to give a full explanation. In fact, these classic forms appear in the *Idylls* only in parody. The poem is the most complete expression of ironic art in Tennyson, perhaps in his time. It manages to attack the substance of each of the other three mythoi: its narrative structure parodies romance; its tone parodies comedy; its characters, particularly its central hero, parody tragedy.

There are, of course, several different kinds of generic questions connected with the *Idylls*, and I should make it clear that I am not primarily concerned here with the important issue of the poem's relation to epic or the even more important issue of Tennyson's use of the term "idyll." [4] For my purposes it is sufficient to note that the obvious epic analogy heightens the irony by suggesting a coherence, a positive scale of values, and conceptions of grandeur which are now absent. Similarly, the term "idyll" brings into view a different order entirely from the one that is present. The "little picture" and its emphasis on leisurely contemplation support very well the parody of romance and its lazy, easy development. [5] We are given, in romance, the illusion of a movement that occurs only in space and thus occupies no time. In the foreground of romance and the *Idylls* is furious action, but the form itself assures us that there is no real development at all.

The narrative discontinuity in the *Idylls*, as in romance, is itself an important virtue, in that it gives a sense of being in an art gallery, glancing slowly from one "little picture" to another. Even the overlaid seasonal progress in the *Idylls* suggests not so much objective, physical time as the spatial representations of time in medieval tapestry or triptychs. This emphasis on space seems to imply the absence of time, which in turn implies the conquest of

4. For the fullest exploration of this term and its implications, see J. M. Gray, "A Study in Idyl," *RMS* 14 (1970): 111–50. A review of the historical confusion attending the term is provided by J. Philip Eggers, *King Arthur's Laureate*, pp. 58–60.

5. Tennyson was perhaps least in sympathy with the genre of romance. According to Edward Fitzgerald, Tennyson said of Malory's *Le Morte D'Arthur*, "There are very fine things in it, but all strung together without art" (*Memoir*, 1:194).

time. In romance, the passage of time is only apparent; there is always room for more adventures. Even the fact that adventures resemble one another and are cast in what appears to be no necessary order supports the illusion of infinite leisure: the reader, it is almost suggested, can go ahead and add some more tales if he likes. The world of romance is the world of the wish-fulfillment dream, where there is motion without destruction, recurrent rather than climactic development.

Tennyson's poem supports all these characteristics of romance, of course, only to belie them: beneath the placid surface is an inexorable and ever more restricting progress. The poem advances one of its most crucial parodies in relation to the timeless "idyll." A strong negative climax is created through a form that is meant to protect us from conclusions; there is no real freedom from the laws of time, especially from the principles of decay and dissolution. Arthur tries to establish a world in which past, present, and future cooperate "as if Time / Were nothing" ("Gareth and Lynette," ll. 222–23), but, despite Arthur, despite even the idyll form, time wins.

Time and a great many other forces conspire to destroy the city that "is built / To music, therefore never built at all, / And therefore built for ever" ("Gareth and Lynette," ll. 272–74). These central lines occur in the midst of a speech by Merlin, wherein he mocks the rationalistic and empirical assumptions of Gareth and his companions. Merlin is no relativist, but he realizes that there are some who will be satisfied only with the deceptive truths of materialism: "And here is truth; but an it please thee not, / Take thou the truth as thou hast told it me" (ll. 252–53). If they are not "pleased" with the one central truth, the only and single truth, they are welcome to the "truth" they already possess, such as it is. Tennyson was so anxious to avoid misunderstanding of this passage and its apparent endorsement of relativism that he added a footnote explaining that Merlin's use of the term *truth* to describe the youth's rationalistic perceptions is "Ironical" (Ricks, p. 1491).

Indeed it is. Merlin is defending the absolute validity and reality of the city built to music that pipes "to the spirit ditties of no tone." The city houses the spiritual and the imaginative, but it is a city and it is *built*. There is no denial of the senses but an incorporation of them into the full harmony of creative life. Camelot is never built at all, Merlin says (partly in jest), only in the eyes of those who insist on the truths (ironical) of rationalism. The secrets of Camelot are not available to those who lack the capacity for exercising the creative imagination; it has no meaning at all for those who have only the tools of logic and the evidence of the senses.

Arthur's world is based on Romantic, especially Coleridgean dualisms, but Arthur is no simple transcendentalist. He insists on a dynamic interplay between ideal and real, reason and imagination, a resolution of apparently hostile forces into an extremely difficult balance. The use of the senses is not part of the danger; only a total reliance on the senses is damaging. An absolute denial of the senses is, in the end, exactly as harmful to Camelot's balanced world as is a dependence on them. This is not an absolutist world defeated by relativism, but a poised and complex world defeated by simplicities.

Arthur is attempting to control rather than to deny change. Above all, Camelot is a dynamic conception whose permanence, like that of music, is fluid, resilient, and unfixed. Almost no one perceives this; even the slippery and cynical Gawain views loyalty merely as stasis: Lancelot's defection seems surprising to him only because it suggests that the presumably constant (which to Gawain means "stationary") knight has *changed:* "Must our true man change like a leaf at last?" ("Lancelot and Elaine," l. 682). To rationalists, all change is evidence of the defeat of Camelot. It is the worldlings, the relativists of Camelot who are, in the end, its rigid absolutists. At the center of Arthur's genuine promise is the figure of the converted Edyrn: "[I] kept myself aloof till I was changed; / And fear not, cousin; I am changed indeed" ("Geraint and Enid," ll. 871–72). The city of music is not built at all, in the sense of being static and unchanging; it is built forever in the sense that it partakes of the growth and variety of the best part of human life.

But in order to realize that best part of life, men must be human; they must ensure a basic coherence so that a dynamic order may be built. The vows bind them only in the way Lancelot is originally bound, to keep the *word* that is "God in man" ("The Coming of Arthur," l. 132). The purpose of this complete trust in words is not the enforcement of mere restrictive honesty but the creation of a bond between word and deed, between past (promise) and future (action), between God and man, that is at the heart of a genuine society. The vows are enemies of chaos only, not of variability and growth. Far from asking for a sacrifice of individuality, they provide a social and personal solidity out of which genuine personality can develop. The direct result of the maintenance of these vows is courtesy, an unforced and natural outward expression of the grace developed within. There is no particular code of conduct, legislated or otherwise, because none should be necessary. Behavior is linked inextricably to being; deception, thus, is impossible and need not be guarded against.

The basis of Camelot's hope is very clearly the basis for its destruction. The kingdom can exist only on the validity of the word, which means that man's best hope can be sabotaged by something as superficial as a lie. As soon as the word is broken, God, who is thus denied, withdraws from the world and human beings cease to be human. Arthur's scheme seems a remarkably simple means for bringing Eden back to man; and it is, but men throw away the only hope they had. Merlin knows that the vows are both necessary and fruitless, that they make almost no demand at all and yet an impossible one: "for the King / Will bind thee by such vows, as is a shame / A man should not be bound by, yet the which / No man can keep" ("Gareth and Lynette," ll. 265–68). The vows will guarantee our humanity; for that reason they will be broken.[6]

The most terrible irony in all the *Idylls* is that there is no real cause for this loss of humanity.[7] As Northrop Frye says, "Tragedy's 'this must be' becomes irony's 'this at least is.' "[8] Instead of the convincing reasons given in tragedy we have a multiplicity of reasons, all inadequate. There are no resounding causes for the fall and no important forces at work against Arthur; he is defeated by triviality. His greatest enemy, in fact, is the natural process of oversimplification. The balance he tries to maintain between the physical and the spiritual, for instance, is destroyed on one side by Tristram and the naturalists, and on the other by the well-meaning search for the Grail. The failure is not one of morality but a pathetic failure of understanding; the world is lost not because it is evil but because it is stupid.

6. There have been a few attempts to dissolve the tension of Merlin's ironic paradox. The most ingenious is Condé Benoist Pallen's *The Meaning of "The Idylls of the King,"* p. 46. According to him, Merlin is talking about "vows which it is a shame for a man not to swear, but vows which no man, simply as man, can keep; for he can fulfill them only by becoming spiritualized."

7. Jacob Korg, "The Pattern of Fatality in Tennyson's Poetry," p. 10, also argues that there is no real cause, that the kingdom "unaccountably" dissolves. He goes on, however, to ascribe this causelessness to an overriding "fatalism," a tragic principle, I would suggest, that is unrelated to ironic action.

8. *Anatomy of Criticism*, p. 285.

Arthur is magnificently heroic, but there is about him the ironic shadow of the relentless and ludicrously ineffective pedagogue whose star pupils misunderstand: the king's grandest and simplest words are presented by a good-hearted reporter, Percivale, whose only comment is, "So spake the King: I knew not all he meant" ("The Holy Grail," l. 916). The entire poem mixes the heroic and the preposterous, the grand and the trivial. The final effect is not to deny the importance of Arthur and Camelot, but rather to insist on both the greatness and the impossibility—even the absurdity—of this dream. The dream is shattered for no particular, or at least no important, reason; most men did not even realize what it was: "the wholesome madness of an hour," according to Tristram ("The Last Tournament," l. 670).

But it is not individuals, finally, who fail Arthur. It makes some sense to say, "Arthur gave the opportunity; only the individual can fulfill the idea presented to him," [9] but in fact no one finds the task that easy. Genuine liberation and growth in Camelot are simple matters only at the very beginning; the world soon closes in and becomes restrictive, very much as it does in *Middlemarch* or *The Trial*, where everyone is caught in complex entanglements he can neither control nor understand. Later, innocent characters like Pelleas and Elaine have no chance at all; they are slaughtered not because they fail to believe in Arthur but because their belief is so pure. Camelot's fall cannot, thus, be traced to people; it is caused by something both larger and more paltry—the very nature of things.

In other words, insofar as Arthur could fight against social bias, immorality, sin, and prejudice, he could win great victories, but he could not win against the natural current of dim sloth and stupidity. The fact that he could, for a time, defeat all natural forces defines his heroism; it also defines the basis of his defeat by the mounting pressure of trivia. The faith in nature or natural impulses is thus bitterly transformed. In comedy, the forces of natural instinct and order overcome rigid and artificial efforts to thwart them. In the ironic form of the *Idylls*, natural forces also win and overcome the king who has tried to impose unnatural virtue, unnatural humanness.

However, the *Idylls* are most often read, or misread, in terms of blame, fault, and causes for decline.[10] The poem itself certainly

9. John R. Reed, *Perception and Design*, p. 157.

10. I do not mean to imply, of course, that it is consistently misread. F. E. L. Priestley's analysis, "Tennyson's *Idylls*," *UTQ* 19 (1949): 35–49, is particularly admirable for its ability

refuses to provide a perspective for finding fault; it engages enthusiastically in denying us this perspective. Despite this fact, it is both natural and common for critics to locate some position anyhow—either inside the poem, with Tristram and the relativists or Percivale's sister and pure spirituality, or outside the poem, usually in some theory of tragic action.

The naturalistic objections to Arthur, stated at various times in the poem by Guinevere, Tristram, and Vivien, are given extremely witty form by a great many commentators. The most colorful is Swinburne's complaint that Tennyson has reduced "Arthur to the level of a wittol." The king's "besotted blindness . . . is nothing more or less than pitiful and ridiculous." Swinburne does at least recognize that he has predecessors in his views and he offers an indirect acknowledgment to his major source: Vivien. He maintains that she is right; "such a man as this king is indeed hardly 'man at all.' " [11]

One must admire Swinburne's heroic consistency; once he finds these realistic grounds for objection, nothing, not even Vivien, will dislodge him. His views are later repeated by G. K. Chesterton[12] and, in modern criticism, most pointedly by Clyde deL. Ryals. Ryals picks up some different points from the poem's rationalists, namely, Tristram's objections to the unreal rigor of the vows ("The Last Tournament," ll. 651–57) and to Arthur's unnatural infringement on his liberties (ll. 678–90). For Ryals, Arthur is "a monomaniac" whose knights are "emotionally exploited" by him.[13]

It is difficult now to escape from this contention that Arthur is somehow at fault. It is a novelistic world in which we (or at least readers of nineteenth-century literature) live, one that is dominated by realistic and pragmatic notions of probable behavior. Tennyson's poem makes very few appeals to that particular set of assumptions, and then only in order to parody them. It is true, of course, that Arthur can never be successful. Merlin says so. To suppose, however, that this means he should have done something different seems to me to reduce greatly the effect of the poem.

---

to state tactfully and precisely the various balanced opposites that hold Camelot together. His argument is the basis for much recent criticism of the *Idylls*, most of which, in fact, departs further from his general position than I do.

11. Algernon Charles Swinburne, "Under the Microscope," in *The Complete Works of Algernon Charles Swinburne*, ed. Sir Edmund Gosse and Thomas James Wise (London: William Heinemann; New York: Gabriel Wells, 1926), 16:405–06.

12. *The Victorian Age in Literature*, p. 167.

13. Clyde deL. Ryals, *From the Great Deep*, p. 81.

The alternative tendency to read the poem in terms of tragic imitation is not reductive, of course, but it is artificially elevating. Some of the most interesting discussions of the *Idylls* are filled with talk of "an unfathomable pattern of universal justice," a purging and cleansing of the world,[14] or the necessity of making Apollonian illusions stand in the face of the Dionysiac beast.[15] There are strong tragic overtones in Arthur's story, but I think they are there, finally, to burlesque genuine tragedy. The death of Arthur confirms no justice, universal or local; the poem ends where *In Memoriam* began: in darkness and uncertainty, without heroism, even without meaning.

The basic form of *Idylls of the King* is very much like that of *In Memoriam* reversed: instead of irony yielding naturally to comedy, here irony subverts comedy. The *Idylls of the King* carefully builds a comic world and then destroys it from within. It is a poem which, at its opposite ends, asserts the alternating visions of comedy and irony. In the middle sections we see the two together, the acidic properties of irony working to dissolve comic values. The three-part structure[16] of the poem corresponds to this division: first, the affirmation of comedy in "The Coming of Arthur," "Gareth and Lynette," "The Marriage of Geraint," and "Geraint and Enid"; next, the parody and dissolution of comedy in "Balin and Balan," "Merlin and Vivien," "Lancelot and Elaine," and "The Holy Grail"; finally, the confirmation of irony in "Pelleas and Ettarre," "The Last Tournament," "Guinevere," and "The Passing of Arthur."

I

The duty of the first section is to establish very clearly and to solidify a comic solution: the complete embodiment of a world with firm and luminous standards, permanent and workable values. The details of this vision of success must be imprinted on the reader's mind so that in the later parts of the poem he can recognize how specific and how complete the parody is. The force of the poem depends very largely on its ability to make its mocking points

14. Henry Kozicki, "Tennyson's *Idylls of the King*," *VP* 4 (1966): 16, 20.

15. William R. Brashear, "Tennyson's Tragic Vitalism," *VP* 6 (1968): 29–49; see also *The Living Will*, passim.

16. Priestley speaks of the three parts of the *Idylls*. He likens the poem to "the three acts of modern drama" ("Tennyson's *Idylls*," p. 47).

concrete and exact; it can do this only by presenting an image of Camelot's success that is so striking it will not leave us, even long after the enemies have taken over.

The first section proceeds very methodically to build that memorable image. The opening poem, "The Coming of Arthur," gives a rational and discursive definition of the bases of the new world, its values and its demands. The second, "Gareth and Lynette," provides a poetic image of that world in action, proving Camelot's power to sustain itself. It is a more or less static image, drawn from the realm of innocence. The world of the last two idylls in this section, "The Marriage of Geraint" and "Geraint and Enid," is the world of experience, and its corresponding image is of dynamic change and repentance. Comedy thus ranges over and metaphorically dominates the total human perspective: from perfection to imperfection, timelessness to the transient, dream to actuality.

"The Coming of Arthur" opens the *Idylls* by posing its most crucial general problem: how do we know, what is the nature of knowledge, what sort of knowledge is authentic? The question is Arthur himself: who is he, where does he come from, how does he operate? Leodogran appears as the reader's surrogate, forced to decide whether or not to yield his being and his love. He must determine what truth is and how one arrives at it. The *Idylls* begins, then, in the most demanding way: with an essay on epistemology. Of course it is all superficially more concrete than this, but Leodogran's search for Arthur's origin and nature leads him into the most basic considerations, those that can be answered only by Merlin's riddling or by the king's dream. It is a search for evidence that ends by rejecting evidence altogether.

Leodogran's most immediate problem is to investigate the nature of evidence, the means by which we find truth. We do learn a great deal about the *nature* of that truth and its *function*, that is, about the nature and function of Arthur, but the central dramatic problem involves the sorting through of evidence that appears to conflict. Leodogran must find how to know before he can worry about the results of knowledge. His dilemma is compounded by the fact that few others seem the least bit troubled by this problem. Almost everyone else is dead certain, most of all the "great Lords and

Barons" (l. 64) of the realm, who are quite clear about evidence: "for lo! we look at him [Arthur], / And find nor face nor bearing, limbs nor voice, / Are like to those of Uther whom we knew. / This is the son of Gorloïs, not the King; / This is the son of Anton, not the King" (ll. 69–73).

This simple faith in the senses is the first faith rejected in the *Idylls*. Mere empiricism is always wrong, self-confident empiricism always dangerous. These assured logicians claim to have *known* Uther, but they knew only his face, bearing, limbs, and voice. Empiricism, the first real enemy in the poem, is now made to seem stupid and irrelevant, for the *Idylls* begins in comedy. But there is a deadly appeal in the empiricist's logic, a simplicity and ease quite attractive when compared with the difficulties Leodogran must endure when he casts away these assurances.

The ultimate answer to the king's problem is given immediately in the poem, in the urgent and dramatic words of Lancelot: "Sir and my liege . . . the fire of God / Descends upon thee in the battle-field: / I know thee for my King!" (ll. 127–29). The phrasing suggests that knowledge involves commitment; Lancelot acknowledges that Arthur is king and pledges his loyalty. He knows because he has experienced Arthur's kingship; it is as simple as that. The test of knowledge and the only genuine source of it is in experience—not necessarily, or even importantly, physical experience, but in the immediate participation in the imaginative life of the thing perceived. Witnesses, then, can be reliable only insofar as they are artists; their logic means nothing and there are no points they can prove, no case they can make. Only insofar as they can re-create the very life of the truth they report can that truth be transmitted. We know, then, in direct imaginative experience.

Leodogran, however, does not yet comprehend this, or at least the experience is not yet available to him; so he turns to witnesses, thinking that he can get at knowledge by empirical means. What he finds in the reports of his chamberlain, of Bedivere, and of Bellicent, is a chaotic jumble of facts that confuses his judgment only to provide him with inward certainty. The real facts of Arthur's birth are so impossible to determine that Leodogran is forced—or allowed—to go beyond facts to the essential truth. The testimony of the three witnesses conflicts wildly but only superficially. Each statement acts to represent the speaker's full belief in

Arthur's legitimacy and spirituality.[17] Leodogran learns from them
to create his own poetry and his own belief. Out of his dream he
fashions an experience that testifies as art testifies: without logic and
proof but with life and power.

His first lessons, however, are negative ones; he has not yet
learned to ask the proper questions. He searches after Arthur's
secrets as if Arthur were a specimen to be traced and classified:
"Knowest thou aught of Arthur's birth?" (l. 146). His chamberlain
very rightly responds that spiritual agencies cannot be discussed in
terms of origins. Only those in touch with magic, Merlin and Bleys,
understand magic events. Leodogran is vexed that he cannot
receive a direct answer to a direct question—"O friend, had I been
holpen half as well / By this King Arthur as by thee today, / Then
beast and man had had their share of me" (ll. 160–62). Such things
as births, he assumes, are surely matters of record, or at least
matters of plain fact. But Arthur is not to be discovered in this way;
"our Arthur's birth," as the chamberlain concludes, is "secret" (l.
158). As J. M. Gray points out, this *our* is the key to the
chamberlain's speech.[18] It indicates that despite his inability to
reply to Leodogran's questions, he has found the answers. From the
very start, then, Leodogran's mode of proceeding is criticized.

The next witness, Bedivere, provides a more subtle criticism of
the logical and empirical proceedings. A clumsy, dull-witted
soldier, he shares Leodogran's pragmatic assumptions. He is
Arthur's first knight, loyal and brave, utterly convinced of Arthur's
spirituality, but his understanding fails completely to grasp what he
knows by experience. He is bold to defend the king against slander
(ll. 175–76), but his own version of Arthur's birth is so gross as
almost to constitute slander. He blithely repeats the gossipy, lurid
tale of how Uther, driven by uncontrollable "heat" (l. 197), so
lusted after Ygerne that he killed her husband. She remarries "with
a shameful swiftness" (l. 204) and begets "all before his time" (l.
210) a son, Arthur.

This inglorious beginning does not bother Bedivere at all; he
cheerfully tells it to *defend* Arthur. How he can imagine that
Leodogran will be much reassured by this thinly disguised story of
rape (Bedivere is no euphemist) is not clear; what is clear is that he

17. This same view is developed by J. M. Gray's "A Study in Idyl," pp. 111–50; also see
Gray's *Man and Myth in Victorian England.*
18. "A Study in Idyl," p. 119.

is unconscious of the effect of the tale not only because he is stupid but because such things do not matter to him. His faith is beyond the need of proof, though his understanding is happy to provide it for the skeptical. Bedivere shows how completely faith and understanding, internal convictions and external verification are divorced in this idyll. Arthur will later strive to bring them into harmony, and will, for a time, succeed. Such a union is, in fact, forecast in Bedivere's story, where Arthur's origin in physical lust is complemented by his mystical training with Merlin. The body and the spirit are thus united, somewhat crudely, of course, but, for Bedivere, appropriately. When there is, as there is in this idyll, a conflict between faith-imagination-experience and logic-reason-proof, however, the first are always held to be superior.

The superiority of imaginative experience is finally stated explicitly by the last witness, Bellicent, whose testimony is most important because her experience is most direct, least affected by superficial judgments: "I was near him" (l. 255), she says, and that one point counts for everything. She does, in fact, tell us a good deal about Arthur, describing his coronation and the participation of the Lady of the Lake, who is the most obvious sign of Arthur's spirituality, his symbolic association with the soul.[19] Bellicent's most important duty, however, is to continue Leodogran's education in the legitimate means of finding truth. Leodogran is very properly moved by her story of Arthur's coronation; he is beginning to learn the truth within him and is secretly glad to receive such vital imaginative confirmation: "Thereat Leodogran rejoiced" (l. 309).

He still is plagued by rationalistic itches, however, and, thinking "to sift his doubtings to the last" (l. 310), returns doggedly to the issue of proof. Bellicent, presumably Arthur's sister, should know the facts if anyone does, he supposes. But she dismisses this approach immediately: "What know I?" (l. 325). She goes on to point out that if he wants ocular proof, it isn't there: "What know I? / For dark my mother was in eyes and hair, / And dark in hair and eyes am I; and dark / Was Gorloïs, yea and dark was Uther too, / Wellnigh to blackness; but this King is fair / Beyond the race of Britons and of men" (ll. 325–30). Arthur is not to be explained in these terms.

19. Tennyson's gloss on this figure's symbolic importance is very direct: "The Lady of the Lake in old legends is the Church" (Ricks, p. 1477).

But there is meaning in what follows, the simple tale of the childhood play of Bellicent and Arthur and of Arthur's sweet comfort to her when she was unjustly punished. Here, Tennyson boldly turns to the naïveté of domestic comedy to define the basis of his epistemology. Bellicent's story not only portrays but transmits the experiential basis of spiritual truth: "he was at my side, / And spake sweet words, and comforted my heart, / And dried my tears, being a child with me. / And many a time he came" (ll. 347–50). The deliberate simplicity of this speech, especially the artless conjunctions, expresses a natural acceptance so basic it resists all but the most childlike language. There are no logical connections in the *ands*, just the marvelous reassurances of fairy tale, of childhood warmth and parental protection. With this inward assurance, precise facts yield to the magnificent non sequiturs of comedy: "But those first days had golden hours for me, / For then I surely thought he would be king" (ll. 356–57).

She does add the tale of Arthur's mysterious birth from the waves, but this story seems to her much less important because it is not a part of her direct experience. It is confirming in a way, and thus makes sense, but she really needs no confirmation. When she asks Merlin, then, if Bleys's story is "true," Merlin taunts her with her basic mistake: "And truth is this to me, and that to thee; / And truth or clothed or naked let it be" (ll. 406–07). In other words, Merlin riddles her to mock her useless (and uncharacteristic) search for single and verifiable external truth. He is not, one must add, suggesting any sort of relativistic doctrine here, at least not a relativism of truth.[20] Truth is single, though it may be expressed, "clothed," in different forms. Tennyson himself glossed the lines as follows: "The truth appears in different guise to divers persons. The one fact is that man comes from the great deep and returns to it."[21]

Tennyson's comments are not always to be trusted, but this one seems appropriate enough. Merlin realizes that Bellicent knows better, and he is simply chiding her. The rationalistic belief in growth into wisdom, echoed symbolically in the opening phrase, "rain, rain, and sun!" (l. 402), and stated directly in "A young man will be wiser by and by" (l. 403), is burlesqued by the actual

20. Many critics so interpret Merlin's song. William Brashear, for instance, says the song expresses "the relativity of all objective truth, or knowledge about 'things'" (*The Living Will*, p. 129).

21. Quoted in Ricks, p. 1480.

dominating cycles: "An old man's wit may wander ere he die" (l. 404); rain may or may not yield to sun: "Rain, sun, and rain! . . . Sun, rain, and sun!" (ll. 408–09). Merlin knows what Bellicent knows and, when he is not "in jest" (l. 419), says that Arthur is beyond mortality: "Merlin in our time / Hath spoken also, not in jest, and sworn / Though men may wound him that he will not die" (ll. 418–20).

Leodogran finally achieves the same inner experience and inner truth, not, significantly, through his understanding but through a dream. Bellicent's poetry has so much power that he immediately clothes the truth in his own myth. In the dream, the "phantom king" (l. 429) is at first surrounded by an obtrusive landscape, filled with carnage, fire, death, and the sound of dissonant, doubting voices. All this, the image of rational judgment, yields finally to pure imaginative actuality: "the solid earth became / As nothing, but the King stood out in heaven, / Crowned" (ll. 441–43). The solid earth, all empirical evidence, becomes as nothing in the presence of authentic experience.

Leodogran's search thus becomes a climactic parable of the search for knowledge. It stands in this first idyll because it represents the central subject of the *Idylls* as a whole. Leodogran's success is important in creating an initial image of the means for finding the experience of truth. Camelot fails because Leodogran's victory is difficult to repeat; later doubters either rest in empiricism, distrust the visions that come to them, or respond hysterically to dangerous, partial visions. The truth is there all along, available, as Bellicent shows, to the most direct and unsophisticated experience. But the world itself becomes sophisticated.

As well as providing this crucial statement on method, the first idyll also does a great deal to define the nature of the spiritual truth with which it is concerned. Though explicitly a spiritual truth, it can find expression only in the physical. *Idylls of the King* carefully puts its mystical perceptions into a concrete, even flatly practical frame. The ideal works through the real; spiritual experience is one with social experience. Arthur is not an enemy of the empirical; at his height, "the world / Was all so clear about him, that he saw / The smallest rock far on the faintest hill" (ll. 96–98). He can also see "even in high day the morning star" (l. 99). He perceives beyond the senses but not around them; he must work in the world, in the body. Thus his need for Guinevere: "for saving I be

joined / To her that is the fairest under heaven, / I seem as nothing
in the mighty world, / And cannot will my will, nor work my
work / Wholly, nor make myself in mine own realm / Victor and
lord" (ll. 84–89). His will is not incomplete without Guinevere; it
just lacks social power: it cannot work to create a realm. Without
her, he is not nothing, but nothing "in the mighty world." By
joining himself to her he is committing himself to social action and
duty, acknowledging himself human. This is the personal reflection
of *ecce homo*, repeated in the divine and comic promise to every man,
the potential for creating a Paradise on earth:

> . . . But were I joined with her,
> Then might we live together as one life,
> And reigning with one will in everything
> Have power on this dark land to lighten it,
> And power on this dead world to make it live.
>
> [ll. 89–93]

Coordinating body and soul, divinity becomes man, giving light
and form to what is now dark and void. Arthur's promise is thus
couched in dynamic, eventually perilous terms: the joining together
of all antagonistic qualities.

The most essential balance is that of body and soul, but all
opposites must unite in the central truth, not only moral and
psychological ones but social ones as well. Before Arthur came,
King Leodogran had been so overwhelmed with the chaos and
brutality of his uncontrolled realm that he had hoped even for the
stability offered by tyranny, "groaned for the Roman legions here
again, / And Caesar's eagle" (ll. 34–35). Arthur offers a balance of
freedom and control, spontaneity and order. The crucial means for
holding the balance is very simple: "man's word." The word is the
symbol of God's gift to man, the ability to give life and permanence
to all concrete and formless objects and acts. Art and life itself are
guaranteed by the power of the word to give lasting coherence.

Arthur extends this gift to the political and social world, giving
meaning to human community by insisting on the permanence of
the word. The word must contain the greatest reality; man's will,
that is, must be larger than circumstances. If God is real, His gift
must have potency; therefore, "Man's word is God in man: / Let
chance what will, I trust thee to the death" (ll. 132–33). No external
evidence is demanded beforehand, not because Arthur is willfully

naïve, not because he is a mystic, and not because Tennyson is working to achieve a "tragic irony" (it is Lancelot, his ultimate betrayer, to whom Arthur speaks). Words must mean more than things; vows more than passing influences. If they do not, there is nothing either divine or human. Arthur has no choice; if he is to offer men the chance to be men, he must build his world on the permanence of complete trust.

He is betrayed in the end by the trivial change, the imperma-nence of all things. Even Excalibur, the symbol of his kingdom and his personal power, has "Cast me away!" written on the side opposite "Take me" (ll. 304, 302). By accepting life, Arthur is forced into transiency. In the manner of all great heroes, however, he refuses to accept this condition. By insisting on constancy, he fails and also succeeds. He is not wrong to demand permanence; though it is impossible, it is man's only hope. Arthur is not just an artist[22] but a comic artist. He opens the wilderness, letting in the sun and making broad, clear paths for all men. He offers men joy, youth, and acceptance, not some gray set of religious prohibitions or renunciations. Camelot is a comic world, and this idyll, like nearly all comedies, ends with a marriage, one that takes the "Sun of May," the springtime and fertility that descend on the married couple, and expands it to all society, promising to "make the world / Other" (ll. 471–72). Arthur first turns on the *senex,* the fossilized parental figure, this time Rome, and dismisses him without tribute, "Seeing that ye be grown too weak and old" (l. 510). Once liberated, the new society is "all one will" (l. 515), harmonious and eternally young. Arthur has "made a realm" (l. 518). The power contained in his truth is the power to re-create the world.

The next idyll, "Gareth and Lynette," provides an illustration of the points made rather directly in "The Coming of Arthur." It is the exemplum for the opening argument. It does not so much define the values of Camelot as create for us an image of the promise it holds: the union of freedom and order. Above all it is an idyll characterized by simplicity and directness. In Gareth's world, there are no real problems.

22. Both Priestley, "Tennyson's *Idylls,*" p. 37, and W. David Shaw, "The Idealist's Dilemma in *Idylls of the King,*" *VP* 5 (1967): 46–47, develop the theme of Arthur as artist.

It is therefore appropriate that "Gareth and Lynette" should have the clearest and most elementary form of any of the idylls. For the first and only time, the society is pure enough to allow the force of innocence to express itself without perversion and compromise. This is the only idyll with a strictly chronological structure. Gareth can move through restriction after restriction to a final victory all the more satisfying because it is, in its major outlines, so very predictable. Such clean and direct progress is never possible again because the medium is never present again. Gareth is able to dedicate himself successfully to abstractions like "honor": simplified desires can work only in a world made simple by purity. Gareth wishes just to serve for glory, and this one resolution can solve all his problems of confinement, identity, and social being, and, symbolically, the problems of the state. Later, much more strenuous and ingenious attempts toward victory will fail in a world made complex by impurity.

At this point Gareth is allowed to present the highest human possibility, "ideal manhood closed in real man" ("To the Queen," l. 38). He represents the likeness of Arthur which passed over the faces of all the knights when they took the vows of obedience. In other words, he is the ideal human imitation of Arthur (and of Christ) and thus is the pattern of the poem. Therefore, though he progresses through a classic comic plot of testing (obscurity, disguise, temptation, final assertion of won identity), the real test is not of Gareth but of his king and his society. Gareth's success proves the authenticity of Arthur and Camelot. The conversion of Lynette, then, is not so much an artful doubling of Gareth's test (though it is that) as it is a symbolic cleansing of the doubt that could corrupt social obedience to Arthur. The real question, in other words, is whether the world can sustain magnificent innocence, and the answer, for the moment at least, is a resounding *yes*.

But in the *Idylls* as a whole it cannot be sustained, primarily because the union of gentleness and manliness celebrated by the marriage of Gareth and Lynette is later disrupted by a rejection of the two principal virtues celebrated by the idyll and its two main themes: obedience and grace, particularly as the latter is manifested in charity, forgiveness, and kindness.

The idyll is a poem of spring in every sense: the opening image of a flooded river suggests renewal and the abundant powers of youth, as well as specific and crucial spiritual qualities. Gareth sees that, despite its apparent abandon, the river "dost His will, / The Maker's" (ll. 10–11). He instantly transcends the evidence of his senses with his intuition of the certainty of divine control. Subtly, this beginning establishes exactly what is lacking in the later empiricists and exactly what Arthur insists on: an assumption of spirituality.

In order to realize this extrarational faculty, Gareth must overcome many obstacles, the first of which is created by his mother, who "holds me still a child" (l. 15). Like all comic heroes, he must assert his manhood in order to begin his real initiation. The fact that Bellicent's demands are so explicitly sexual—she begs him to consider his impotent father, "the yet-warm corpse" (l. 79), who "beside the hearth / Lies like a log, and all but smouldered out!" (ll. 73–74)—really simplifies his problem by stating it so bluntly. The traditional battle with the father has already been won; he must simply escape from his mother. His later prolonged struggle to overcome Lynette's doubts parallels this first difficult fight with his mother and suggests that the real test is not presented by knights (or men) at all. His real triumph is over women, a fact both humorous in its suggestion of triviality and ominous in its anticipation of Guinevere's later frailty.

Gareth, however, has no real dilemmas. He certainly has solved the problem Leodogran had had with doubt. When his mother (the same Bellicent who had convinced Leodogran) tentatively raises rationalistic worries about Arthur's origins in order to poison Gareth's mind—"wilt thou leave / Thine easeful biding here, and risk thine all, / Life, limbs, for one that is not proven King?" (ll. 125–27)—he deals with her very shortly: "Who should be king save him who makes us free?" (l. 136). So much for proof! Gareth sees that the liberator is defined by the process of liberation; the king is he who forms subjects and continually is in the process of defining himself as king. He is always making us free. The existential answer is the one later given by Merlin and by the *Idylls* as a whole, though Gareth is one of the few embodiments of the central creed: that the proof of spiritual fact comes unbidden and never totally through the senses; it is guaranteed by faith, obedience, and charity.

Gareth demonstrates these qualities at once by agreeing to Bellicent's trial, which provides him the opportunity to enact a ritual testing. He recognizes that "his only way to glory lead / Low down through villain kitchen-vassalage" (ll. 156–57). Gareth must

submit to the central paradoxical action of Christianity: losing
himself in order to find himself. He sees that "the thrall in person
may be free in soul" (l. 162) and declares, "I therefore yield me
freely to thy will" (l. 165). The renunciation of personal will allows
him not only personality but freedom, and Gareth has, in fact,
pronounced the key to the success of Camelot.

In the Christian tradition so strongly marked in this poem,
Gareth's renunciation, obedience, and eventual glory are an
imitation of Arthur's own initial obscurity (he "rode a simple
knight among his knights" in "The Coming of Arthur," l. 51) and
eventual triumph and, of course, of the Christ whom Arthur
suggests. The Christ-like character of Gareth's own action is
implied very quietly but nonetheless very firmly. He travels to
Arthur at Eastertime and later acts among his fellow kitchen-thralls
in such a way "that first they mocked, but, after, reverenced him"
(l. 497). In any case, Gareth comes to Camelot already possessed of
the mysteries that could preserve its glories; he arrives not really to
be initiated but to demonstrate the possibilities of Arthur's rule.

In one sense all he has to do is to be young—to assert first the
power and then the magnificence of youth. Even Merlin, the
prophetic voice of doom throughout the *Idylls*, provokes Gareth's
proper scorn. It is true, of course, that Merlin's statement that the
vows are those by which men must be bound but which "no man
can keep" (ll. 265–68) expresses the central ironic vision of the
entire poem. But he is wrong in applying that prophecy to Gareth,
who will temporarily belie the wizard's grim truth. It is not only the
temporary irrelevance of the vision that causes Gareth to dismiss
Merlin, however; Merlin is also old, and the comic form now
evident in the idyll sees all the old as enemies—pompous, windy,
and tyrannical. It is difficult, in other words, to keep a hollow, dusty
ring out of Merlin's voice. There is no artistic inappropriateness
here; prophecies of doom are simply incongruous in comedies.
When, as happens here, their truth is later revealed, it comes with
additional force.

The other blocking agent and emissary of the old is Sir Kay,
Gareth's temporary master and, in his lack of generosity, an enemy
of all that comedy values. He hates the young simply because he is
old. Perhaps more significantly, his insensitivity is decidedly out of
place in Camelot: he promises to take Gareth and "Like any pigeon
. . . cram his crop, / And sleeker shall he shine than any hog" (ll.

449–50). Lancelot very properly responds, "A horse thou knowest, a man thou dost not know" (l. 453). Camelot has been built to avoid just this confusion of man and animal and the perilous invasion of the human by the bestial. But again the darkness of the reference is not stressed, and Sir Kay is really cast as an officious buffoon, like one of Dickens's comic magistrates, temporarily a nuisance but not ultimately dangerous. Gareth easily throws him over when the time comes, having passed the test of obedience and humility.

The quest that he undertakes, then, arises straight from the center of the comic vision: "Let be my name until I make my name!" (l. 562). He proceeds with no name because he believes in the grand power of the human will to create its own personality and being. The rest of the idyll, in one sense, illustrates the truth of that perception.

It must persuade us and, of course, Lynette, who is in her way as pure as the hero. But she is initially so committed to the evidence of the senses (even her single joke is based on Gareth's smelling of the kitchen) that she is unable to recognize that her knave might be something other than he seems. She is, however, as educable as he is, and she undergoes the most important testing in the poem. She learns that man is defined by perpetual being, not by stable externals. Tennyson manages to include this education within one of the oldest of comic themes. Lynette comes on the scene as shrilly as Shakespeare's Kate, presuming even to lecture the king: "Why sit ye there? / Rest would I not, Sir King, an I were king" (ll. 582–83). The reasons for the satisfactions found in the shrew-taming theme are seldom stated so bluntly: "an I were king."

Lynette, like all shrews, threatens the process of the creation of personality by her desire to assume all personality unto herself. More specifically, she threatens all manhood. But her very excesses help ensure the gentleness of the comedy, and they provide the certain traditional clues that she will, in the end, be tamed. In addition, her impulses are basically proper; she asks Arthur to clear the land and create order. In consonance with the form, her sister is threatened with nothing worse than marriage to a brute. Further, even these enemies that surround Lyonors are the traditional enemies of comedy, not only "fools" (l. 620) but of "the fashion of that old knight-errantry" (l. 614). In other words, they, like Sir Kay, are outdated members of an obsolete order which Gareth, like Arthur, must do away with.

The final three-part battle (death turns out not to be a test)
recalls Red Cross's three-day fight with the dragon as well as
Spenser's allegorical model, the three-day period from Christ's
crucifixion to his resurrection. All three knights whom Gareth fights
suggest some form of compromise or temptation that would make
the purity that Arthur demands impossible.[23] The first, the
Morning Star, carries a single crimson banner, suggestive of the
passion of youthful ardor and lack of control. The fight is quickly
over, Gareth having long ago conquered the impatience and
frustration he showed at the opening of the idyll. The second
combatant, the Noonday Sun, carries with him suggestions of the
traditional Romantic and Victorian association of the sun with
reason as opposed to the imaginative moon. Here, reason is seen
specifically as the empirical reason that threatens to blind one to
the real truth (even "Gareth's eyes had flying blots / Before them
when he turned from watching him" [ll. 1005–06]). Though later
one of the most dangerous enemies, he is no real threat to Gareth
and here defeats himself: "The hoof of his horse slipt in the stream,
the stream / Descended, and the Sun was washed away" (ll.
1020–21). The illusion of materialism is no match for spiritual fact.
The Evening Star, apparently naked but actually wrapped in the
skin of beasts, has become one with the animals,[24] and he represents
to Gareth the greatest danger and the most difficult enemy. For
here Gareth is struggling against what he might become (see ll.
1100–04), the inhuman old man, animalistic and egocentric, the
largest threat to comic and Christian society. At this point,
incidentally, Lynette is converted, admits that she is "shamed" (l.
1135), and humbly asks his pardon. By undergoing a form of
Gareth's own humiliation, she becomes courteous and presents a
double for the pattern of perfection this idyll illustrates.

The final enemy, Death, provides the clearest indication of the
comic nature of the idyll. Gareth has just been defeated by
Lancelot, suggesting the puncture of his last enemy, Pride, and
illustrating the key Christian theme that only those who lose egos
can find selves: "Victor from vanquished issues at the last, / And
overthrower from being overthrown" (ll. 1230–31). He goes on to a

23. Shaw points out that the four antagonists (counting Death as one) also suggest the
Four Horsemen of the Apocalypse, thus adding an extra dimension of joy to Gareth's
triumph ("Gareth's Four Antagonists," *VN*, no. 34 [1968], pp. 34–35).
24. This same point is made by Buckley, *Tennyson*, p. 184.

last battle which, of course, is no battle at all. In one of the most brilliant of twists, Tennyson does not extinguish Death in the pattern of old comedies but turns him into life itself: "the bright face of a blooming boy / Fresh as a flower new-born" (ll. 1373–74). Gareth and Lynette have not won eternal stasis but rather a life so pure and rich it contains only the present. The happiness is so great that Tennyson succeeds, for perhaps the only time in his poetry, with a tone of coyness: "And he that told the tale in older times / Says that Sir Gareth wedded Lyonors, / But he, that told it later, says Lynette" (ll. 1392–94). It is the final joke on the old, this time turned against Malory himself. "So large mirth lived" (l. 1391), the poet says. Gareth has accomplished for a time the great social goal of all comedy: he has made joy the one fact of existence.

The next two idylls, "The Marriage of Geraint" and "Geraint and Enid," are conveniently treated together; they were, in fact, one long poem until 1873, when Tennyson made the division into the present form. The division makes a good deal of sense, since it preserves tonal and generic continuity within this first general section of the *Idylls*. "The Marriage of Geraint" is an idyllic comedy with some suggestions of turbulence and darkness about its edges; "Geraint and Enid" completes the transition into the world determined by the canons of realism, the world of instability, lapses from grace, doubt.

These are idylls of change and regeneration, idylls of experience. "Gareth and Lynette" had sought to preserve a natural Eden; these next poems seek to recapture an Eden that is lost. Though the permanent confidence that had infused "Gareth and Lynette" is now gone, it is a mistake to overstress the darkness of the Geraint-Enid idylls. The pastoral innocence of the earlier time, the marriage, is carefully structured so as to be contained within the dynamic testing and renewal of Geraint, but to argue that the effect of this structure "is to surround the idealization of the first meeting with the grim details of the present reality" [25] seems to me to misrepresent the form. The *experience* contained in the image of the first meeting could just as well be seen as rendering the doubts of the present trivial.

25. Lawrence Poston III, "The Argument of the Geraint-Enid Books in *Idylls of the King*," *VP* 2 (1964): 270.

The power and undoubted validity of the love perceived in the
main section of "The Marriage of Geraint" act to diminish the
effect of the doubts and to suggest that they are only temporary.
The decision to begin the poem with Enid's unfortunate fragment—
"I fear that I am no true wife" (l. 108)—and Geraint's subsequent
mistrust seems an appeal to a traditional comic structure, where the
movement is always from disarray to harmony. The initial disorder
is played off against the experience of past love; because the doubts
are merely rational and the love full, vital, and a part of experience,
we know, from the values already established in the *Idylls*, that the
doubt cannot last. The past order will reassert itself. The dominant
effect is not darkness but the pleasant tension that arises from
waiting for the good times to come again—for they certainly will
come.

In structure and values these idylls are strongly comic. Of course,
comedy is more difficult to maintain now than it was in "Gareth
and Lynette." Gareth had only to confirm what he was, perma-
nently and unshakably; Geraint must, in the deepest sense, re-form
himself. The journey Geraint takes into the wasteland is a journey
of self-discovery, a journey into his own moral and psychological
being.[26] Selfhood is no longer a constant; it must, like Camelot
itself, be continually rediscovered and reaffirmed. The loss of
guaranteed personal stability is a major one, but it is compensated
for by the affirmation of the power of renewal, particularly the
power of the human will to triumph over circumstances, even the
circumstances of its own decay.

The static and innocent world of "Gareth and Lynette" becomes
the dynamic world of experience. Ironic forces are present, but they
are soundly defeated. Leodogran's dream, that imaginative experi-
ence which provided truth and personal identity, is now seen as
transient but also infinitely repeatable. One can find again that
vital experience which makes knowledge and being possible. It is
Geraint, then, even more than Gareth, who is the primary model on
which later idylls reflect. Geraint suggests the ability of fallen man
to find his way back to Paradise: a more complex but, in its way,
more hopeful suggestion than that in the preceding idyll. Geraint is

26. Reed (*Perception and Design*, pp. 58–69) explores this aspect of the journey motif fully,
explaining many of the details of the poem in terms of Geraint's psychology and his
psychological development.

the last comic answer to the world of ironic experience, the image of repentance and regain that ought to preserve Camelot.

Through Geraint, Tennyson shows the corrupting force of rational doubt and the ability of man to find and destroy the source of that doubt. It is not Geraint's doubt of his wife but his doubt of the queen's loyalty—that is, elementary doubt itself—which emasculates him and makes him into a being without will, one "whose manhood was all gone" ("The Marriage of Geraint," l. 59). This doubt removes him entirely from the promise and values of Camelot—"Forgetful of his promise to the King" (l. 50)—consequently from all pleasure, and finally from his true self—"Forgetful of his glory and his name, / Forgetful of his princedom and its cares" (ll. 53–54). He must rebuild a self that has lost touch with primary experience and thereby reaffirm the meaning of his *name*. Names in Camelot, like all words, must have permanent meaning, so that the world may be made artistically coherent. The assertion "Man's word is God in man" assumes the stability of all its terms, not only *God* and *word*, but *man* as well.

Geraint must show that identity is solid, even if that solidity demands vigilance and great struggles. Geraint and Enid live in a world of fluctuations, of slippery movements and deceptions, and they must master that world lest they be caught by it. The great strength of a central experience that provides love and faith is enough to allow them to delight in change and make it serve a larger constancy: "And as the light of Heaven varies, now / At sunrise, now at sunset, now by night / With moon and trembling stars, so loved Geraint / To make her beauty vary day by day, / In crimsons and in purples and in gems" (ll. 6–10). The sources of this confidence and love are the subject of "The Marriage of Geraint"; "Geraint and Enid" is concerned with the disappearance of that experience and the ability of man to recapture it.

Tennyson uses two motifs to carry the burden of this theme: the need to express meaning in the permanent and authentic word, and the struggle to bring the senses into conjunction with the spiritual world of experience. "The Marriage of Geraint" presents a harmony of sense and spirit, meaning and word. Geraint appears as another Gareth, duplicating Arthur's function and thus proving his divinity. Like Arthur, Geraint is letting in the light and creating new worlds. By defeating the sparrow hawk, Edyrn, he brings justice to the region and liberates the people from the narrow dominance of their fear. In the process he finds liberation himself: the voice of Enid strikes him suddenly, suspending his normal activity and providing a crucial imaginative experience. He is transformed by her song and decides, "Here, by God's grace, is the one voice for me" (l. 344). It is not that he is falling in love with merely a voice but that he is struck with a profoundly new experience. His is not a shallow and sensual reaction; the beauty of Enid's voice blends with the comic burden of her song and the power of the particular moment to create, for Geraint, a transfiguring perception.

Enid's song on Fortune, or rather *against* Fortune, is the center of the poem. She denies the power of circumstance to affect the essential lives of man: "For man is man and master of his fate" (l. 355). The song proclaims man's ability to remain constant and true even in a changing and ironic world: "Turn, Fortune, turn thy wheel with smile or frown; / With that wild wheel we go not up or down" (ll. 350–51). This is the final comic hope of the poem as a whole, and it is to this hope that Geraint responds. Upon seeing Enid, Geraint reacts in the only way possible: "Here by God's rood is the one maid for me" (l. 368). Hearing and seeing do not determine his love; they support it. The proper exercise of the senses is to reinforce and confirm imaginative experience. So long as the experience is still potent they do so, but when the experience fades and is not renewed, the senses achieve an improper dominance.

But for now Geraint is quite wonderfully captivated by comedy. He goes on to defeat Edyrn, that archetypal enemy of all that is generous (in his first great crime he had taken advantage of Earl Ynoil's extreme hospitality, ll. 453–56), young, free, and good. He is also, appropriately, not really very wicked. His fall, like Gareth's earlier defeat at the hands of Lancelot and like Geraint's own later sickness-unto-death, is a necessary part of growth. Though he does not realize it, Geraint is helping to set the necessary pattern for all positive development, a pattern he must soon trace himself. Edyrn's story foreshadows and gives an externalized version of Geraint's own inner collapse and recovery. Edyrn, no less than Geraint, demonstrates that man has the ability to create his own comedy; he "slowly drew himself / Bright from his old dark life" (ll. 594–95).

Nothing in this idyll seems to be troubling Geraint's life, except for his curious worries about Enid's apparel. In one sense it is fitting that he should want only Guinevere to dress his wife. Though this

alliance later causes him much uneasiness, Enid is, and should be, a
legitimate double for Guinevere. Enid and Geraint are duplicating
the marriage of Guinevere and Arthur, expanding the realm and
showing the cumulative harmony of body and soul. Enid's pro-
longed frettings about the dress are not frivolous but quite
appropriate demonstrations that externals should mesh with spirit-
ual reality. Her willingness to remove her old dress repeats the
theme of obedience and trust to the power of inner experience. She
is rewarded, significantly, with a glorification, not a mortification of
the senses. The only thing ominous about the test is that it *is* partly
a test. Geraint admits that, even with the strength of the experience
behind him, he could still doubt a little, enough so as to conduct a
kind of laboratory experiment on Enid and her loyalty. Even
though his doubts are stilled for a moment, then, his assurances are
false—"Now, therefore, do I rest, / A prophet certain of my
prophecy, / That never shadow of mistrust can cross / Between us"
(ll. 813-16)—and he is certain to be attacked at his weakest point:
his lingering faith in evidences.

"Geraint and Enid" shows us that attack, the destruction and
rebuilding of a personality. Having constructed this superficial and
meaningless test, Geraint himself must be tested, and very rigor-
ously. Becoming more infested with doubt, he soon finds himself in
a chaotic and dissonant world, where the evidence of the senses jars
against spiritual intuitions. He therefore turns hysterically against
the senses and constructs another malign test for his wife, telling her
to ride ahead of him, never to look back, and, above all, to keep
silent the voice that first won him. By denying his senses entirely he
is also blocking his way to regaining that initial experience of love
that had come from the senses. He claims that he is one "With eyes
to find you out however far, / And ears to hear you even in his
dreams" (ll. 428-29), but actually he has no valid knowledge of any
kind, not even from the senses. His wife tells him so: "Yea, my lord,
I know / Your wish, and would obey; but riding first, / I hear the
violent threats you do not hear, / I see the danger which you cannot
see" (ll. 418-21). Willfully cutting himself off from all sources of
truth, he has only himself. He puts his wife first, and she leads him
back into himself.

There he finds total incoherence. He charges Enid to be silent, to
utter no word; thus he creates ironies for himself and for her:
obedience, for instance, means disobedience. He immediately turns

Arthur's world upside down, assuming disloyalty and inconsistency everywhere. As he prepares for the first battle in the woods, he cynically tells Enid, "If I fall, cleave to the better man" (l. 152).

But it is Enid's constancy that saves him from himself, even from the ludicrously self-indulgent part of himself symbolized by Limours. The subtle identification of Limours with Geraint is indicated by Geraint's acts of slovenly and insulting overpayment at this point in the poem. He lazily gives a horse and arms to a boy in return for food ("You overpay me fifty-fold" [l. 220]) and offers five horses and their armor for lodging (which so amazes the wily host that he is "suddenly honest" [l. 410]). Geraint is as surly in his lethargy (he responds to an invitation, "If he wants me, let him come to me" [l. 237]) as the most yellow decadent. He is, at this point, Limours. His attempt to kill the word and the constancy it implies leads him to the whirlwind of rioting. He approves the way Limours "told / Free tales, and took the word and played upon it, / And made of it two colours" (ll. 290–92). There is no meaning at all at this level of self. Tennyson shows the maudlin self-concern and self-pity at the heart of Geraint's pose of wounded manhood, the ugly sentimentality in his possessiveness; it is Limours being described, but Limours is only a heightened and purified version of this aspect of the hero: "At this the tender sound of his own voice / And sweet self-pity, or the fancy of it, / Made his eye moist" (ll. 348–50).

From rioting, then, Geraint passes to silence, to the true death of the word. Suffering from a secret wound, he falls unconscious "without a word" (l. 508). Here, just at the point of death, he finds his own inner chaos, Earl Doorm, a figure of wordless animalism: "And all the hall was dim with steam of flesh: / And none spake word, but all sat down at once, / And ate with tumult in the naked hall" (ll. 602–04). This is the black climax of the serious testing. From this depth he is rescued and once again transformed by Enid's voice, this time in the form of a bitter and helpless cry. He immediately beheads Earl Doorm and thus rids himself of doubt.

Tennyson then evokes specific images of the Eden that has been rewon: "And never yet, since high in Paradise / O'er the four rivers the first roses blew, / Came purer pleasure unto mortal kind / Than lived through her" (ll. 762–65). She moves back into Eden, Geraint "hers again" (l. 767). The key word is *again*. There they meet the other symbol of regained happiness and personality, Edyrn, who insists over and over on the principal theme of these idylls: "I am changed" (ll. 824, 872). "By overthrowing me you threw me higher" (l. 791), he says. Arthur himself reinforces the point, maintaining that such reform is far more marvelous and important than is mere consistency. It is a dynamic world now, one that requires continual renewals. The Edyrns, therefore, are most significant. And so, of course, are the secret Edyrns, such as Geraint. Arthur does not know it, but his words about Edyrn apply even more profoundly to Geraint, Edyrn's complement. Even though Geraint feels uncomfortable about the queen (an ominous sign, of course, for the future), "he rested well content that all was well" (l. 951). The magical Tennysonian phrase "all is well" comes to a troubled, changeful world and is therefore all the more comforting.

II

"Geraint and Enid" shows the limits of hope in an ironic world. With "Balin and Balan" the hope has disappeared, and the rest of the *Idylls* traces the decay of Arthur's comic society and the resurgence of that bestial irony which had reigned before Camelot. The middle four idylls—"Balin and Balan," "Merlin and Vivien," "Lancelot and Elaine," and "The Holy Grail"—demonstrate how comic expectations are foiled by an ironic actuality. These idylls presage the fall of Camelot and offer, by the way, preliminary analyses of the reasons for that fall. Hopeful values are still widespread in these idylls, in the sense that many characters still hold to them. But the values themselves seem progressively less in accord with reality, and the comic assumptions seem more and more to be illusions. Fewer and fewer people cleave to Arthur until, by the time of "The Last Tournament" in the next section, the prevailing temper is cynicism. Only Arthur and the fool still believe. Comedy is still present, at least on the periphery of the four idylls in the center of the poem, but its vital life is gone.

The first poem in this section, "Balin and Balan," is by far the least popular poem of the *Idylls*; Valerie Pitt, for instance, dismisses it as an "abominable wreckage" of Malory's story.[27] Only J. M. Gray makes a successful attempt to come to grips with the poem's details, and does so in such a way as to make us recognize the full

27. Pitt, *Tennyson Laureate*, p. 188.

coherence that it is very easy to miss.[28] Despite a heavy, sometimes overinsistent allegorical framework, "Balin and Balan" works very well as an inversion of many of the principal themes and values of the Geraint-Enid books. The central theme in all three poems is repentance, but in "Balin and Balan" it is repentance gone wrong. The first ironic poem traces a dual failure, a failure within and without. It shows the inability of man to find genuine renewal and rehabilitation. Both Balin and Geraint retreat into the wilderness of their own selves. Both annihilate the beast within; but for Geraint that death is preliminary to a new and purified life, for Balin it is final. Balin parodies the comic re-creation of self.

The tale follows the same pattern as Geraint's, except that none of the consequences hold, none of the lovely comic solutions arrive. Arthur's playful overthrowing of Balin and Balan should result in the same humility and reformation that works with Edyrn. Arthur obviously thinks it will, for he invokes the same moral: "Rise, my true knight. As children learn, be thou / Wiser for falling" (ll. 72–73). The court prepares to welcome Balin as "The Lost one Found" (l. 78); all nature joins in the festivity: "With joy that blazed itself in woodland wealth / Of leaf, and gayest garlandage of flowers" (ll. 79–80).

Balin, like Edyrn, is, or should be, taught and subdued by gentleness and courtesy. As a result of this training he should learn the control and patience that come from recognizing the ultimate harmony of things: "all the world / Made music, and he felt his being move / In music with his Order, and the King" (ll. 206–08). He has "fought / Hard with himself, and seemed at length in peace" (ll. 233–34). By force of will, it appears, he has mastered circumstances and overcome his own animalism and egocentricity. This is exactly the point of Enid's lovely song on the irrelevance of Fortune and all external circumstances; it is really the point of the Geraint-Enid idylls. But in "Balin and Balan" external and trivial circumstances finally conquer the human will entirely, and the parallels are maintained only to be mocked. The emphasis on crude chance and improbable coincidence in the narration of Balin's fall may have an allegorical point, but it also functions to highlight the utter triviality of his death.

28. J. M. Gray, *Tennyson's Doppelgänger*; see also the same author's "Fact, Form and Fiction in Tennyson's *Balin and Balan*," *RMS* 12 (1968): 90–107.

Such a victory of mere circumstance is possible because the unity of the world is disrupted. "Balin and Balan" is a poem that deals with unnatural and fatal divisions. The most obvious form of this split, of course, is that between the two brothers, the divorce of the rational and social man from the instinctive and private one. Behind this rupture is the shadow of the rumored separation of Guinevere from Arthur, body from soul. The idyll's emphasis on lying or slander continues the important motif of the *word*. Creation falls apart in a lie, since a lie destroys all coherence and denies the ability of man to create a permanent order.

All this is obvious enough. But there are splits in "Geraint and Enid" too, and they are healed. The more central question in "Balin and Balan" is why the healing process will no longer work, why instinct and reason meet in mutual destruction rather than reunification. As in "Geraint and Enid," this is the fallen world, the world of experience. It may be *more* fallen, I suppose, but still, Balin's ordeal is nothing like Enid's. Enid has almost infinite stability, whereas Balin cracks hysterically when he sees Guinevere blush. "How to deal with moral outrage" seems a reductive formulation of the poem's problem, but it is the concrete form by which the narrative handles the more general issue of how to live in a fallen and imperfect world. Enid needs only to be patient and she will emerge from the wasteland into the ordered world of Camelot. For Balin, there is no other world waiting; he sees chaos in the very heart of order. The only legitimate pattern of response—patience, courtesy, forgiveness—is unavailable to him because the ethical and moral life has been removed entirely from the practical and the instinctive.

The only alternatives Balin seems to have take him into extremes: unnatural spirituality or unnatural and cynical empiricism. The demon in the woods is not slander but revenge, the unbalanced response of an isolated hatred of injustice. The demon symbolizes all ethical discontinuity, the irrational measures man is forced to when he finds no external coherence, no just scheme to which to appeal his cause. In a chaotic world the search for justice leads to a self-destructive separation from the general scheme of things, chaotic and unjust as they may be. The demon was "driven by evil tongues / From all his fellows, lived alone, and came / To learn black magic, and to hate his kind" (ll. 122–24). He is the type of those who, searching for purity in an impure world, are forced into indiscriminate and wild attempts to invoke order and cleanliness where none exist.

This is not a poem on extremism; it is not at all clear that Balin is wrong, and it is certainly not clear that he has any choice. It is a sad and ironic poem on the absurd disjunction of things, a disjunction that leaves man no reasonable choices. We are less likely to judge Balin, then, than to judge both the condition of the world that drives him to such wildness and the power of chance that can so easily overcome the best intentions. Thus, the poem opens not on Balin but on the ascetic Pellam, a man who, like the demon, has retired from a society he no longer feels part of. He seeks for inner coherence and looks for a purity there he cannot find outside himself. Ironically paralleling Balin, the demon, and, later, Vivien and Garlon, he is the heightened and most ludicrous symbol of the mistaken reaction to a fallen world. Camelot exists on the perilous and creative balance of spirit and body, ideal and real. Pellam is the first of many who misunderstand and destroy the balance.

Balin similarly tries to defeat his own pollution, not with proper controls, which are symbolized by his absent brother, but with a perverse and extreme obsession with purity, an obsession he unluckily but naturally attaches to the queen. That is why he can be shattered by the single glance he sees exchanged between Lancelot and Guinevere. The conversation preceding that blush interestingly forecasts Balin's wild search for an answer. It also bids farewell to comedy. Lancelot calls forth an image of extreme purity much like Pellam's. He has a dream of a maiden saint and her "spiritual lily" (l. 259). She is "perfect-pure" in her absolute whiteness; "As light a flush / As hardly tints the blossom of the quince / Would mar their charm of stainless maidenhood" (ll. 261–63). Surely this is a denial of life; so extreme a wish to preserve purity reveals its motivating fear. Guinevere's response seems not only healthier but in full accord with comedy: "Sweeter to me . . . this garden rose / Deep-hued and many-folded! sweeter still / The wild-wood hyacinth and the bloom of May" (ll. 264–66). But full acceptance is possible only in a harmonious world; Guinevere's hearty openness now is made to sound suspicious, causes her to blush, and utterly destroys Balin's faith. The ironic world's strength is brilliantly indicated by making a comic affirmation the signal of doom.

Balin immediately perceives the crack in the world: "Queen?

subject? but I see not what I see. / Damsel and lover? hear not what I hear" (ll. 276–77). Guinevere and Arthur are sundered, sense is divorced from spirit. He has no way to accept the implications of what he has seen (or thinks he has seen, since the senses no longer connect with truth) and retain purity, even sanity. His reaction is destructive, but it is the only one possible for him. He seeks the devil, then, in order to purify himself: "To lay that devil would lay the Devil in me" (l. 296). But there is no purity and no external devil. The devil is, of course, himself, the disjoined and misanthropic idealist.

It is quite appropriate that Balin finds Pellam's castle, where he meets the two opposite but similar errors that will destroy Camelot: ascetic mysticism and skeptical empiricism. Pellam, of course, has totally denied the senses; his nephew, Garlon, can ask sneeringly, "Hast thou eyes?" (l. 353) because he trusts nothing but eyes. Garlon's doubts can infect Balin now because doubt is the reigning principle in the world. The poem had begun with Pellam's refusal to pay tribute, that is, to obey the chief dictum of Camelot, which Arthur repeats again: "Man's word is God in man" (l. 9). The poem is, as Clyde deL. Ryals says, in one sense "an exemplum on [this] text." [29] Because the word no longer has meaning, God has disappeared, and Garlon's ironic cynicism has taken over.

Balin leaves, discarding the shield with its emblem of Guinevere. This act causes his death (Balan fails to recognize him without it and attacks him by mistake), but Balin has no alternative. The shield was his one protection, but he could no longer believe in it or use it. Nor, perhaps, should he have. When he leaves it behind, however, he naturally meets Vivien, Guinevere's parody. The queen's springlike beauty and fertility become, in Vivien, wantonness and lust. Vivien sings of sun-worship, of a mindless unity of carnality and violence. Guinevere's mild conception of nature and natural objects is twisted into the dark and threatening nature that is to dominate the rest of the *Idylls*. Vivien's easy lies about Lancelot and Guinevere strike the defenseless Balin immediately as valid. "It is truth" (l. 519), he says—and in a way it is. Tennyson carefully confounds lying and truth to depict the chaos of the world. Vivien's lies contain the truth, while the honorable Balan dies violating the word with a reassuring but false statement: "Foul are their lives;

29. *From the Great Deep*, p. 181.

foul are their lips; they lied. / Pure as our own true Mother is our Queen" (ll. 605–06). Liars tell the truth; truthful men lie.

Vivien's epitaph on the two slain brothers indicates the pointlessness and brutality of the ironic world that is in control: they "butt each other here, like brainless bulls, / Dead for one heifer!" (ll. 568–69). But the idyll is not finally this cynical. The two brothers wake for a moment and, with "a childlike wail" (l. 585), "all at once they found the world, / Staring wild-wide" (ll. 584–85). There is a slight but fine ambiguity here: two children suddenly wake and stare at a world that is blankly staring back at them. All their innocence and trust mean nothing now; they can only promise one another a reunion in heaven. Comedy has been pushed altogether out of this world.

"Merlin and Vivien" is less dramatic, more diagnostic, less an image than an anlysis of Camelot's fall. What saves the idyll from didacticism is that it is, in the end, a parody of didacticism. It pretends to find reasons for Merlin's fall but finally reduces all reasons to triviality.[30] In such a world, calamities are natural; there need be no causes. Again, as in the two preceding idylls, there is a retreat into "the wild woods" (l. 202), no longer to reclaim them from the beast but to confirm the triumph of the wilderness. Merlin's defeat by Vivien signals the end of hope: the architect of Camelot and the representative of all wisdom is lost. Merlin is the artist[31] who could once sustain the imaginative life and support the balance of the spiritual and the physical. He had provided the continuity for the creative word. His fall, as F. E. L. Priestley points out,[32] does not represent just the defeat of reason by passion, or even the larger victory of the senses over wisdom (Priestley's terms). True wisdom has now lost touch with the proper working of the senses and thus upsets the dynamic balance on which Camelot is built. The victory does not belong to the senses but to a perversion of the senses.

30. Jacob Korg ("The Pattern of Fatality," p. 10) also argues that Merlin gives in to Vivien for no "logical" reason. He further suggests that this supports a "fatalistic" pattern in the poem.

31. A point discussed by Lawrence Poston III, "The Two Provinces of Tennyson's *Idylls*," *Criticism* 9 (1967): 372–82, and by Fred Kaplan, "Woven Paces and Waving Hands," *VP* 7 (1969): 285–98.

32. "Tennyson's *Idylls*," p. 40.

To put it less abstractly, the victory is Vivien's, who surely provides the poem with whatever concrete narrative force it has. Whatever one may say of Vivien, she is no abstraction; she is "about the most base and repulsive person ever set forth in serious literature," if one is to believe Swinburne.[33] She enters Merlin's life, just as in the last idyll she had entered Balin's, as both a symptom and a cause of disillusionment. She is the naturalistic and logical representative of pure irony, coming into the *Idylls* as its chief spokesman just at the point where the poem becomes ironic. She is Arthur's antithesis, bringing her assumptions into competition with his world: "Then as Arthur in the highest / Leavened the world, so Vivien in the lowest" (ll. 138–39). She strives to dislocate Arthur's bonds, to rend body from soul. She loves to burlesque comedy, passing herself off as a champion of its values, of love and loyalty: "In Love, if Love be Love, if Love be ours, / Faith and unfaith can ne'er be equal powers: / Unfaith in aught is want of faith in all" (ll. 385–87).

Vivien is cynical here, of course, but she is deeply sincere when she speaks to Mark, invoking against Arthur's purity the awesome force of nature: "This Arthur pure! / Great Nature through the flesh herself hath made / Gives him the lie! There is no being pure" (ll. 49–51). She is the representative of the new and increasingly threatening natural world. For the most part, the *Idylls* agrees with her: all of nature *is* on her side. Arthur is not betrayed by a single sin but by the indifferent dishonorableness of nature herself. All this does not, of course, make Arthur less heroic, rather more so, nor does it in any way reduce Vivien's vulgar and immense evil. She is an agent of death iself—"born from death was I / Among the dead and sown upon the wind" (ll. 44–45)—out to destroy all comedy and all hope.

Because she is so nearly accurate in her cynical way of explaining things, she has a frightening power that is increasingly denied the idealists. This is not to say that she understands the truth; she understands nothing. She is simply more in tune with the bestial world that is crowding back into Camelot. Tennyson uses this very combination of stupidity and unwitting perspicacity to discredit very carefully what might otherwise seem to be reasonable arguments. It is the reptilian Vivien who is made to state the best

33. "Under the Microscope," p. 408.

arguments against Arthur: that he is naïve, absurdly unreal, actually at fault for his kingdom's failure, and, in the end, a fool: "Man! is he man at all, who knows and winks? / Sees what his fair bride is and does, and winks?" (ll. 779–80). She says she "Could call him the main cause of all their crime; / Yea, were he not crowned King, coward, and fool" (ll. 786–87).

This about sums up the charges that have been made against Arthur, from Swinburne to the present. By anticipating them in this way and putting them in the mouth of Vivien, Tennyson shows how crudely naturalistic the bases of these arguments usually are, how narrow and unsubtle in their relentless, cocky logic. Vivien discredits such simple rationalism and draws our attention to the enormous demands Arthur's new kingdom makes, not only on will but on intelligence. Merlin may smile at her "blind and naked Ignorance / [Which] Delivers brawling judgments, unashamed" (ll. 662–63), but it is this crude, self-assured vulgarity that is about to inherit the earth.

The poem opens with a completed picture of this absurd invasion:

> A storm was coming, but the winds were still,
> And in the wild woods of Broceliande,
> Before an oak, so hollow, huge and old
> It looked a tower of ivied masonwork,
> At Merlin's feet the wily Vivien lay.
>
> [ll. 1–5]

The huge oak, the national symbol of stability and endurance that meant so much to Tennyson, is now old and hollow, lacking its firm heart and thus helpless against the impending storm. The single question posed by the idyll is "why?" Why does Merlin yield? The answer is that there is no answer. There is no adequate cause, just a series of trivial and wildly inappropriate "reasons." Tennyson makes Vivien's words and wiles so elaborately unsubtle that it would take no wizard to see through her, much less wisdom personified.

That, of course, is the point: Merlin is never really fooled. He knows what Vivien is but yields anyway. Deliberate references to the fall of man are inserted in the tale—Merlin tells Vivien he "stirred this vice in you which ruined man / Through woman the first hour" (ll. 360–61), for example—along with echoes from Book 9 of *Paradise Lost*,[34] but these allusions only highlight the irony. Merlin does not choose "love," [35] or Eve, certainly not uxoriousness; he simply gives in, without making any choice at all. There is no conflict of loyalties or values—all loyalties and values alike are overthrown.

In fact, Tennyson parodies these tragic and grand themes while emphasizing the grotesque irony of another allusion: the January / May theme. Merlin is originally drawn to Vivien by mere flattery and allows this physical flattery to overtake his judgment again and again. It is not his great melancholy, the foresight of Camelot's fall, that causes him to yield to her. He foresees the fall distinctly, but that vision fades in the presence of Vivien's gorgeous sexuality, which he says has "broken up my melancholy" (l. 265). "Your pretty sports," he claims, "have brightened all again" (l. 303). One can almost see the glinting eye, the nervous, palsied hand, the drool. Time and again, Tennyson forces the physical contrast between Merlin and Vivien on our attention: Vivien "Clung like a snake; and letting her left hand / Droop from his mighty shoulder, as a leaf, / Made her right a comb of pearl to part / The lists of such a beard as youth gone out / Had left in ashes" (ll. 240–44). Tennyson deliberately associates the venerable sage with perhaps the least dignified of all literary archetypes in order to impress on us the ironic pointlessness of his fall. This is not only Adam being expelled from Paradise; it is also Chaucer's befuddled carpenter crashing to the ground.

These ironies are all sharpened and brought into focus at the poem's climax. Tennyson first has Vivien lose her composure and give herself away completely, revealing "How from the rosy lips of life and love, / Flashed the bare-grinning skeleton of death!" (ll. 844–45). The pure ironic principle of death-in-life stands exposed, and Merlin understands completely what Vivien is. There is no disguise now, no real deception possible. Nonetheless, Vivien wins. She merely flatters him some more and half-heartedly adopts some set postures of sexual allurement. Merlin then simply folds; he is weary: "he let his wisdom go / For ease of heart" (ll. 890–91).

34. Traced by Thomas P. Adler, "The Uses of Knowledge in Tennyson's 'Merlin and Vivien,'" *TSLL* 11 (1970): 1397–1403.

35. Ibid., p. 1400.

Heaven's warning lightning strikes, but nothing can touch Merlin now; for he is caught by her sexuality: "The pale blood of the wizard at her touch / Took gayer colours, like an opal warmed" (ll. 947–48). Man loses his best hope in this act of mockery, a profanation of sexuality, of beauty, grace, and reason.

The storm that follows suggests not only the natural chaos now in control but, on the coarsest narrative level, the grotesque coupling of Merlin and Vivien. All man's wisdom is in the shape of the goat who, satiated and worn, tells Vivien the secret of the charm. The final irony is contained in Vivien's triumphant howl that she has "made his glory mine" (l. 969). She has, in fact, obliterated all glory. She can gain no fame because she has wrecked the social fabric that creates fame. She has destroyed the world and is thus captured more fully than she knows. Merlin was, as he says, the last who could read the *words* that could establish contact with the mysterious. He was the last who could build the comic city. All the hopefulness one might possibly see at the end of "The Passing of Arthur" cannot erase the image of Wisdom himself ludicrously betrayed by the balance he had sought to maintain, caught in eternal silence.

"Lancelot and Elaine" just as clearly acts to cancel any hope, now or later. Comic expectations are presented here in their purest and most justifiable form, but they are flatly denied. Lancelot, by turning his back on Elaine, confirms her death and the death of Camelot. "Lancelot and Elaine" makes the same *point* about the dissolution of comedy as "Merlin and Vivien," but it does so in a very different vein. Instead of emphasizing grand events and moving in the direction of generalization this idyll deliberately simplifies and concentrates entirely, almost naïvely, on the details of its narrative. "Lancelot and Elaine" is a domestic idyll, quite different in scope and manner from the poems surrounding it. One of the unique virtues of the *Idylls* is its ability to support the ironic vision on various levels and in various forms, showing how it controls all perspectives. It is also important that the tendency toward abstraction we see in "Merlin and Vivien" and "Balin and Balan" be balanced by a poem that is highly particularized. "Lancelot and Elaine" restores the concrete base to the symbolic motifs running through the poem. It takes the images of cosmic disjunction and refocuses them on a personal basis. "Lancelot and

Elaine" is still a poem on ironic disharmony, but it sees this disharmony in its most simple social form: personal disloyalty.

The idyll emerges from a single evocative statement in Malory: "she cast such a love unto sir Launcelot, that she could not withdraw her love, wherefore she died." Tennyson expands the fragment into a narrative of more than fourteen hundred lines, but he does not lose the force of its simplicity, particularly the calculated naïveté of "wherefore she died." The enormously suggestive and illogical connection between love and death is made the subject of Tennyson's irony. Once Camelot has decayed, love equals death, even when that love is directed toward the very best man of all. The poem has one major theme, betrayal, and one major direction: the search for a cause that leads only to the recognition that there is no cause, no fault. There is no one to blame, since everyone is caught in the same trap.

Least of all can Elaine be blamed. The poem is so deliberately plain that explication might be mostly a matter of pointing out the obvious but for the existence of the now popular notion that Elaine herself at least shares the responsibility for her own doom. She is, one is told, overly idealistic, naïve, consumed by fantasy, suicidal, willful, absurdly empircal.[36] She thus is the victim of her own nature, as well as of Lancelot's guilty and dishonorable alliance with Guinevere. Such interpretations add other interesting ironies, but I think the Victorian critics were, in this case, more sensitive. Gladstone, for instance, called the poem "a new 'Maid's Tragedy,' "[37] and I think he is right. Elaine is as guiltless as Aspatia. She dies only because she loves.

"She lived in fantasy" (l. 27) with Lancelot's shield, of course, creating an imaginary past for him from the markings on the shield and further changing and embroidering it by "her wit" (l. 10). *Fantasy* may suggest illusion, but it can just as well suggest legitimate creative activity. Elaine's illusions are only that Camelot is Camelot, that Lancelot is what he appears to be, and that the word providing coherence to the world has not been broken. She is herself an artist, and she has an artist's faith in Arthur's poetic creed.

36. See, for example, W. David Shaw, *"Idylls of the King," VP* 7 (1969): 182–83; Ryals, *From the Great Deep*, pp. 133–35; and Eggers, *King Arthur's Laureate*, pp. 146–49.

37. "Tennyson's Poems," p. 474.

It is also true that she was won by Lancelot's voice "before she looked" (l. 242), but a precedent for just this response had already been established and approved with Geraint. As with Geraint, Elaine falls in love not just with a sound but with the total being suggested by the voice; the voice is the impetus to imaginative re-creation, not only a legitimate but a necessary activity. Geraint hears Enid's lovely song about Fortune; Elaine hears Lancelot's noble and modest words about fellowship and courtesy. Neither Geraint nor Elaine is an empiricist; they are artists, using their senses to serve, not dominate, their imaginations. The difference between the two is that in Geraint's world sense and spirit are united, in Elaine's they are not. She sees in Lancelot's manner a unity that is not in fact there: "There brake [from Lancelot] a sudden-beaming tenderness / Of manners and of nature: and she thought / That all was nature" (ll. 326–28). Manners and nature are now severed; the courtesy that had once tamed Edyrn and by outward discipline taught him an inward peace has now become a habit unrelated to true grace. Elaine is mistaken only in assuming that there is what there most certainly should be: a unity of manners and nature. Lancelot, however, has become a dissembler.

Not that Elaine is blind to the real Lancelot. On the contrary, she has the penetrating artistic gift that enables her to see what he really is:

> As when a painter, poring on a face,
> Divinely through all hindrance finds the man
> Behind it, and so paints him that his face,
> The shape and colour of a mind and life
> Lives for his children, ever at its best
> And fullest. . . .
>
> [ll. 330–35]

Like all artists, she gives life by perceiving full vitality. She does not falsify; she essentializes, piercing through superficialities. She does so, one notes, divinely. She shares the artistic godlike assurances that are Arthur's: the trust that man's word, in art as elsewhere, is permanent.

But it is no longer a divine world. It no longer serves to cast aside superficialities; superficialities are all that remain. Elaine, then, is miscast as a comic artist in an ironic world. That is her only fault.

The union of red and white in her favor indicates very pointedly her willingness to join body with spirit.[38] She is not Edenic nor merely "innocent," much less blind. She is a creature of the fallen world, prizing love over convention: "And never woman yet, since man's first fall, / Did kindlier unto man" (ll. 854–55). Like Enid, she has the virtues of experience: patience and compassion.

Elaine is contrasted to the pathetic Guinevere, who simply does not understand. At the heart of Camelot is this blank ignorance, the inability to get beyond the simplicities of naturalism. Guinevere is like a naïve critic, prattling on about "probabilities" and "believable characters." She unwittingly repeats most of Vivien's arguments: Arthur is too remote and inhuman: "That passionate perfection, my good lord— / But who can gaze upon the Sun in heaven?" (ll. 123–24); he is at fault for "swearing men to vows impossible" (l. 130); in fact, he *is* the problem: "He is all fault who hath no fault at all" (l. 132).[39] She misses her only chance to be genuinely human, throwing it away with jejune flippancy.

Lancelot's defects are largely moral ones, but even he is presented as ironically dim. He sees that love now involves lying, but he is entirely untouched by the ironic point, being vexed only "at having lied in vain" (l. 102). He wonders how he will be able to mend the lie, "Before a King who honours his own word, / As if it were his God's" (ll. 143–44). The whole point of Arthur's pledge to Lancelot was that man's word *is* God in man. It is God, not a fanciful equivalent for him. Lancelot's substitution indicates both moral and intellectual laxity. He is an honorable man, insofar as he understands honor, but he sees it only as proximate, not total, and he is therefore bound to be a breaker of words.

Tennyson carefully constructs parallels between this poem and earlier idylls in order to heighten these ironies. Lancelot retires both into the physical waste of the hermit's castle after the battle and also, periodically, "into wastes and solitudes" (l. 251) within. Also like Geraint, he is awakened from a point near death by the cry of one who loves and is faithful to him. But Enid's faithfulness is fruitful; Elaine's is arid. Lancelot is not reborn; he simply rejoins his earlier condition: "His honour rooted in dishonour stood, / And

38. The importance of these symbolic colors throughout the *Idylls* is examined by Richard Adicks, "The Lily Maid and the Scarlet Sleeve," *The University Review* 34 (1967): 65–71.

39. Priestley rightly calls this "the false but comforting doctrine of the fallen" ("Tennyson's *Idylls*," p. 40).

faith unfaithful kept him falsely true" (ll. 871–72). These terms are not paradoxical but ironic. For Lancelot, honor is dishonor; loyalty, treachery.

It is not coincidental, then, that he is tied symbolically to the hermit in the woods or to Gawain, who visits Elaine in search of him. Together, the hermit and Gawain represent the opposite extremes of Camelot's divisions: false asceticism and empiricism. Having given in to the senses, Lancelot must then, like the hermit, deny their proper use. The destructive opposites meet in Lancelot. By keeping himself faithful to Guinevere, he denies true faith and reveals a heartless insensitivity even worse than Gawain's "a diamond is a diamond" (l. 691). As it turns out, a diamond for Lancelot is also only a diamond.

He is so caught in his loyal disloyalty that, at the poem's climax, he can only play the part of a *senex,* denying love and standing against youthful life, armed with all the clichés of sterile age. Again Tennyson evokes incongruous comic echoes to make more emphatic the pointlessness of his ironic climax. With grand and impassive callousness, Lancelot offers to give Elaine any present for saving his life, never imagining that a genuine, nonmaterialistic demand may be made on him. She asks for love, even if it does not include marriage. His response creaks with banality: "Nay, the world, the world, / All ear and eye, with such a stupid heart" (ll. 935–36). It is the bigot's appeal to others' bigotry.

She senses immediately that there is no hope: "Alas for me then, my good days are done" (l. 942). Eager to blunt the potential tragic pathos of all this, Lancelot drones on with the consolations known to all the emotionally wizened: "This is not love: but love's first flash in youth, / Most common: yea, I know it of mine own self" (ll. 944–45). He does recognize the impotence of all this, though, and he has no wish to be unkind. Like Elaine, Lancelot is trapped in the impossible situation. The greatest of all romantic knights is reduced to sounding like everyone's dull grandfather. He ends by again offering money and land, the final, pointless gesture. "Of all this will I nothing" (l. 961), says Elaine, confirming by her death the futility of more words. The "wordless man" (l. 171) who accompanies her funeral barge suggests the final death of the word, of art, and of Camelot.

As always in these ironic idylls, Tennyson adds a coda, a turn of the screw; here it is the meeting between Lancelot and Guinevere.

Lancelot presents the diamonds he has won to Guinevere with the finest words he can manufacture: "Take, what I had not won except for you, / These jewels, and make me happy, making them / An armlet for the roundest arm on earth, / Or necklace for a neck to which the swan's / Is tawnier than her cygnet's" (ll. 1174–78). The artificiality of this language strikes even Lancelot, who turns from it embarrassed: "these are words" (l. 1178). They are, as he says, only words, and words no longer really signify. Any speaking, therefore, is a kind of sin (ll. 1179–82), an act of deception, since the coherence that underlies genuine speech has been lost. The queen, unconsciously tearing away leaves from a vine and surrounding them with the wreakage of youth and hope, fails to respond at all to Lancelot's gift or to his flattery. She denies that they have any permanent bond between them, since there are now no permanent bonds of any kind. In pure spite she throws away the diamonds he nearly died for, assuring the absurdity of the quest and of Elaine's death.

Arthur's final verdict is very clear: Elaine was shaped "By God for thee alone" (l. 1356). Lancelot has rejected all that was divine in man. His attempt to wriggle out of Arthur's scrutiny—"free love will not be bound" (l. 1368)—is met immediately with Arthur's important comment on the nature of self and society, freedom and obedience: "Free love, so bound, were freest" (l. 1369). Lancelot turns away, answering nothing because he is beyond the reach of Arthur's truth. The only knowledge that comes to him is the dusty knowledge of irony: he has lost a world and a life, perhaps for nothing, not even for love but for "Dead love's harsh heir, jealous pride" (l. 1387). He now desires to reject his name, but he cannot bring himself to renewal or repentance, even now. In a moment of bitter clarity he sees that he can never leave his terrible prison; he has become accustomed to the pain: "I needs must break / These bonds that so defame me: not without / She wills it: would I, if she willed it? nay, / Who knows?" (ll. 1409–12).

As Elaine drifts by on her barge, some of the ignorant Camelot society think that she may be that fairy queen "come to take the King to Fairyland" (l. 1249). In a way, they are right. Lancelot's failure to make Elaine a second queen—she achieves that distinction only in being buried "like a queen" (l. 1325)—is a sign that the centrifugal growth of Camelot, suggested so clearly in the unions of Gareth and Lynette, Geraint and Enid, has been stopped at its source. There is now no growth except the growing awareness of decay.

The next idyll, "The Holy Grail," represents the last great attempt to save man from bestiality, to recover the values that are already lost: "tell thy brother knights to fast and pray, / That so perchance the vision may be seen / By thee and those, and all the world be healed" (ll. 126–28). The imbalance is simply shifted from Garlon to Pellam, from empiricism to mysticism. The well-meant search for the Grail assures the divorce of the sensual from the spiritual life as certainly as Vivien's victory over Merlin. Tennyson is willing to allow for the reality of the Grail and the legitimacy of its vision in a proper life;[40] what devastates the realm is the separation of this spiritual reality from any other. The Grail quest is a quest for harmony that in the end helps to destroy the comic society. Like Bosola, in Webster's equally ironic *The Duchess of Malfi*, it proceeds with the best intentions to murder that which it had sought to preserve.

Tennyson's vehicle for this tale of ironic heroism is a variation on the dramatic monologue: in the main it is made up of *two* dramatic monologues. Sir Percivale's reconstruction of the story and his defense of the quest is presented for the admiration and awe of Ambrosius, Percivale's brother monk, who occasionally interrupts with very pointed questions and exclamations. The poem builds its tensions between the poles of these irreconcilably different speakers. Tennyson himself, Hallam says, "would . . . call attention to the babbling homely utterances of the village priest Ambrosius as a contrast to the sweeping passages of blank verse that set forth the visions of spiritual enthusiasm." [41]

Both men, Ambrosius and Percivale, are in touch with a different version of reality. They are warm, loving friends, but they fail even remotely to understand one another. Words in this poem go nowhere and make no contact. Ambrosius can wonder at Percivale's account of spiritual enthusiasm, but that is all; Percivale is alike impervious to Ambrosius's instinctive warmth and to Arthur's statements on the proper spiritual life. The heroic comedy of

40. "I have expressed there my strong feeling as to the Reality of the Unseen" (*Memoir*, 2:90).

41. Quoted in Ricks, p. 1661.

Percivale is disjoined completely from the domestic comedy of Ambrosius, almost as in *The Princess*. But here, the values dear to the individual ego fight against and destroy the values that bind men together. "The Holy Grail" is a story of fruitless beauty and grandeur. Arthur's vision of integration is a lonely and alien one: it gets no response, only these two good men chatting away and ignoring the destruction around them.

It has been customary, ever since Clyde deL. Ryals's startling arguments in defense of Ambrosius as "Arthur on a smaller scale," [42] to take sides between the two speakers. The form of the dramatic monologue, at least in Tennyson's use of it, seems to me to disallow such judgments. The values held by the two main speakers are in opposition, but neither is victorious. The third voice in the poem, that of Arthur, does not encourage judgments; it emphasizes the distance between an integrated life and the lives implied by both of the equally compelling monologues to which we had been listening. Like all dramatic monologues, "The Holy Grail" works on a tension between sympathy and judgment, though our sympathies are this time split. The necessity for judgment is very strong: a whole kingdom is being thrown away. But the immediacy and force of the monologues and the melancholy resignation of Arthur's final speech all act to freeze judgment. It is all very well to argue that Percivale and Ambrosius are complementary and need to be combined,[43] but the whole force of the poem goes to convince us that there is no possibility of effecting this coalition.

The poem is the most subtle of Tennyson's exercises in ironic rhetoric. He insists everywhere on the moral and rational framework whose validity he is just as emphatically denying. "The Holy Grail" shows us the destruction wrought by good men, and Tennyson manages a unique irony by making us acknowledge not only that these men are good but that they are, in their way, right. Instead of every choice being the wrong choice, every one is correct. By a refinement of irony, then, Tennyson again makes judgment both essential and trivial. Everyone except Gawain is treated sympathetically. It is a poem which defends the good intentions of the killers.

42. Ryals, *From the Great Deep*, p. 166; see pp. 161–66. Historical support is given to Ryals's argument by Robert D. Hume and Toby A. Olshin, "Ambrosius in 'The Holy Grail,' " *N&Q*, n.s. 16 (1969): 208–09.

43. See Reed, *Perception and Design*, pp. 95–96.

Though Arthur himself sees very clearly that the quest is destructive, he also grants that it is authentic, that salvation may and will be obtained through the Grail. Percivale's sister has originated a new order that both complements and mocks Arthur's. Though her desire to cleanse and reunify the kingdom is exactly the king's own desire, her means for accomplishing that cure are too impatient, too partial. The ardor of her wish for the return of the healing Grail derives from "a fervent flame of human love, / Which being rudely blunted, glanced and shot / Only to holy things" (ll. 74–76). Her own incomplete life, the denial of her natural human love, leads her to a holy but disastrous compensation.

The quest for the Grail is entirely a negative one, unconsciously conceived as a substitute and sworn to by Percivale and his fellow knights, it is emphasized, because they had *not* seen the Grail: "Then when he asked us, knight by knight, if any / Had seen it, all their answers were as one: / 'Nay, lord, and *therefore* have we sworn our vows" [italics mine] (ll. 283–85). All of these men are driven by the same desperate sense of spiritual inadequacy, the same perception of loss and fragmentation that had infused Percivale's sister. When Galahad hears of her vision, "His eyes became so like her own, they seemed / Hers" (ll. 141–42). This recalls exactly the earlier creation of the Round Table, when the momentary likeness of the king had passed over the faces of all the knights. The new order, however, is one of fanaticism and dissolution, not unification. It is based on spiritual truth and an acute perception of the rapid disappearance of the spiritual life. For all this, it is a disaster. The point is that in an ironic world the search for comedy only thickens the prison walls.

"The Holy Grail" once again repeats the wasteland motif, the image of elementary inner chaos that one must conquer. The theme of losing oneself to find a new self is not at all submerged in this idyll, nor are the means to that salvation ineffective. Galahad, Bors, and Percivale, perhaps others, do see the Grail. But now, without a background of social harmony, salvation acts to make man unfit for social life. One emerges from comic testing into a world that has no place for comedy. This process of rejuvenation, the same undergone by Gareth, Edyrn, and Geraint, was once essential to the life of society; now it becomes a source of its destruction. By defending the Quest, then, Tennyson emphasizes the decay of the Arthurian society and the terrible sickness of an order attacked by its own legitimate and necessary supports.

This disruption is signaled by continually heightened discontinuities, principally those between Percivale and Ambrosius, of course. The fact that Ambrosius, an unworldly and secluded monk, should defend communal values while Percivale, from the very center of the social world, expresses the values of the solitary, is more than a neat specific irony. It emphasizes further the dissociation of man from his experiences and suggests his inability ever to learn, even from what is directly around him. Even a monk cannot understand what a spiritual life means; even a member of the Round Table itself cannot understand community. Neither is wrong, nor are they especially limited people. On the contrary, they are eloquent and sensitive.

Percivale can sometimes appear rigorously single-minded and prosaic, but he is also capable of great exaltation, as, for instance, in the passage beginning "O brother, had you known our mighty hall" (l. 225) and ending with a description of Arthur's statue on the top of the hall: "till the people in far fields, / Wasted so often by the heathen hordes, / Behold it, crying, 'We have still a King' " (ll. 243–45). The center of the poem is occupied by Percivale's impassioned description of his trials. These are not, as is often stated, "temptations." [44] It is rather Percivale, as Jacob Korg points out, who brings "waste and destruction wherever he rides." [45] His journey into the wasteland can be seen as a symbolic attack on the values of comedy, particularly domestic comedy. Specific aspects of that form are deliberately and successively annihilated. Running brooks and apples on fertile lawns turn to dust in his hands; a woman, gracefully spinning, opens her arms to welcome him, but innocent and expansive hospitality is also turned to dust; the plowman (interestingly, the same image Arthur uses at the end of the poem to invoke the perfect, balanced life) dies at his plow, the milkmaid in her milking; all productive and simple unity is destroyed. Beauty, in the form of a jewelled casque and golden armor, offers itself to him, but it is also destroyed by Percivale's touch.

44. See Lawrence Poston III, "The Two Provinces," p. 380, and Ryals, *From the Great Deep*, pp. 170–71.
45. "The Pattern of Fatality," p. 11.

Out of all this, though, he still finds holiness. After further testing in the chapel, ensuring his humility and the loss of his old self, he goes on to see the Grail. There is no doubt of this. Tennyson insists on the reality of his salvation and on its terrible effects; for, after seeing the Grail, Percivale comes on a lady whom he had once loved. She now offers to renew that love, expressing the same directness and openness as Elaine: "And calling me the greatest of all knights, / Embraced me, and so kissed me the first time, / And gave herself and all her wealth to me" (ll. 594–96). He refuses love, not because of sin or guilt, as Lancelot did, but because of virtue.

Percivale is given the opportunity to carry on, like Gareth and Geraint, the expanding force of Camelot, the re-creation of the pattern set by Arthur and Guinevere's wedding, the union of soul and body that should connect and unify the kingdom. The lady's people cry to Percivale to "Wed thou our Lady, and rule over us, / And thou shalt be as Arthur in our land" (ll. 604–05), but he must turn his back on them and break the Arthurian chain and the Arthurian promise. He remembers the holy vow, which, in turn, allows him to forget his lady: "Then after I was joined with Galahad / [I] Cared not for her, nor anything upon earth" (ll. 610–11). Nothing on earth now has any connection to the Grail, for spiritual values have withdrawn utterly from life. Thus, Percivale has no choice; the love he is offered cannot be fulfilled in a world that denies love. It is not Percivale who is criticized.

Ambrosius's own song, his dramatic monologue, is subversive of Percivale's values, but it does not supplant them. Ambrosius's great simplicity, his earnestness, and his emotional honesty are extremely well-caught. They are undeniably made attractive, especially when they are added to his ability to ask the most uncomfortable and piercing questions quite innocently: "Tell me, what drove thee from the Table Round, / My brother? was it earthly passion crost?" (ll. 28–29) or "What is it? / The phantom of a cup that comes and goes?" (ll. 43–44). He peppers Percivale's speech with these deflating remarks, bringing to bear on religious mysticism the simple and naïve skepticism of humanitarian values.

It is, of course, an intuitive skepticism; Ambrosius is not Tristram, but a warm and loving man of the earth. He has imagination and he certainly has creative powers: he can even create a love in Percivale by the very force of his own warmth (ll. 9–12). Still, his artistry is of a very limited kind. He is amazed by the Grail story, stunned by a notion of spiritual reality so far beyond him. Again, he is not Tristram, but if we take his naïve doubts about the Grail—"these books of ours . . . seem / Mute of this miracle" (ll. 65–66)—too seriously, we are responding to the poem as Tristram would.

For Ambrosius does not control the poem and give it a new unity; he supports, indeed partly creates, its theme of disunity. By the very power of his dramatic monologue, he helps demonstrate the inadequacy of the purely spiritual life, just as the power of the Grail legend itself renders insufficient his own domestic naturalism. Ambrosius is the spokesman for the values of "The May Queen," but he is speaking in the world of "Tithonus." Full approval and great force are given to the life he leads, but it is not the life to heal Camelot. It can only emphasize how far beyond cure Arthur's kingdom is. At the height of Percivale's eloquent recitation of the Grail quest, Ambrosius interrupts to stress by contrast his own world and, therefore, the radical disjunctions that now exist:

> . . . [I love to] mingle with our folk;
> And knowing every honest face of theirs
> As well as ever shepherd knew his sheep,
> And every homely secret in their hearts,
> Delight myself with gossip and old wives,
> And ills and aches, and teethings, lyings-in,
> And mirthful sayings, children of the place,
> That have no meaning half a league away:
> Or lulling random squabbles when they rise,
> Chafferings and chatterings at the market-cross,
> Rejoice, small man, in this small world of mine,
> Yea, even in their hens and in their eggs—
>
> [ll. 549–60]

His capacity for joy, for a full and imaginative participation in the life about him, is given rich expression in order to show how incapable of full extension that capacity is. The love of man he values is no longer the love of God, since the word, that is, God in man, has been violated. Percivale's quest for God, therefore, necessarily takes him away from man:

> "O brother [said Ambrosius,] saving this Sir Galahad,
> Came ye on none but phantoms in your quest,
> No man, no woman?"

> Then Sir Percivale:
> "All men, to one so bound by such a vow,
> And women were as phantoms."

[ll. 561–65]

At the end of the poem, Arthur surveys the tithe of his men that have returned and the mutilation wrought on his kingdom by this last search for order. The king turns *sharply* (l. 736) away from Percivale when the knight announces that the sight of the Grail has made it necessary for him "to pass away into the quiet life" (l. 735). Quiet is now all that is possible for holiness; as in "Merlin and Vivien" the poem moves toward frozen stillness. Fully aware of the largeness of the ironies that surround him, Arthur turns just as sharply on Gawain's shallow ridicule of the quest. He then makes one last statement of the image of ideal balance: the hind who dedicates his life to immediate duty and for that reason—in the very immersion in common duty, not in escape from it—finds the superfluity of the purely physical—"this earth he walks on seems not earth" (l. 908)—and a confirmation of God and self: he "knows himself no vision to himself, / Nor the high God a vision, nor that One / Who rose again" (ll. 913–15).

These last lines, which Tennyson called "the (spiritually) central lines of the Idylls," [46] are also the saddest; for they are uttered by a king who no longer believes in the efficacy of utterance. They once constituted the hope that built a permanent kingdom; they are now only words that go nowhere and teach nothing: "So spake the King: I knew not all he meant" (l. 916). Percivale uses the past tense *knew*, surely, not to suggest that he now does know, but to imply that the matter is now just part of the past, something he has long since ceased to think about.

III

The last section—"Pelleas and Ettarre," "The Last Tournament," "Guinevere," and "The Passing of Arthur"—allows no more comedy, no more positive judgments, not even of the limited and subversive kind that prevailed in "The Holy Grail." These final poems represent the nightmare stage of irony; images of absolute bondage, cynicism, and utter waste dominate. The last

---

46. *Memoir*, 2:90.

glimpse of hope, in Pelleas, is crushed brutally and unmercifully. After that, only Arthur and the fool hold out.

"Pelleas and Ettarre" is a bleak parody of the initiation stories that open the *Idylls*. Pelleas himself is the last figure of comic exuberance we hear of in the poem: it is almost as if the news had not reached him out there in the wilds. This time the story opens with the wasteland already conquered; Pelleas enters as a fully realized person, with nothing to prove, no need to be tested. Much like Gareth, he is there to affirm his developed being and the authenticity of Camelot. He comes in as part of a new wave of knights, recruited "to fill the gap / Left by the Holy Quest" (ll. 1–2) and to give new life to Camelot. Arthur even holds a "Tournament of Youth" to inaugurate the kingdom's new beginning, but, as Pelleas shows, there are to be no new beginnings, only a reiteration and confirmation of waste. Pelleas develops a unified being whose very completeness and harmony unfit him for this world.

Tennyson projects this ironic absurdity as a burlesque of comedy, making Pelleas seem not only alien to his environment but ludicrously so. By a very subtle management of tone, Pelleas's comic expectations are made to appear absurd and simple-minded. It is only gradually that we perceive the full bitterness of this parody. The tone and theme are exactly those reflected in an epigram Tennyson wrote at about the same time:

I ran upon life unknowing, without or science or art,
I found the first pretty maiden but she was a harlot at heart;
I wandered about the woodland after the melting of snow,
"Here is the first pretty snowdrop"—and it was the dung of a crow!

Pelleas seems silly only to those who, like Tristram or Vivien, no longer can feel what it was to live in harmony with the king and with themselves. His expectations have the effect of a certain kind of off-key singing that seems hilarious until we realize that it is, in fact, a beautiful melody rendered discordant by the theater and our own ears. It is true, a great deal of critical ingenuity has been used to demonstrate that Pelleas is merely a "deluded lover" who "loves love," "a dupe," an idolator guilty of "willful blindness," a secular "courtly lover," a "coward, traitor, and beast." [47] This tendency to

47. See, in order, Ryals, *From the Great Deep*, pp. 135–38; R. B. Wilkenfeld, "Tennyson's Camelot," *UTQ* 37 (1968): 287–91; W. David Shaw, *"Idylls of the King,"* p. 181; Lawrence

cast blame about is the natural tendency to try to locate the jailer. It seems to me, however, that Pelleas is defeated *because* he is guiltless. It may be, perhaps, that the incomplete Balin should have further resisted the ironic implications of his environment, but Pelleas really has no choice. The world he faces is not the tantalizing and deceptive world of Balin but a merciless and animalistic one. The beasts are back in charge. Instead of virtuous Lynette or even ambiguously blushing Guinevere, he finds only the vicious Ettarre.

Pelleas moves into this world, incongruously accompanied by "the sweet smell of the fields / . . . and the sunshine" (ll. 5–6). He brings with him all of natural comedy, not realizing or having any way of realizing that nature and human hopes are mutually inimical. His single speech to Arthur, "Make me thy knight, because I know, Sir King, / All that belongs to knighthood, and I love" (ll. 7–8), fixes his purity and expansive confidence. He can afford to love so openly, without qualification or even object, because he believes this is a world of love. He bestows his love on Ettarre, a harlot who is, appropriately, also a "great lady"; this is not an exceptionally unfortunate choice but rather a typical one for this time. Pelleas is not tragically doomed because he chooses to love Ettarre but because he loves at all. She is one with the world in which she lives. He meets Ettarre and her lovely attendants, confused "because the way was lost" (l. 57). Pelleas walks out into the light, Ettarre sardonically comments, to be their "pilot-star" (l. 60). But instead they drag him down into their own confusion and darkness.

He immediately mistakes Ettarre's physical beauty for spiritual beauty: "the beauty of her flesh abashed the boy, / As though it were the beauty of her soul" (ll. 74–75). This is a mistake, but it should not be. Pelleas is simply making the wrong assumptions about the nature of the world. Geraint made no mistake in trusting his imaginative picture of Enid, we recall. Now, however, the body and soul are split, and Pelleas's innocent action has the same consequences as the similar action of the equally innocent Elaine.

Poston III, " 'Pelleas and Ettarre,' " *VP* 4 (1966): 203; F. E. L. Priestley, "Tennyson's *Idylls*," p. 48; Reed, *Perception and Design*, p. 106. Among Pelleas's few defenders is William Brashear, who claims that the knight is totally innocent; there simply "is no atmosphere in which the spirit of youth can prosper" (*The Living Will*, p. 145). This, it seems to me, is the more fruitful and accurate reading.

He is also an artist, responding to a unity that should be but is not there.

By the very exuberance of his spiritual energy, Tennyson makes clear, Pelleas seals his own doom: "For as the base man, judging of the good, / Puts his own baseness in him by default / Of will and nature, so did Pelleas lend / All the young beauty of his own soul to hers" (ll. 76–79). Ettarre, practiced in the breaking of words and skilled in the deceptions now prevalent in the discordant land, chides him for not knowing "the fashion of our speech" (l. 96). He knows as yet only an integrated and coherent speech, imported, significantly, from the wasteland, which is now closer to God than Arthur's society. Ettarre later keeps him away from her "so that he could not come to speech with her" (l. 198). She must avoid him because he speaks a different language: that of the comic and spiritualized word. When she at last breaks out in her own angry and chaotic words, slandering the vows and the king, Pelleas "was stricken mute" (l. 243). He faces, finally, an emptiness.

His humiliation at the hands of Ettarre, he thinks, is a test. But now there are no educations in Camelot; no change of any kind, just static disloyalty. He refuses to leave Ettarre and love, properly resisting all the combined evidence of his senses—properly, that is, from a comic point of view. Only Gawain, emissary of Arthur himself and of the most basic union that binds the order together, convinces him of his error. Pelleas can, as the song he recalls says, easily accept the thorns with the rose, but not the cancerous worm. He is not defeated by a mixed, imperfect world but by a hellish one. Like Arthur and Dagonet, he becomes a divine "fool" (ll. 465, 466), made so by his own love. Turning from that company, he has no choice but complete cynicism: "Love?—we be all alike: only the King / Hath made us fools and liars. O noble vows! / O great and sane and simple race of brutes / That own no lust because they have no law!" (ll. 469–72). He learns, ironically from the pure Percivale, that the heart of Camelot is split. If Guinevere is false, nothing is left: " 'Is the King true?' 'The King!' said Percivale. / 'Why then let men couple at once with wolves' " (ll. 525–26). To Pelleas it seems as if all the world, led by Arthur, were in a conspiracy against him. He is right about the conspiracy, but wrong about Arthur, who is victimized as much as he.

Finally, in an inversion of Gareth's creation of his own personality, Pelleas specifically renounces his own being: "No name, no name" (l. 553), he shouts to Lancelot. He loses personality and manhood, answering Guinevere's attempt to calm him with a "fierce" eye and a hissing, "I have no sword" (l. 589). He then springs "from the door into the dark" (l. 591). There is now nothing but this dark—and the silence: "And all talk died, as in a grove all song / Beneath the shadow of some bird of prey; / Then a long silence came upon the hall" (ll. 594–96).

"The Last Tournament" ends with an explicit comment on the death of comedy: "I am thy fool, / And I shall never make thee smile again" (ll. 755–56). Arthur is at last overcome by the trivial and the unmeaning. The truth of irony, first available to the stupid Vivien, is about to touch Arthur's genuine wisdom. Arthur is the last to know, not because he is naïve but because ironic "truth" is an inversion of real truth. When cynicism becomes actuality, the idiots are the best informed. Surrounded by a world that failed to understand, Arthur refuses to give in to the absurd *facts* that eventually defeat him. Arthur establishes his kingdom on the assumption that human beings are truly human: he is defeated by this self-evident yet false proposition. Evidence is reduced entirely now to the empirical, and humans prove themselves, in the end, to be nonhuman. The lonely figure of Arthur, whose heroism now seems perverse or even ludicrous, is at the center of nineteenth-century irony. His fight seems almost pointless; human beings are not worth saving: "my brother fool, the king of fools" (l. 354), Dagonet calls him, "Conceits himself as God that he can make / Figs out of thistles, silk from bristles, milk / From burning spurge, honey from hornet-combs, / And men from beasts—Long live the king of fools" (ll. 355–58).

There is no longer even a Pelleas or a Tournament of Youth; there are not even comic assurances to be burlesqued. Pelleas comes, bringing springtime with him, but now there is only the dry thunder of autumn: "then one long roll / Of Autumn thunder, and the jousts began: / And ever the wind blew, and yellowing leaf / And gloom and gleam, and shower and shorn plume / Went down it" (ll. 152–56). The double meaning of "The Tournament of the Dead Innocence" is acknowledged by everyone in Camelot. "The Last Tournament" is self-conscious and overt in its sarcasms. Everyone in Arthur's kingdom except the king has become an ironist: a representative, anonymous maid, for instance, cries,

"Praise the patient saints, / Our one white day of Innocence hath past, / Though somewhat draggled at the skirt. So be it. / The snowdrop only, flowering through the year, / Would make the world as blank as Winter-tide" (ll. 217–21). Only ironic materials are available. "All courtesy is dead" (l. 211) now; even the outward forms of it are disappearing. The world has been sick for some time; people are naturally tired of complaining.

The chief spokesman and apologist for this new world is Tristram, that self-acknowledged and proud "worldling of the world" (l. 691). Tennyson awakens the great romantic echoes of the Tristram-Isolt tale in order to parody, not romantic love but tragedy. Tristram's love is the type of the new loyalty; it is subject to the new law, "Mark's way." Mark, the voiceless, sneaking, immaterial specter, is the central force in a world without a word. His murder of Tristram is not even an act of revenge, nor does he either love or hate his wife. It is simply Mark's way, the way of the world, to slaughter.

Mark's way is now even the way of Arthur's men. Their victory over Pelleas, as the Red Knight, is the clearest sign of their defeat. Pelleas has been most viciously attacked by the dissimulations of the decaying Camelot and has sought, in his continuing innocence, to dissolve the tensions of irony. He does so in the only way available to him, through a parody of Arthur's promise. Since Camelot is no longer open and real, he establishes a black Camelot: "My tower is full of harlots, like his court, / But mine are worthier, seeing they profess / To be none other than themselves—and say / My knights are all adulterers like his own, / But mine are truer, seeing they profess / To be none other" (ll. 81–86).

Pelleas is another murdered innocent, and his reactionary inversion of Camelot is the last cry of the pure in a perverted world. He is so much the antithesis of Arthur's knights and so incapable of disguise that he cannot even stay on a horse long enough to maintain the combat. He falls off in a drunken stupor, whereupon Arthur's men complete the slaughter of innocence: they "roared / And shouted and leapt down upon the fallen; / There trampled out his face from being known, / And sank his head in mire, and slimed themselves" (ll. 467–70). The massacre that follows is a parody of knightly conquest, and the fire Arthur's followers raise is "like the live North" (l. 478)—the North of the heathen, the beast, and Satan. The narrator's sardonic comment, "So all the ways were safe from shore to shore" (l. 484), reminds us sadly of the earlier glorious defeat of the heathen. Only now the heathen are within.

The last holdout against the beast is Dagonet, Tennyson's version of the holy fool. He suggests, in a stunted and pathetic form, the image of Geraint and Edyrn, the last of the redeemed: "The dirty nurse, Experience, in her kind / Hath fouled me—an I wallowed, then I washed" (ll. 317-18). There is to be no more cleansing. "I have had my day and my philosophies" (l. 319), he says sarcastically, putting the fall of man into Tristram's blithe, relativistic terms. His "philosophies" were not systems at all, but, in the end, a generous faith that gave him the ability to see.

In an ironic world, those who can see seem blind, however, so that Dagonet's wisdom becomes idiocy. He still speaks the *word*, but the coherence of language and universe is gone and Dagonet's words emerge as riddles that no one understands. He asks Tristram if he is able to see the star called the harp of Arthur; Tristram naturally (it is natural to Tristram) says he cannot see it in open day. Dagonet's response is the final statement of the truth that Arthur has promoted and the perception he has mistakenly insisted on: "Nay, nor will: I see it and hear. / It makes a silent music up in heaven, / And I, and Arthur and the angels hear" (ll. 348-50). Dagonet is "the wisest knight of all" (l. 248), but he is the last knight, absurdly impotent, illustrating the futility of all wisdom.

Tristram can never see the star. He has, Dagonet says, reopened the old doubts about Arthur's legitimacy. One of the darkest ironies in this tale is that the new man of experience is unable to learn from, even to make contact with, genuine experience. Tristram is a pragmatist with no feeling for evidence, even direct evidence. The simple answer of Gareth, "Who should be King save him who makes us free" (l. 136), is lost on Tristram, who goes rummaging about in the dusty rationality of formal legitimacy. It is the presumably liberated Tristram—"free love—free field" (l. 281)— who is bound to trust only an experience he cannot understand. He is caught absolutely in the very chaos he promotes, in "Mark's way."

He wins the lawless tournament; rightly so, since he is indeed at the center of this world. Only the fool and Arthur differ from him very much. Lancelot's attempt to draw a distinction between himself and the brutal Tristram is met with a completely just rebuke: "Great brother, thou nor I have made the world; / Be happy in thy fair Queen as I in mine" (ll. 203–04). The gentle and courteous Lancelot has made himself one with this man who parodies courtesy. Tristram is, as he claims himself, a figure of untransformed nature, willing to accept the world, he supposes, just as it is. He completes the collapse of the balance Arthur had once maintained so well. His dream, which, like all dreams in the *Idylls*, is a vision of the dreamer's true self, reveals clearly that destructive imbalance.

Tristram dreams of a quarrel between his two Isolts, struggling for the ruby-chain he has won in the Tournament of the Dead Innocence. Isolt of Breton points to her rival and says, "Look, her hand is red! / These be no rubies, this is frozen blood, / And melts within her hand—her hand is hot / With ill desires" (ll. 411–14). The point of the dream is not, however, related to the evils of lust. The two, between them, manage to ruin the chain: "Followed a rush of eagle's wings, and then / A whimpering of the spirit of the child, / Because the twain had spoiled her carcanet" (ll. 416–18). The essential problem is the radical split of body and soul, sense and spirituality: the two Isolts. Innocence is torn to shreds by a false competition. Tristram cannot balance the two forces, so he chooses carelessly, and he chooses Isolt of Ireland—the body, irony, and Mark.

The climactic scene between Tristram and Isolt demonstrates the impossibility now of permanent values or contracts. Isolt recalls the old word—"My God, the power / Was once in vows when men believed the King!" (ll. 643–44)—but she is herself pathetically forsworn, as Tristram is able to point out: "Vows! did you keep the vow you made to Mark / More than I mine?" (ll. 650–51). There is no solidarity, nor, according to Tristram, should there be. His reasons are those of Vivien; they are, like hers, compelling in their free and articulate very common sense. "The vow that binds too strictly snaps itself" (l. 652), he declares; Arthur has violated nature. He points to his own arm, vigorous and pounding with blood, as, in itself, sufficient refutation of Arthur's inhuman and naïve rigors: "can Arthur make me pure / As any maiden child? lock up my tongue / From uttering freely what I freely hear? / Bind me to one? The wide world laughs at it" (ll. 687–90). There are no boundaries to their love, he says, because there are no bonds, a sophistication that directly echoes the earlier conversations between Lancelot and Guinevere.

Tristram sprinkles other arguments and other appeals in with the main one as they occur to him. He is willing to admit that the vows had a certain temporary pragmatic value—"They served their use, their time" (l. 671)—and he remembers to add the old rationalistic doubts about the king's origins: "They failed to trace him through the flesh and blood / Of our old kings: whence then? a doubtful lord / To bind them by inviolable vows" (ll. 681–83). Tristram is not even concerned with logical consistency. He accepts a world of no consistency at all and is, therefore, not even a materialist or a rationalist. He is only, as he says, a "worldling," giving himself up to an ironic world. Against the liberating will of Arthur, we have the new passive and defeated will of the ironic nonhero. By loving this man, Isolt is already giving herself to Mark; for Tristram is every bit as violent and unprincipled: he "had let one finger lightly touch / The warm white apple of her throat, [and] replied, / 'Press this a little closer, sweet, until—' " (ll. 710–12).

Mark's act of murder is the appropriate climax to the love of Tristram and Isolt. They have no bonds and acknowledge no loyalties. Isolt leaves Mark and cleaves to Tristram for no human reason: "What rights are his that dare not strike for them?" (l. 525), she asks, invoking standards of mere power and ownership. Only force and brutality are recognized by these two. Since Mark does "dare strike" for his rights, according to Isolt's own standards he now deserves her. Mark and Isolt, bound by violence, suspicion, and hatred, stand as the ironic counterparts to the marriage of Arthur and Guinevere. They turn the comic world inside out. All that remains is the alien word, the "voice" (l. 753) that clings sobbing to Arthur's feet and utters its last pronouncement: Camelot is dead.

"Guinivere" apparently had quite a spectacular effect on many Victorians.[48] It seems astonishing, for instance, that the idyll "made George Eliot weep" when Tennyson read it.[49] These days the idyll is more likely to seem an unaccountable lapse on Tennyson's part. Less open about our emotions and also less struck by the novelty of domestic realism, we are prone to blame the whole episode on

48. Certainly not all, as is pointed out by Ann Gossman and George W. Whiting, "King Arthur's Farewell to Guinevere," *N&Q*, n.s. 6 (1959): 446–48.
49. *Memoir*, 2:109.

sexual prudery. In any case, it seems thematically narrow, generi-
cally and tonally inappropriate. Idyll after idyll appeared to be
promoting the point that there was no cause for Arthur's fall, no
blame to be assigned since the forces against him were both so large
and so insignificant as to be beyond blame altogether. But now
Arthur himself comes pronouncing "judgment" (l. 418). In this
idyll, irony nearly relaxes into melodrama: we have a cause, a
reason, plenty of blame and forgiveness, even gestures toward the
emotions of tragedy. "Guinevere" is all too close to being like a
pratfall in the middle of *Antigone*; it releases some of the tension,
which perhaps helps to explain the tears—even George Eliot's.

Arthur, as many have noted, now seems less the mythic king than
the outraged husband, speaking with a too personal bitterness and
desire to hurt: "Thou hast not made my life so sweet to me, / That I
the King should greatly care to live" (ll. 448–49). He is even
capable of tremulous self-pity: "but rather think / How sad it were
for Arthur, should he live, / To sit once more within his lonely hall"
(ll. 492–94). Here, the balance between the concrete and the
allusive tips dangerously toward the concrete, as Arthur almost
loses dignity and—more important—symbolic stature. When he is
reduced to the level of saying, "I was ever virgin save for thee" (l.
554), it is difficult to bear in mind his mystical birth or indeed any
of his symbolic attributes.

Nor is it only Arthur who is often merely angry; the dominant
tone of the idyll is one of simple anger. Cool and complex
detachment is dropped for the uncomplicated, childish pleasure of
indignation—Arthur's and, very clearly, Tennyson's. Arthur's as-
tonishing definition of "the worst of public foes" (l. 509) as a man
who shields an erring wife has a symbolic aptness, I suppose, but it
is put so bluntly that it recalls Tennyson in his worst reactionary
moods, railing at Zolaism and the moral decline. The entire poem
moves far too close to the diffuse articulation of clichés that had
been used in "The Miller's Daughter." The prattling novice has a
function parallel to that of Ambrosius, but instead of the subtle
interconnections between speakers established in "The Holy Grail,"
"Guinevere" does all it can to make its ironies entirely superficial,
overt, and elaborate. The narrator arranges the novice's questions
and exclamations so as to give us plenty of rhetorical winks. Like
too many domestic idylls, this is designed to make very few
demands.

All this is true, but it is not the whole truth. The idyll seems weak principally because of its context. What is important is its failure to support the full weight of the entire poem's complex themes, and that failure is only relative. Neither Tennyson's sense nor his artistic powers desert him entirely in "Guinevere." Its own kind of artistry and its own fitness must be acknowledged.

There are, for instance, important and subtle echoes of past motifs: Guinevere reverses the action of the early poems, moving into, rather than out of, the wasteland. Instead of finding a name and proper speech, she learns to curse her name and to accept a life of silence. She is no mere empiricist, but the novice's questions force her, again and again, to take refuge in the shallow arguments of Tristram. Guinevere talks to her companion about Lancelot and the king, ending with an important comic truism: "For manners are not idle, but the fruit / Of loyal nature, and of noble mind" (ll. 333–34). The novice is not slow to see the conflict between this code and Lancelot's behavior: the prince of courtesy is also "the most disloyal friend in all the world" (l. 338). Guinevere is caught by the fundamental divisions she has helped to create and can only appeal, like Tristram, to "the world": "What knowest thou of the world, and all its lights / And shadows, all the wealth and all the woe?" (ll. 341–42). In the absence of genuine standards, "the world," the chaos of undifferentiated and unordered experience, has to do.

In the end, though, the queen is treated with compassion, as a victim rather than a villainess. She is trapped by her own nature, her lack of understanding, most importantly by Arthur's impossible scheme for making human beings human. In the very midst of her repentence, her sincere pledge "not even in inmost thought to think again / The sins that made the past so pleasant to us" (ll. 372–73), her mind slips back to those lovely "golden days" (l. 377). She cannot help herself; those days seemed so much like Eden: she and Lancelot "Rode under groves that looked a paradise / Of blossom, over sheets of hyacinth / That seemed the heavens upbreaking through the earth" (ll. 386–88). They *looked* a paradise, *seemed* the heavens. She was trapped by forces much larger than herself, forces that obviously do not connect with simple notions of sexual prudery.

Adultery, in fact, is hardly the issue. On the narrative level the great sin is disloyalty; more generally, Guinevere's defection suggests the failure of physical actuality to support and give life to spiritual truth. Despite his few lapses into self-indulgent and self-pitying ire, Arthur's real charges against her are social, not personal. She has ruined not him but law and civilization: "The children born of thee are sword and fire, / Red ruin, and the breaking up of laws, / The craft of kindred and the Godless hosts / Of heathen swarming o'er the Northern Sea" (ll. 422–25). Guinevere is finally blamed for being the agency of irony; Arthur says so explicitly: through Guinevere, he says, "the loathsome opposite / Of all my heart had destined did obtain" (ll. 488–89).

Guinevere finally does see the basis of her error and the nature of the promises she has broken. The full force of what has been thrown away so stupidly breaks upon her only when it is already gone: "No light: so late! and dark and chill the night! / O let us in, that we may find the light! / Too late, too late: ye cannot enter now" (ll. 172–74). But there is no special reason why it is too late, why she should not have seen earlier. Irony does not depend on clear reasons, but rather on the absence of reasons. Guinevere comes to perceive the central point about Camelot and about the *Idylls* as a whole: "now I see thee what thou art, / Thou art the highest and most human too" (ll. 643–44). This simple truth, a refutation of all rationalistic objections, has escaped her entirely until now. Her dedication to the senses was so complete she did not understand even them; she could only see and therefore was blinded. She has, thus, lost everything. Her only hope now for renewal and new chances lies in heaven. And even that hope is uncertain: she lives the rest of her life "still hoping, fearing 'is it yet too late?' " (l. 685).

The hope for heaven is made both uncertain and generally unreal. What matters is that Arthur has been unable to create heaven on earth. All spiritual values are now so alien and so little a part of man that heaven is more distant than ever. God has retreated altogether from the world, leaving only the mists and confusion that control the final poem in the *Idylls*, "The Passing of Arthur." Arthur's last battle acts not to dispel but to ensure this bewilderment: "and even on Arthur fell / Confusion, since he saw not whom he fought. / For friend and foe were shadows in the mist, / And friend slew friend not knowing whom he slew" (ll. 98–101). All order and meaning are gone; friends and foes are alike since there is now no stable personality. The word has been replaced by "shrieks / After the Christ, of those who falling down / Looked up for heaven, and only saw the mist" (ll. 110–12).

The idyll is dominated by bewilderment. All hope vanishes
without leaving behind a trace of having been there. No one even
understands. Exactly as Arthur says, "all my realm / Reels back
into the beast, and is no more" (ll. 25–26). The striking central
image of the poem is not of the dying Arthur but of the last initiate
staring blankly, without comprehension, at his disappearing king.
The cycle is complete and nothing remains of the best hope offered
to man. It is a bitter and entirely pessimistic close.[50] The ideal itself
is not dead, perhaps, but it is lost to mankind. It may be that other
promises will be made in the future—the poem does leave open that
possibility—but there is no chance at all that human beings will
ever be able to accept that promise. Arthur may come again,
though that is far from certain, but he is sure to find the same
absurd fate and the same mixture of sloth, hysteria, common sense,
and plain stupidity that so ingloriously defeated him before. There
may be future cycles but, at very best, they will be cycles of
futility—like the one just completed. At its very greatest moments,
the *Idylls* suggest, mankind rises to trivial absurdity.

The poem opens on the arresting and very important vision of the
future: the aged Bedivere, now "no more than a voice" (l. 3),
speaking to "new faces, other minds" (l. 5). The pure voice, the *word*
that had built a comic society, now is alien and alone, about to
disappear. The poem's opening, then, helps to deny any small hope
that may be contained in its slightly ambiguous conclusion. Arthur
leaves only Bedivere behind, and Bedivere makes no converts. The
promise of Camelot has had no lasting effect whatsoever.

Arthur at least partly recognizes this, and his complaints have
about them a new bitterness. He is almost an ironist himself, nearly
captured by the new world, at least insofar as he can distort the
purity of the word to a form of sarcasm: "I found Him in the
shining of the stars, / I marked Him in the flowering of His
fields, / But in His ways with men I find Him not" (ll. 9–11). The
suggestion that God is in nature, not in man, exactly reverses the
point of *In Memoriam*[51] and of the *Idylls* themselves. The great

50. For alternative views, see Reed, *Perception and Design*, passim; Priestley, "Tennyson's
Idylls," p. 46; W. David Shaw, "The Idealist's Dilemma," pp. 52–53; Ryals, *From the Great
Deep*, p. 110. Samuel C. Burchell's interpretation of the ending, in "Tennyson's 'Allegory in
the Distance,'" *PMLA* 68 (1953): 418–24, is even darker than my own.

51. Also, incidentally, what we know to be Tennyson's own beliefs: "I believe in God, not
from what I see in Nature, but from what I find in man" (*Memoir*, 2:374).

humanitarian transcendentalist bitterly reverts to the exploded argument from design. Something worse than the beasts, he sees, is taking over. He suggests that a spiritual kingdom of weeds might be a possibility, but not one of men. Only man is vile. The highest and most human, therefore, is forced to kill that which is human; Arthur must slaughter his own knights and destroy his own kingdom: "Ill doom is mine / To war against my people and my knights. / The king who fights his people fights himself" (ll. 70–72). Things have become so distorted that the ideal and the real have become deadly enemies.

The central ironic narrative, the story of the casting away of Excalibur, is a parable of ignorance and disloyalty and also a deliberate absurdist reduction of tragic grandeur. Instead of a dignified passing, a sustained mood of heroic elegy, we have something like a parody of the *Beowulf* tone. Arthur is reduced to the near ludicrous position of a man unable to get himself buried, haggling with an underling while an audience (i.e. the reader), expecting tragedy, looks on with embarrassment.

Bedivere's inability to perform the simplest task neatly summarizes the *Idylls* and ironically deflates their grand themes. Bedivere is first distracted from duty by the effect of the sword's material beauty on his senses: "For all the haft twinkled with diamond sparks, / Myriads of topaz-lights, and jacinth-work / Of subtlest jewellery. He gazed so long / That both his eyes were dazzled as he stood" (ll. 224–27). He denies his king for these *twinklings*. So he lies. The next time, he succumbs to the argument that the sword would be handy to have around as evidence to convince those who doubt Arthur's existence and his might. Arthur is diminished to empirical proofs or to superstitious magic; the continuity and permanence that had once been assured by the word are now pathetically sought for in fame and materials.

Recognizing just what is left of his kingdom—"I see thee what thou art" (l. 291)—Arthur finally is forced to use absurd threats of physical violence: "if thou spare to fling Excalibur, / I will arise and slay thee with my hands" (ll. 299–300). Bedivere understands only this language. Arthur himself is forced to enter the animalistic world briefly in order to wring some kind of obedience from his follower. The power, even the dignity, of Camelot shrinks finally to the image of a sputtering old man. Bedivere goes through a ritualistic and meaningless performance, like a parrot who has been taught to say mass.

It is a frightening conclusion, where, as in a dream, human faces slowly dissolve into the features of pigs and all humanity seems a bizarre joke. Arthur is exactly "Like one that feels a nightmare on his bed / When all the house is mute" (ll. 345–46). He is now in utter silence, surrounded by the bleak and mocking signs of irony: the "icy waves," "barren chasms," and a "bare black cliff" (ll. 345–46). Even the three queens cry out, "like a wind that shrills / All night in a waste land, where no one comes, / Or hath come, since the making of the world" (ll. 369–71).

Bedivere, who is tagging along behind Arthur into this world, finally perceives that his king is about to leave him. His reaction is the lost and hopeless cry of the deserted child, aware only that "the true old times are dead" (l. 397). His plea to the king for new counsel is cast in the simplest and most poignant terms: "Ah! my Lord Arthur, whither shall I go?" (l. 395). The fall of all the world is contained in Bedivere's great sense of simple loneliness: "And I, the last, go forth companionless, / And the days darken round me, and the years, / Among new men, strange faces, other minds" (ll. 404–06).

Arthur does what he can to give comfort: "The old order changeth, yielding place to new" (l. 408). But this cyclic argument is a platitude so inappropriate that Arthur cannot allow it to stand: "Comfort thyself: what comfort is in me?" (l. 411). This line is, in its implications, the most horrible and in some ways the most important in the *Idylls*. Arthur cannot make a world or promise hope; he cannot even, in the end, offer consolation. He asks for Bedivere's prayers, *almost* sure he is going to Avalon: "But now farewell. I am going a long way / With these thou seëst—if indeed I go / (For all my mind is clouded with a doubt)—" (ll. 424–26).

If Arthur is unsure, Bedivere is absolutely confounded. He has intimations both of doubt and hope; what is certain, though, is that he is left with "the stillness of the dead world's winter dawn" (l. 442). He saw, "Or thought he saw, the speck that bare the King, / Down that long water opening on the deep / Somewhere far off, pass on and on, and go / From less to less and vanish into light" (ll. 465–68).

The King may, though it is not certain, have his victory, but it is a triumph distant from men. The angels may welcome Arthur, but that does Bedivere little good. With Arthur's passing, heaven removes itself entirely from the world, and lonely Bedivere is left without comfort. He can only tell his tale to the uncomprehending. This knight who never understood is the only one left to try to re-create Arthur's world out of the silence. The *Idylls* trails off dismally, leaving behind the absurd image of Bedivere, telling of magical deeds, disappearing swords, and waving hands to those "new men, strange faces, other minds," who yawn and nudge each other. There are no new beginnings, only the mockery of renewal by a cruel and deceptive nature: "And the new sun rose bringing the new year."

Appendix

The Minor Poems

The Political and Public Poems

In this category fall those poems which are self-consciously public in nature: the Horatian verse epistles, the official Laureate poems, and various other poems on political and nationalistic themes. One could make a case for the real distinction of many individual poems in the first two categories, but not, I think, for the highly charged political poems that issued from Tennyson's wrath and indignation regularly throughout his career. These are *not* the Laureate poems. When Tennyson became Laureate he was forced to find for the official poems a different, more comprehensive and inclusive point of view, and a more detached stance, all of which made for much more interesting and powerful poetry. He did continue during this period to publish his "real feelings" without the softening of much art or distance, but he did so anonymously. It is this unquestionably inferior category which is, unfortunately, most revealing for my purposes. The fine poems in the first two categories can be given only a nod in passing.

First, the Laureate poems. Despite the excellence of Valerie Pitt's analysis of them, it is not easy to accept her very high estimate of their quality. It is true that in the great Wellington Ode one can see how skillfully Tennyson creates an elegiac community, a unity of sorrow in "hamlet and hall" (l. 7) and of all those in the "long long procession" (l. 15). Surprisingly, he strives first to increase the community's sorrow and sense of loss: "The last great Englishman is low" (l. 18), but, having uttered this, he immediately turns from it—the next line says "he *seems* the last" [my italics]—and begins to build a new unity. The cohesiveness is provided by the power of the society to give honor and thus give life:

> And through the centuries let a people's voice
> In full acclaim,

A people's voice,
The proof and echo of all human fame,
A people's voice, when they rejoice
At civic revel and pomp and game,
Attest their great commander's claim
With honour, honour, honour, honour to him,
Eternal honour to his name.

[ll. 142–50]

It is not a new idea to suggest immortality through fame, of
course, but Tennyson gives it quite a special emphasis by focusing
not so much on the continuance of the dead man's name as on the
power of *the people* to grant that continuance. It is the "people's
voice," as the recurrent phrase insists, that endures through the
ages. The poem subtly promotes not the immortality of Wellington
so much as the immortality of a unified and disciplined people. The
duke finally becomes explicitly a "great example" (l. 220), showing
that "the path of duty was [and will be] the way to glory" (l. 202)
and teaching discipline, union, and peace. One sees, in other words,
that the poem is rhetorically subtle and highly controlled. But one
can also see how this and the other Laureate poems work
deliberately to restrict their area of concern and to establish it both
impersonally and abstractly. The impulse to cleanse, rejuvenate,
and solidify is there, as it is in the major comedies, but it seems
contained and modest in comparison to the boldly ambitious *The
Princess*, *In Memoriam*, and *Maud*.

Much the same point may be made in relation to Tennyson's
undoubted mastery of epistolary verse, where again the emphasis is
on controlled grace and perfect felicity of phrasing. The most
famous example is the sophisticated and charming ending of "To E.
FitzGerald":

And so I send a birthday line
Of greeting . . .

.   .   .   .

. . . which you will take
My Fitz, and welcome, as I know
    Less for its own than for the sake
Of one recalling gracious times,
    When, in our younger London days,
You found some merit in my rhymes,

> And I more pleasure in your praise.
> [ll. 45–46, 50–56]

The warm "My Fitz" is balanced by the self-depreciating "rhymes," the deliberate understatement of "some merit," and the quiet word *pleasure*. The emotion is expressed by being unexpressed, so that the commonest words, like *gracious*, become remarkably expansive when used to cover a whole range of emotional experience: *gracious times*. There is a warm sense of mutual understanding, of scarcely needing to state what is so well understood, that gives new life to simple language and includes the reader in its familiarity and sophistication. The last lines of "To the Rev. F. D. Maurice" achieve the same restrained warmth through the use of a slight, happy ambiguity: "Nor pay but one [visit], but come for many,/ Many and many a happy year" (ll. 47–48).

Again, while these epistolary poems are obviously expressions of a comic impulse, they are, like the Laureate poems, expressions of a very restrained, ordered comedy. The multiplicity and abandon associated with comedy are played down in order to emphasize the great control. Even the "Ode on the Death of the Duke of Wellington" works by deliberately *simplifying* our response in order to specify our emotional attitude and create a restricted unity. Many diverse emotions are raised in the poem (it opens, we recall, by focusing our grief), but they are finally brought into a closed form, cast out, or superseded by the overriding force of oneness. This can be seen as a part of a great comic tradition, and no one can say that the tradition is in any sense deficient.

But it does seem that by the nineteenth century more chaotic, multitudinous strategies were beginning to prevail. The old, coherent certainties are gone, and even Dickens, who we can sense would have had a wonderful time manipulating vices and virtues, does not stay with the simplifying strategy for long. *The Pickwick Papers* begins that way, but before long Sam and Tony Weller appear, spraying subversive comments everywhere and disallowing —in fact attacking—the crystalline rhetoric and clear unity the novel had seemed to be advocating. Though there are no Wellers in Tennyson, his solutions in the long comic poems tend toward the same deliberate denial of simplicity and unity that we find in *The Pickwick Papers*. Only in these minor poems does he reach a level of assured public statement by a highly skillful process of selection and focusing.

Beneath this level of confident and sophisticated art in Tennyson
runs a kind of subterranean stream that feeds the direct political
poems in the third category. These poems are made up of dark fears
that are to the comic impulse approximately what a jungle howl is
to a symphony. Critics often express astonishment that the same
mind could produce both "St Simeon Stylites" and "The May
Queen"; there is, surely, an equal distance between "Ode on the
Death of the Duke of Wellington" and "Riflemen Form!". I am
aware that no one would deny this; the only reason for discussing
these poems is that they represent an interesting perversion and
reduction of many of Tennyson's major themes and generic
preoccupations. Though trivial, they are revealing.

Like most modern comic poets, Tennyson almost always envi-
sioned the ideal social unit as the family, not the nation. But there
was a part of him that had national opinions, very deeply held
opinions on political issues accompanied by a deeply felt compul-
sion to express them. It is often said that Tennyson was not very
intelligent in these matters, that "he really did hold a great many of
the same views as Queen Victoria, though he was gifted with a
more fortunate literary style," [1] or that he was, in a general way,
"undoubtedly the stupidest" of English poets.[2] To read his "views"
in the *Memoir* or in his wife's and son's various recordings of his
"Sayings" is a tedious and depressing business.[3] But the quality of
his intelligence is really not the problem; rather, it is the depth of
uncontrolled, primitive feeling welling over in the poems that
makes an unsympathetic reader think, not so much of defective
intelligence as defective emotions, not a dull schoolteacher but a
drunk in a bar declaiming on the moral decline. The poems are not
unintelligent; they operate beneath the level of intelligence alto-
gether. It was this plain primitivism, no doubt, that caused John

1. G. K. Chesterton, *The Victorian Age in Literature*, p. 162.

2. W. H. Auden, Introduction to *Poems*, p. x.

3. This is not to deny the testimony of contemporaries like Thackeray, who said that
Tennyson was "the wisest man he knew" (*Memoir*, 1:419). It is likely, I think, that Thackeray
was using the word *wisdom* in a very Tennysonian (and nineteenth-century) sense, referring
not to his capacity for conceptual, analytical thought but to his more intuitive and
imaginative powers.

The best discussions of Tennyson's political views are by Joseph Solimine, "The Burkean
Idea of the State in Tennyson's Poetry," *HLQ* 30 (1967): 147–65, and by Robert Preyer,
"Alfred Tennyson," *VS* 9 (1966): 325–52. For a general defense of the political poems, see G.
Wilson Knight, "Excalibur: An Essay on Tennyson," in *Neglected Powers*, pp. 419–29.

Stuart Mill to wonder if "they are meant for bitter ridicule of vulgar nationality," "if they are to be taken seriously." [4]

The vulgarity and bitterness Mill perceived in the early volumes continue to dominate these poems until Tennyson's death. There is absolutely no development, a fact which certainly suggests that they had no connection with Tennyson's notions of his duties as Laureate; similarly, the violence of the language suggests that neither were they connected with high-minded views of social duty, apostolic or otherwise. One can hardly imagine the Apostles countenancing such things as the hysterical reference to the French in the original version of "Riflemen Form!": "Ready, be ready! the times are wild! / Bearded monkeys of lust and blood / Coming to violate woman and child!" (see p. 1779 in the Ricks edition). This is extreme even for Tennyson, but it suggests the level of simplicity, even brutality, on which much of his political poetry operates.

This poetry is dedicated to "law and order" in the peculiarly modern sense that slogan has acquired: it is reactionary, cautious, and terribly afraid. It meets the cataclysmic change of the nineteenth century with a childish, mocking jeer. The price Tennyson paid for his great poetry was this barbarous counter-strain, where he could, apparently, blow off steam and gather his resources for his important efforts. He relaxed from irony and comedy into poetry that was made as simple as possible so that the tension could be released. The political poetry is, perhaps, an artistic and emotional drainage system.

It is significant that when, as in "The Charge of the Light Brigade," Tennyson was stirred by public events to write ironically, he tried in revisions to dispose of the irony. In the 1855 version Tennyson changed the poised and tonally ambiguous ending to one that is bland and unidirectional.[5] He also dropped the famous line,

---

4. Review of *"Poems, Chiefly Lyrical* and *Poems* (1833) [1832]," *London Review* 1 (July 1835): 42.

5. The original ending was:

> When can their glory fade?
> O the wild charge they made!
>   All the world wondered.
> Honour the charge they made!
> Honour the Light Brigade,
> Noble six hundred!

It was replaced in 1855 by:

> Honour the brave and bold!
> Long shall the tale be told,

"Some one had blundered." John Ruskin wrote to him about this subversive line, urging him to restore it: "It was precisely the most tragical line in the poem," [6] he said. It is, in our sense, precisely the most ironic line. Though Tennyson later did restore it, the 1855 revision is interesting, in that it suggests not so much timidity as Tennyson's need for emotional simplification in this genre. This statement is just the sort that would have infuriated Tennyson, but the truth is he cared very little for political life or even for the conception of "England" as a political unit. He could, after all, use them in this necessary but quite offhand way, releasing his tensions onto them so he could turn his mind to genuine work. The poems are sincere, of course; they have the sincerity of emotional doodles.

There is, as I have said, no discernible development throughout them. "English Warsong" in the 1830 volume might have been published at any time. Its shrill purpose is to convince any waverers that fear of death is shameful, deserving "withering scorn" (l. 5), and that, in any case, the enemy who will force us to confront death will hardly be able to manage it: "He is weak! we are strong; he a slave, we are free" (l. 30). One would suppose that the thought of death need hardly arise if "The child in our cradles is bolder than he" (l. 27), but one is not encouraged to *suppose* anything. The poem is full of such gaps, constantly returning to slogans and the obsessive "we are free." This word *free* is the key term in all of Tennyson's national songs, popping up in chorus after emotional chorus. The comic principle of freedom is continually stated but never realized, since the motive of the poem is so obviously a fear that the vaunted freedom is or soon will be gone.

The poems strive for comedy without any optimism, and they spend an enormous amount of energy playing what might be called "Find the jailer." The perception of bondage is reduced to a search for a cause, and since there is no real cause, the political poems can only use symbolic villains that are quite inadequate. Most often the scapegoat asked to bear the weight of responsibility for the frustration is France[7]—"For the French the pope may shrive

---

       Yea, when our babes are old—
       How they rode onward.
  6. Quoted in *Memoir*, 1:411.
  7. Harold Nicolson caustically comments, "And indeed, in all Tennyson's considerations on foreign policy there is this tinge of prejudice against our Gallic neighbours" (*Tennyson*, p. 95).

'em, / For the devil a whit we heed 'em" ("National Song")—or, even better, Napoleon Buonaparte: "He thought to quell the stubborn hearts of oak, / Madman!—to chain with chains, and bind with bands / That island queen who sways the floods and lands / From Ind to Ind" ("Buonaparte," ll. 1–4).

When actual war threatened in 1852, Tennyson rose to the challenge with vigorous attacks on all complexities. The one thing, he urged, was to "Arm, arm, arm!": "Is this a time to cry for peace, / When we should shriek for rifles?" ("The Penny-Wise," ll. 34–35). "Shriek" indeed. All those who stood in the way of the arming and the rifle clubs, war plans, and, one supposes, an invasion of the Continent, were quickly dismissed: the "O babbling Peace Societies" ("The Penny-Wise," l. 32); the tradesmen and "niggard throats of Manchester" ("The Third of February, 1852," ll. 43–45), whom Tennyson more than suspected of promoting peace in order to build profits; the House of Lords for their niggling economies; and all those who foolishly urged religious, moral, or practical scruples against war.

Everything must be concentrated on the search for and the elimination of the villain: "Let your reforms for a moment go! / Look to your butts, and take good aims! / Better a rotten borough or so / Than a rotten fleet and a city in flames!" ("Riflemen Form!", ll. 15–18). In the end, the major enemies are logic, reason, and especially prudence: "For her there lie in wait millions of foes, / And yet the 'Not too much' is all the rule she knows" ("Suggested by Reading an Article in a Newspaper," ll. 59–60). Tennyson's snarling attack on British "respectability" and his inflamed defense of extremism make us aware that we are up against a kind of temporary hysterical paranoia, therapeutic to the writer, no doubt, but not conducive to great art. Poems like these are at the opposite pole from the poised reasonableness of the Laureate poems.

There is no evidence that Tennyson, for all his morbidity, was paranoid, but these poems do project a sense of betrayal on all sides. The political poems are only the crudest expression of the feeling of loss, an attempt to find a central enemy so that the ironic tension may be dissolved. Tennyson keeps returning in the later poems, not only in *Maud*, to the term "liar"—"peace-lovers we—but who can trust a liar?" ("Britons, Guard Your Own," l. 14)—and Arthur's kingdom stands and falls on its central belief in absolute honesty.

Again, this political expression seems to be a reduction of what in the *Idylls* is a sense of great cosmic trickery. The ironic apprehensions, then, are present in the political poems, which are not so much superficial politics as mistaken attempts to solve the ironic dilemma by reducing it to manageable, discreet terms.

What is remarkable, then, is not that Tennyson was attracted to simple escapes from his vision but that he was attracted to them so little. One might say that these poems are inferior only because Tennyson's ironic perception was so strong yet delicate that he could not put labels on the villains at all convincingly. In any case, a few poems on British hearts of oak are a small price to pay for *Idylls of the King.*

The Domestic Idyls

Unlike the stationary political poems, these poems do show development. Anyone who reads through the poems chronologically up to about "Edwin Morris" or "The Golden Year" (both most likely written in 1839) will, I think, notice a steady improvement. From that point on, there is a decline that is just as steady, until one reaches the level of "Happy" or "Charity" (written between 1888 and 1890), exercises so perfunctory they seem to parody themselves. I do not pretend to know why such a curious decline took place: it may be that Tennyson lost interest in the form, did not need the therapy so much, learned to produce these popular things mechanically, or was simply draining off the sentimentality from the great, tough, and unsentimental *Idylls* he was writing at the same time. All of these reasons seem possible and none is very convincing. What is more interesting is the initial improvement, the movement through 1842 toward greater compression, subtlety, and obliquity. Though Tennyson begins with a very loose joining of pastoral, ballad, and novelistic traditions, for a brief time he achieves some minor but quite definite triumphs.[8] This development also suggests that the domestic idyls are, on the whole, much more complex and

8. It is not customary for critics to do much more than sneer at those poems. Of those who attempt more, Jerome H. Buckley (*Tennyson: The Growth of a Poet*) has some sympathetic, if very brief, analyses; Philip Drew, in " 'Aylmer's Field,' " *Listener* 71 (2 April 1964): 553, 556–57, suggests an approach to the poems through a consideration of "pace and scale"; and T. J. Assad has some acute comments on the idyls that appear in the *Enoch Arden* volume: "On the Major Poems of Tennyson's 'Enoch Arden' Volume," *TSE* 14 (1965): 29–56. A general discussion of Tennyson's domestic vision is found in William E. Fredeman's " 'The Sphere of Common Duties,' " pp. 357–83.

interesting than the political poems, which in motive and function
(that is, psychological function) they perhaps resemble. The fact is
that the domestic idyls are more than simple therapy; they touch
on, and now and then join with, Tennyson's quite genuine
apprehension of comedy, an apprehension which at the time was
not being expressed in the major poems.

The earliest domestic idyls are so diffuse that diffusion seems to
be their very essence. Some are vaguely happy, some are vaguely
sad; but they seem anxious to avoid raising any emotion at all
which is sharpened or defined. They induce—or strive to induce—a
pleasant sort of murky warmth that is much the same whether the
subject is death or a picnic. They work by establishing a heightened
mood through a dramatic event, and then gradually taking the
edge off that mood by repetition, long digressions, gentle and ornate
embellishments. One can see this diffusive process very clearly at
work in the early and popular "The May Queen." The potential
harshness of the poem's reversal, from the girl's confident expecta-
tion of life in May to her equally confident expectation of death in
December, is oddly muted by the long final section entitled
"Conclusion."

The poem had seemed already to have reached a fitting and
symmetrical conclusion at the end of the second section ("New-
Year's Eve"), where the first line of the poem is echoed with an
obvious and melodramatic switch. Lively Alice is about to die. But
in the Conclusion Tennyson almost risks humor by having little
Alice still around in the spring, prosing on about angels, heaven,
and God. This part, which seems at first glance, if not ludicrous at
least superfluous, is longest of all the three sections, precisely
because it has the most important job to do: it must drain off the
effect of the melodramatic contradiction and the thought of
youthful death. The conclusion softens the poem not so much by its
talk of religious consolation, though that no doubt helps, but just by
talk—and lots of it. The main effect of poems in the ballad tradition
is exactly reversed here; in place of the heightening of shock we
have the relaxation produced by verbosity. In fact, with the
exception of unusual poems like "Dora" and "Forlorn," these early
idyls might be seen as the antithesis of the ballad. The ballad's
tendency toward elliptical statement, suggestive gaps, and verbal
irony is replaced by a tendency to explain everything several times,
by fullness and elaboration. If there is any shock at all in these idyls,

or in "The May Queen" in particular, it is only a preliminary step on the way to lassitude.

Another early poem, "The Gardener's Daughter," captures the same effect more subtly, this time by contrasting two styles: a superfluous ornateness with a deliberate use of rather flat clichés. Tennyson later added a headnote apologizing for the over-richness of the poem's language, but his apology is hardly to the point. It is not that lines like "She stood, a sight to make an old man young" (l. 140) or phrases like "She, a Rose / In roses" (ll. 141–42) are too ornate; it is that they are unparticularized. Any emotion they might evoke is completely unfocused. Words like *heart* and *love* and *rose* occur over and over, floating along without a real context, seeking to call forth the most undifferentiated response possible. The poem is, in other words, a deliberate cliché. Take, for instance, its romantic climax:

> Requiring at her hand the greatest gift,
> A woman's heart, the heart of her I loved;
> And in that time and place she answered me,
> And in the compass of three little words,
> More musical than ever came in one,
> The silver fragments of a broken voice,
> Made me most happy, faltering, "I am thine."
>
> [ll. 224–30]

This is not "ornate"; it is simply the language of the Annuals, of the love sonnets of any haberdasher. The poem rises to a climax which is the most inclusive possible, since it asks for no particular response, just a pleasant sense of recognition. At the end of the poem the speaker suddenly reveals that the Gardener's Daughter is now merely a picture, alive only in memory: "the most blessèd memory of mine age." It is pretty certain that no reader—Victorian or modern—has reacted to this last "shock" with any fundamental change of response. The fact of death is covered completely by the pleasant sentimentality of the speaker—who seems, like a mellowed or senile duke of Ferrara, rather to enjoy it all—and by the real ornateness of the closing language. Even the fragment quoted above—"the most blessèd memory of mine age"—displays the blurring machinery at work, in the vague religiosity of "blessèd" and the deeply comforting "*mine* age."

What these early poems aim at, then, is stasis and relaxation.

They work best when the theme is a cliché, when it is obscured as much as possible, or best of all, when there is no theme. Even if, as in "Lady Clara Vere de Vere," there is a certain theme—marriage for money rather than love, a theme, furthermore, which presumably obsessed Tennyson—we can see that the poem does a good deal to occlude the issue by denying its logic. Most of the poem, it is true, develops the central idea that "Kind hearts are more than coronets, / And simple faith than Norman blood" (ll. 55–56) by depicting Lady Clara's coldness and haughty viciousness circling back to destroy her. But, instead of completing this circle and this theme, the poem turns from it at the end, first by terming as "pranks" (l. 64) actions that we thought were hideous, and then, in the last stanza, by exhorting Lady Clara to reform: "Oh! teach the orphan-boy to read, / Or teach the orphan-girl to sew" (ll. 69–70). Even the elementary pleasure of seeing the proud brought low is too specific, it seems, and we find it blunted by and mixed with that curious Victorian reaction to doing-good. It is as if Sir Willoughby Patterne had suddenly been struck with the virtue of humility. Lady Clara Vere de Vere is no villainess, it turns out, just another Miller's or Gardener's Daughter or Queen of the May.

For a time, though, Tennyson allowed his ironic instincts to mix with this form and thus brought it much closer to the symbolic indirectness of the ballad. Poems like "Walking to the Mail," "Audley Court," "Edwin Morris," and "The Golden Year," written in proximity to one another, achieve a quiet and understated suggestiveness missing from the earlier idyls. These are meditative and highly finished poems, whose theme is not blunted but hidden, and whose emotional quality is not diffused but subtle and difficult to locate.

"Walking to the Mail," for instance, appears to be a kind of naturalistic experiment. Two men, whose principal interest, quite clearly, is simply getting to the Mail, pass the time walking there in idle gossip concerning a neighbor, Sir Edward Head, about whom they really do not know very much. He has run away, it seems, and they speculate about possible reasons, but with an air of indifference and with long and egoistic digressions that clearly show how vague and impersonal their interest is. He may have had trouble with his wife; he may have been driven to a kind of madness by the Reform Bill agitations and his fear for his position. It is hard to say, and it really does not matter much, not to these speakers. One of them,

James, offers a personal analogy to explain the problems connected with the Reform Bill. In a long digression he proceeds to illustrate, he says, the point that there are essentially only two parties: "those that want, and those that have" (l. 70). But what he really gives is a story that has nothing to do with genuine need or want. It is a tale of schoolboy callousness: robbing a farmer, being caught and flogged, and retaliating by stealing and hiding a sow and taking her young from her one at a time.

Behind all of this irrelevance and pointless arrogance lies the shadowy but always present figure of Sir Edward Head, who was driven by some unknown extremity to a desperate escape. The poem finally becomes a statement on the indifference, inhumanity, and egoism that divide man from man and make us, as John (the other speaker) says in summary, "mimic this raw fool the world, / Which charts us all in its coarse blacks or whites, / As ruthless as a baby with a worm" (ll. 96–98). But John neutralizes even this wisdom by dropping all concern when more immediate issues press. His excited description of the Mail shows what really attracts them: "here it comes / With five at top: as quaint a four-in-hand / As you shall see—three pyebalds and a roan." This is the first passionate utterance from either speaker; it ends the poem and quietly confirms its theme.

Even gentler is "Audley Court," where the realization of the joys of pastoral beauty is played off against the quiet certainty that this vision of Eden cannot be maintained, that it is, in fact, already gone. The poem simply shows two friends on an uneventful picnic. They move through unexceptional political and topical discussions —sometimes agreeing, sometimes not—to a pair of songs that express a level of desire beyond reason and argument. The first friend sings of a life that rejects the external demands of war, commerce, politics, and marriage for pure liberation—"let me live my life"—while the second accepts a world of calm and love. Together, the two visions form a perfect comic union. But the day ends, and the friends walk toward the peaceful bay, which is now symbolic of an ideal completion but which also signals, one is led to suppose, a return out of the comic center to the world of everyday concerns. This day, it turns out, occurred once in the past, a time more leisurely and happy both for the speaker and his friend (see ll. 75–78). The present, by implication, is something very different. Still, the irony is gentle; the day is gone but it is deeply valued. The

poem ends with a simple affirmation of the value of that moment of
happiness: "we were glad at heart."

"Edwin Morris" [9] achieves a similar balance and treats a similar
theme. The pastoral-melodramatic narrative is distanced both by a
frame, in which the narrator looks back sadly and wryly on the
past, and by a mocking, even a self-mocking tone. The theme of the
forced marriage is still there, and it is quite serious; but it is
presented with controlled, often fine humor:

> . . . "Leave," she cried,
> "O leave me!" "Never, dearest, never: here
> I brave the worst:" and while we stood like fools
> Embracing, all at once a score of pugs
> And poodles yelled within, and out they came
> Trustees and Aunts and Uncles. "What, with him!
> Go" (shrilled the cotton-spinning chorus); "him!"
> I choked. Again they shrieked the burthen—"Him!"
>
> [ll. 116–23]

Notice that the satire attacks not only the mob of galloping animals
and trustees, but the speaker as well: his language is deliberately
excessive, and the "worst" he promises to brave turns out to be very
little indeed, though it is enough to rout him. This poem returns to
the diffuse elaborateness of the earlier poems, but it still achieves
the ironic balance of "Walking to the Mail" or "Audley Court,"
this time by allowing for a much higher degree of self-consciousness
and a much greater tonal ambivalence. Even at the end, the
speaker admits that Letty has been pardoned not, as we might
sentimentally suppose, for her own sake but for the speaker's. In the
midst of a dusty and ugly life, "those fresh days" have a real
meaning and give real pleasure. These needs, then, work through
memory and purify Letty.

After a long break, Tennyson again returned to these domestic
idyls and very largely returned to his earlier manner. Poems like
"Enoch Arden" and "Aylmer's Field" are more demanding than,
but not fundamentally different from, "The Gardener's Daughter."
They seem to me, despite their length, popularity, and prominence,
to represent interruptions in Tennyson's career. But they are very

9. This poem is also defended by Christopher Ricks, "Tennyson's Methods of Composi-
tion," pp. 225–27, who shows how Tennyson parodies himself in the poet Edwin Morris.

close to being fine ironic poems. Particularly with "Aylmer's Field," is it possible to make the poem sound much more interesting and effective than it is. The ironic ingredients are there, most notably in the structure and even in many of the details, but they are unfortunately neutralized by the tendencies of the early idyls toward expansion and diffuseness. Consider the poem's form: the image of dead stagnation with which the poem begins—"the same old rut" created by "the same wheel" (ll. 33–34)—is broken up by those who can bring new life to the land, Edith and Leolin, symbols of growth and flexibility (Edith's beauty, even, is remarkable for "varying to and fro" [l. 73]).

By throwing their youth and life against this "dull sameness" (l. 115), however, they move into a trap. Those who might be saved turn on their rescuers (ll. 499–500) and finally destroy them. In true ironic fashion, then, the deaths are made meaningless; there is no redemption but only the bitter and arid recognition by the parents of what they have done in killing off their only hope for preservation. The climactic sermon serves to drive home the irony, to show that there is no hope, no lesson to be learned; only, as the text of the sermon repeats over and over, the awful image of a house made desolate. The story comes from a "grizzled cripple . . . / sunning himself in a waste field alone" (ll. 8–9), a grimly appropriate source for this tale of fruitless life and waste and desolation. This opening image of barrenness is picked up at the end: the Aylmer's house disappears, "and all is open field" (l. 853), leaving triumphant the wasteland, the droppings of hawks, field animals, "the thin weasel," and "the slow-worm" (l. 852).

I think this is a valid outline, but it distorts the actual effect of the poem, which has almost no ironic force at all, though it might have if it were cut drastically—say by four lines out of every five. As it is, melodrama keeps intruding, especially in the long, long passages on the "Indian kinsman" and Leolin's pointless jealousy of him. The Indian kinsman does, of course, introduce the knife with which Leolin later stabs himself, but this sort of thing, surely, indicates the problem Tennyson had in trying to write "domestic tragedy." Tragic incidentals must, it seems, not be softened but heightened enormously in an attempt to make tragic paraphernalia do for the lack of tragic heroism. It is *Othello* with the handkerchief, and perhaps Desdemona, but without Iago and the Moor. The specific ironies become so resoundingly obvious that they are entirely of the surface, without resonance of any sort.

In addition, there is the old idyl tendency to cancel or subdue strong emotion. Thus, we have extended descriptions of Edith's ministering to the poor or, to choose the most absurd example, thirteen lines devoted to Leolin's program for maintaining physical fitness while studying for the law. Even the sermon takes care to minimize the general ironic pattern by reducing it to an exemplum of "pride," which pretties up the theme and minimizes it by offering in its place very easy cliché alternatives. One cannot entirely ignore the power of the submerged ironic pattern or of fine details like the picture of the tyrant Sir Aylmer Aylmer finally seeing death as an "escape" from "his keepers" (ll. 838–39). But the old idyl is just as clearly reasserting its murky self.

"Enoch Arden" [10] is especially infected. A poem that moves toward several ironies becomes, in the end, a popular piece of sensationalism, with detachable set-pieces. It comes very close to being an attack on middle-class values[11] but ends by reinforcing them. The poem is deeply disappointing and perhaps needs to be attacked, but the most famous attack it has received, that by Walter Bagehot, seems to me to put us off the track. Bagehot's objections to the language of the poem are based on very naïve assumptions about verisimilitude and "realism": Tennyson, he says, "tells us a great deal about the torrid zone, which a rough sailor like Enoch Arden certainly would not have perceived." [12] All this seems mere unsophisticated snobbery, though Bagehot does perhaps hint, in his assault on the poem's ornate style, at what is indeed central: the ability of the poem to deny its ironies and make difficult things easy. This is not, as Bagehot suggests, a matter of diction or description; it is a matter of rhetoric: "Enoch Arden" uses all of the idyl's protective and covering devices.

Extension and elaboration are everywhere; heightened "tragic

10. There are good treatments of this poem by Martin Dodsworth, "Patterns of Morbidity: Repetition in Tennyson's Poetry," in *The Major Victorian Poets*, pp. 7–34, and by P. G. Scott, *Tennyson's Enoch Arden*.

11. Assad ("Tennyson's 'Enoch Arden' Volume," pp. 44–53) nearly says that it *is*. He discusses its assault on materialism, even Enoch's materialism. I wish he were right, but I think he is responding to a single ironic strand of the poem and overlooking the neutralizers of this irony.

12. "Wordsworth, Tennyson, and Browning; or Pure, Ornate, and Grotesque Art in English Poetry," in *Literary Studies*, 2:352.

ironies" that go nowhere and act to dilute the genuine ironic
structure (the business with the seaman's glass and the misunder-
stood biblical prophecy are the most prominent) are made much of;
secondary themes—particularly those involving popular religiosity
—are introduced to counter major ones. And then there is Philip
Ray, a character whose victory ought certainly to be a subject for
irony, as he has nothing but the opposite of heroic qualities:
extreme reticence, prudence, weakness, and the kind of morbid
tenacity one associates with creeping plants. But he is, I suppose,
made a hero.

Against all this, still, is the strong ironic frame, the attack on the
materialistic and prudential values of the middle class. According
to this reading, the potentially heroic Enoch falls victim to the
bourgeois cliché, restraining his wildness and working carefully "To
save all earnings to the uttermost, / And give his child a better
bringing-up / Than his had been" (ll. 86–88). The poem is filled
with comfortable talk of riches, shops, security, and the like—all of
which comes to nothing. Even darker is the hint that perhaps
Annie's child died because "her business often called her from it" (l.
263). Enoch, the faithful materialist, reaches a kind of materialist's
hell, an Eden where nothing is missing but people.

Trapped in this "eternal summer" with the useless riches he went
to find, Enoch is the image of the archetypal ironic victim. He is
finally rescued, presumably, from this bondage and becomes "the
dead man come to life" (l. 754). But it is a mock resurrection only;
he moves into a more horrible trap at home, where he is more "lost"
(l. 712) than he had been on the island. The final two lines—"And
when they buried him the little port / Had seldom seen a costlier
funeral"—then, could be seen as a bitter and fitting completion of
the pattern: the victory of slimy Philip Ray, whose money pays the
undertakers, and the defeat of Enoch by the very money he sought.

Everyone recognizes, though, that this is a wild misreading.
Philip is kind to children and loves to go nutting. Enoch is not
really the archetypal ironic victim; he is not, it seems, even alone on
that deserted island: he has "Spoken with That, which being
everywhere / Lets none, who speaks with Him, seem all alone" (ll.
615–16). These are among the clumsiest lines in Tennyson, but they
do the job of tearing down the irony. Even when Enoch returns and
the trap closes at home, "He was not all unhappy. His resolve / Up-
bore him, and firm faith, and evermore / Prayer from a living

source within the will, / . . . Kept him a living soul" (ll. 795–97, 800). One could argue that the popularity of the poem is (or was) a direct result of Tennyson's incredible skill in raising specters and then wiping them out, in turning the shock of irony into the mild and comfortable sensationalism of "domestic tragedy."

In the later idyls, irony is less often present, so no denials are necessary. We are back to the straight presentation of the domestic, with one difference: Tennyson seems to be, perhaps with an unconscious humor, pushing the genre to its limits. The search for everyday events to make into tragedy becomes the search either for the bizarre, which naturally means the trivial, or else for the trivial, which it is necessary to heighten by the bizarre. What all these poems present is a kind of Ripley's "Believe It Or Not" irrelevance. Tennyson certainly understood the passage in Aristotle concerning the difference between fact and probability,[13] but he desperately ignores it here, appending endless headnotes to assure us that poems like "In the Children's Hospital" (subtitled "Emmie") are "true," or were at least told to him by some highly reliable person who said they were true.

The picture of the Laureate riffling through newspapers for ghastly and embarrassing oddities is not edifying, but it may be accurate. There are not so many of these late idyls, of course, only seven or eight, but some of them must have made even Mrs. Tennyson gasp. "In the Children's Hospital" can be written off as typical Victorian sentimentality, but there is nothing at all typical about a poem like "Charity" (founded on a true story, he tells us) or, especially, "Happy: The Leper's Bride," further than which one cannot go. In fact, it may be that the poem crosses the line, arguing a bit like Mark Twain's sardonic atheists, that "Now God has made you leper in His loving care for both, / That we might cling together, never doubt each other more" (ll. 91–92), and achieving a morbid parody of sexual passion: "A little nearer? Yes. I shall hardly be content / Till I be leper like yourself, my love, from head to heel" (ll. 87–88).

13. In fact, he marked the "analysis" of the relevant passage (chap. 9) in a copy of the *Poetics* he owned and which is now in the Tennyson Research Centre at Lincoln: *Aristotle's Treatise on Rhetoric, also The Poetics of Aristotle*, trans. Theodore Buckley (London: Bell and Daldy, 1872). The passage was rendered: "But it is evident from what has been said, that it is not the province of a poet to relate things which have happened, but such as might have happened, and such things as are possible according to probability, or which would necessarily have happened."

These two categories—the public and political verse and the domestic idyls—do not comprise all of Tennyson's minor poems, but they contain a great many and, more important, they demonstrate by their clarity and enforced simplicity some of the qualities that imbue the major poems, where these alternate impulses are joined. There is a third group of poems, which might be called Tennyson's satiric or funny works; but poems like "The Goose," "To Christopher North," or "O Darling Room" detain no critics nor, I gather, readers. There are, however, the dialect poems, which some admire very much. Sir Charles Tennyson, for instance, a very moderate and careful commentator on his grandfather's poems, presents an able defense of them and calls a poem like "The Grandmother" a triumph.[14] All the same, with the exception of "The Northern Farmer" and "The Village Wife," poems that are not so much comic as ironic anyhow, these dialect poems seem to me quite minor expressions of Tennyson's comic art.

14. *Alfred Tennyson*, p. 351. A very articulate and interesting treatment of these dialect poems is found in Charles Wilson's "Mirror of a Shire," *Durham University Journal*, n.s. 21 (1959): 22–28.

Bibliography

Although extensive, the following bibliography is meant to be suggestive, certainly not complete. It indicates some of the criticism and scholarship that has been most useful to me in this study.

Adey, Lionel. "Tennyson's Sorrow and Her Lying Lip." *Victorian Poetry* 8 (1970): 261–63.

Adicks, Richard. "The Lily Maid and the Scarlet Sleeve: White and Red in Tennyson's *Idylls*." *The University Review* 34 (1967): 65–71.

Adler, Joshua. "The Dilemma in Tennyson's 'The Hesperides.'" *Studies in English Language and Literature*. Ed. Alice Shalvi and A. A. Mendilow. Jerusalem: The Hebrew University, 1966, pp. 190–208.

Adler, Thomas P. "The Uses of Knowledge in Tennyson's 'Merlin and Vivien.'" *Texas Studies in Literature and Language* 11 (1970): 1397–1403.

Alaya, Flavia M. "Tennyson's 'The Lady of Shalott': The Triumph of Art." *Victorian Poetry* 8 (1970): 273–89.

Antippas, Andy P. "Tennyson, Hallam, and *The Palace of Art*." *Victorian Poetry* 5 (1967): 294–96.

———. "Tennyson's Sinful Soul: Poetic Tradition and 'Keats Turned Imbecile.'" *Tulane Studies in English* 17 (1969): 113–34.

Armstrong, Isobel, ed. *The Major Victorian Poets: Reconsiderations*. Lincoln, Neb.: University of Neb. Press, 1969.

Assad, Thomas J. "On the Major Poems of Tennyson's 'Enoch Arden' Volume." *Tulane Studies in English* 14 (1965): 29–56.

———. "Tennyson's 'Break, Break, Break.'" *Tulane Studies in English* 12 (1963): 71–80.

———. "Tennyson's 'Courage, Poor Heart of Stone.'" *Tulane Studies in English* 18 (1970): 73–80.

———. "Tennyson's 'Tears, Idle Tears.'" *Tulane Studies in English* 13 (1963): 71–83.

———. "Tennyson's Use of the Tripartite View of Man in Three Songs from *The Princess*." *Tulane Studies in English* 15 (1967): 31–58.

———. "The Touch of Genius in Tennyson's Earliest Lyrics." *Tulane Studies in English* 16 (1968): 29–47.

Auden, W. H., ed. *A Selection from the Poems of Alfred, Lord Tennyson*. Garden City, N. Y.: Doubleday, 1944.

August, Eugene R. "Tennyson and Teilhard: The Faith of *In Memoriam*." *PMLA* 84 (1969): 217–26.

[Bagehot, Walter.] "Tennyson's Idylls." *National Review* 9 (October 1859): 368–94.

———. "Wordsworth, Tennyson, and Browning; or, Pure, Ornate, and Grotesque Art in English Poetry." In *Literary Studies* (London: Longmans, 1898), 2: 326–81.

Bakaya, K. N. "Tennyson's Use of the Dramatic Monologue." *Essays Presented to Amy G. Stack*, edited by R. K. Kaul, pp. 95–110. Jaipur: Rajasthan University Press, 1965.

Baker, Arthur E. *A Concordance to the Poetical and Dramatic Works of Alfred, Lord Tennyson.* New York: Macmillan, 1914.

Ball, Patricia M. *The Central Self: A Study in Romantic and Victorian Imagination.* London: Athlone Press, 1968.

———. "Tennyson and the Romantics." *Victorian Poetry* 1 (1963): 7–16.

Basler, Roy P. *Sex, Symbolism, and Psychology in Literature*, pp. 73–93. New Brunswick: Rutgers University Press, 1948 [on *Maud*].

———. "Tennyson the Psychologist." *South Atlantic Quarterly* 43 (1944): 143–59.

Battaglia, Francis Joseph. "The Use of Contradiction in *In Memoriam*." *English Language Notes* 4 (1966): 41–46.

Baum, Paull F. *Tennyson Sixty Years After.* Chapel Hill: University of North Carolina Press, 1948.

Benziger, James. "Tennyson." *Images of Eternity: Studies in the Poetry of Religious Vision from Wordsworth to T. S. Eliot*, pp. 138–63. Carbondale: Southern Illinois University Press, 1969.

Bergonzi, Bernard. "Feminism and Femininity in *The Princess*." In *The Major Victorian Poets: Reconsiderations*, edited by Isobel Armstrong, pp. 35–50. Lincoln, Neb.: University of Nebraska Press, 1969.

Berry, Francis. "The Voice of Tennyson." *Poetry and the Physical Voice*, pp. 47–65. London: Routledge and Kegan Paul, 1962.

Bishop, Jonathan. "The Unity of *In Memoriam*." *Victorian Newsletter*, no. 21 (1962), pp. 9–14.

Bloom, Harold. "Tennyson, Hallam, and Romantic Tradition." *The Ringers in the Tower: Studies in the Romantic Tradition*, pp. 145–54. Chicago: University of Chicago Press, 1971.

Boas, F. S. "*The Idylls of the King* in 1921." *Nineteenth Century* 90 (1921): 819–30.

Bose, Amalendu. *Chroniclers of Life*, pp. 189–94; 227–68. Bombay: Orient Longmans, 1962 [on *In Memoriam*].

Boyd, John D. "*In Memoriam* and the 'Logic of Feeling.'" *Victorian Poetry* 10 (1972): 95–110.

Bradley, A. C. "*A Commentary on Tennyson's In Memoriam*." 3d ed. London: Macmillan, 1910.

———. *The Reaction Against Tennyson.* The English Association Pamphlet no. 39. London: Oxford, 1917.

Brashear, William R. *The Living Will: A Study of Tennyson and Nineteenth-Century Subjectivism.* Studies in English Literature, vol. 52. The Hague: Mouton, 1969.

———. "Tennyson's Third Voice: A Note." *Victorian Poetry* 2 (1964): 283–86.

———. "Tennyson's Tragic Vitalism: *Idylls of the King.*" *Victorian Poetry* 6 (1968): 29–49.

Brooks, Cleanth. *The Well-Wrought Urn: Studies in the Structure of Poetry.* New York: Reynal and Hitchcock, 1947.

Buckley, Jerome H. *Tennyson: The Growth of a Poet.* Cambridge, Mass.: Harvard University Press, 1960.

———. "Tennyson's Irony." *Victorian Newsletter,* no. 31 (1967), pp. 7–10.

Bufkin, E. C. "Imagery in 'Locksley Hall.'" *Victorian Poetry* 2 (1964): 21–28.

Burchell, Samuel C. "Tennyson's 'Allegory in the Distance.'" *PMLA* 68 (1953): 418–24.

———. "Tennyson's Dark Night." *South Atlantic Quarterly* 54 (1955): 75–81.

Bush, Douglas. "Tennyson." *Mythology and the Romantic Tradition in English Poetry,* pp. 197–228. Cambridge, Mass.: Harvard University Press, 1937.

Byatt, A. S. "The Lyric Structure of Tennyson's *Maud.*" In *The Major Victorian Poets: Reconsiderations,* edited by Isobel Armstrong, pp. 69–92. Lincoln, Neb.: University of Nebraska Press, 1969.

Cadbury, William. "Tennyson's 'The Palace of Art' and the Rhetoric of Structures." *Criticism* 7 (1965): 23–44.

———. "The Utility of the Poetic Mask in Tennyson's 'Supposed Confessions.'" *Modern Language Quarterly* 24 (1963): 374–85.

Cannon, Garland. "'The Lady of Shalott' and 'The Arabian Nights' Tales." *Victorian Poetry* 8 (1970): 344–46.

Carr, Arthur J. "Tennyson as a Modern Poet." *University of Toronto Quarterly* 19 (1950): 361–82.

Chandler, Alice. "Tennyson's *Maud* and the Song of Songs." *Victorian Poetry* 7 (1969): 91–104.

Chesterton, G. K. *The Victorian Age in Literature.* London: Williams and Norgate, n.d. [1913].

Chiasson, E. J. "Tennyson's 'Ulysses'—A Reinterpretation." *University of Toronto Quarterly* 23 (1954): 402–09.

Collins, Joseph J. "Tennyson and the Spasmodics." *Victorian Newsletter* no. 43 (1973), pp. 24–28.

Collins, Winston. "Tennyson and Hopkins." *University of Toronto Quarterly* 38 (1968): 84–95.

Crawford, John W. "A Unifying Element in Tennyson's *Maud.*" *Victorian Poetry* 7 (1969): 64–66.

[Croker, John Wilson] Review of *Poems* (1833). *Quarterly Review* 49 (April 1833): 81–96.

Dahl, Curtis. "A Double Frame for Tennyson's Demeter?" *Victorian Studies* 1 (1958): 356–62.

———. "The Victorian Wasteland." *College English* 16 (1955): 341–47.

Daiches, David. "Imagery and Mood in Tennyson and Whitman." In *English Studies Today*, edited by G. A. Bonnard, pp. 217–32. Berne: Francke Verlag Bern, 1961.

Danzig, Allan. "The Contraries: A Central Concept in Tennyson's Poetry." *PMLA* 77 (1962): 577–85.

———. "Tennyson's *The Princess*: A Definition of Love." *Victorian Poetry* 4 (1966): 83–89.

D'Avanzo, Mario L. "Lyric 95 of *In Memoriam*: Poetry and Vision." *Research Studies* (Washington State University) 37 (1969): 149–54.

Devlin, Francis P. "Dramatic Irony in the Early Sections of Tennyson's *In Memoriam*." *Papers on Language and Literature* 8 (1972): 172–83.

Dodsworth, Martin. "Patterns of Morbidity: Repetition in Tennyson's Poetry." In *The Major Victorian Poets: Reconsiderations*, edited by Isobel Armstrong, pp. 7–34. Lincoln, Neb.: University of Nebraska Press, 1969.

Donahue, Mary Joan. "Tennyson's *Hail, Briton!* and *Tithon* in the Heath Manuscript." *PMLA* 64 (1949): 385–416.

Dowden, Edward. "Mr. Tennyson and Mr. Browning." *Studies in Literature 1789–1877*, pp. 191–239. London: Kegan Paul, 1878.

Drew, Philip. " 'Aylmer's Field': A Problem for Critics." *Listener* 71 (2 April 1964): 553, 556–57.

Duncan, Edgar Hill. "Tennyson's *Ulysses* and Translations of Dante's *Inferno*: Some Conjectures." In *Essays in Memory of Christine Burleson in Language and Literature by Former Colleagues and Students*, edited by Thomas G. Burton, pp. 13–26. Johnson City, Tenn.: East Tennessee State University, 1969.

Eggers, J. Philip. *King Arthur's Laureate: A Study of Tennyson's Idylls of the King.* New York: New York University Press, 1971.

———. "The Weeding of the Garden: Tennyson's Geraint Idylls and the *Mabinogion*." *Victorian Poetry* 4 (1966): 45–51.

Eliot, T. S. "In Memoriam." *Essays Ancient and Modern*, pp. 186–203. New York: Harcourt, Brace, 1936.

Elliot, Philip L. "Imagery and Unity in the *Idylls of the King*." *Furman Studies* 15, no. 4 (1968): 22–28.

Ellmann, Mary Joan. "Tennyson: Revision of 'In Memoriam,' Section 85." *Modern Language Notes* 65 (1950): 22–30.

Engbretsen, Nancy M. "The Thematic Evolution of *The Idylls of the King*." *Victorian Newsletter*, no. 26 (1964), pp. 1–5.

Engelberg, Edward. "The Beast Image in Tennyson's *Idylls of the King*." *ELH* 22 (1955): 287–92.

Estrich, Robert M., and Sperber, Hans. "Personal Style and Period Style:

A Victorian Poet." *Three Keys to Language.* New York: Rinehart, 1952.

Ferguson, John. "Catullus and Tennyson." *English Studies in Africa* 12 (1969): 41–58.

Findlay, Leonard M. "Swinburne and Tennyson." *Victorian Poetry* 9 (1971), 217–36.

Fleissner, Robert F. "Tennyson's Hesperidean Xanadu: The Anagogical Thread." *Research Studies* 39 (1971): 40–46.

Foakes, Reginald Anthony. "The Rhetoric of Faith: Tennyson's *In Memoriam* and Browning's *Men and Women.*" *The Romantic Assertion: A Study in the Language of Nineteenth Century Poetry*, pp. 111–37. New Haven: Yale University Press, 1958.

Fredeman, William E. " 'A Sign Betwixt the Meadow and the Cloud': The Ironic Apotheosis of Tennyson's *St. Simeon Stylites.*" *University of Toronto Quarterly* 38 (1968): 69–83.

———. " 'The Sphere of Common Duties': The Domestic Solution in Tennyson's Poetry." *Bulletin of the John Rylands Library* 55 (1972): 356–83.

Freeman, James A. "Tennyson, 'Lucretius' and the 'Breasts of Helen.' " *Victorian Poetry* 11 (1973): 69–75.

Frye, Northrop. *Anatomy of Criticism: Four Essays.* Princeton: Princeton University Press, 1957.

Fulweiler, Howard. "Mermen and Mermaids: A Note on an 'Alien Vision' in the Poetry of Tennyson, Arnold, and Hopkins." *Victorian Newsletter,* no. 23 (1963), pp. 16–17.

———. "Tennyson and the 'Summons from the Sea.' " *Victorian Poetry* 3 (1965): 25–44.

Gibson, Walker. "Behind the Veil: A Distinction Between Poetic and Scientific Language in Tennyson, Lyell, and Darwin." *Victorian Studies* 2 (1958): 60–68.

Gladstone, W. E. "Tennyson's Poems." *Quarterly Review* 106 (1859): 454–85.

Golffing, Francis. "Tennyson's Last Phase: The Poet as Seer." *Southern Review,* n.s. 2 (1966): 264–85.

Gossman, Ann, and Whiting, George W. "King Arthur's Farewell to Guinevere." *Notes and Queries,* n.s. 6 (1959): 446–48.

Gransden, K. W. *Tennyson: In Memoriam.* Studies in English Literature, no. 22. London: Edward Arnold, 1964.

Grant, Stephen Allen. "The Mystical Implications of *In Memoriam.*" *Studies in English Literature* 2 (1962): 481–95.

Gray, Donald J. "Arthur, Roland, Empedocles, Sigurd, and the Despair of Heroes in Victorian Poetry." *Boston University Studies in English* 5 (1961): 1–17.

Gray, Jon M. "The Creation of Excalibur: An Apparent Inconsistency in the *Idylls.*" *Victorian Poetry* 6 (1968): 68–69.

————. "Fact, Form, and Fiction in Tennyson's *Balin and Balan*." *Renaissance and Modern Studies* 12 (1968): 91–107.

————. "Knightly Combats in Malory's Tale of Sir Gareth and Tennyson's 'Gareth and Lynette.' " *Notes and Queries* 16 (1969): 207–08.

————. " 'The Lady of Shalott' and Tennyson's Readings in the Supernatural." *Notes and Queries* 12 (1965): 298–300.

————. *Man and Myth in Victorian England: Tennyson's The Coming of Arthur*. Tennyson Society Monograph no. 1. Lincoln: Tennyson Research Centre, 1969.

————. *Organicism in the Evolution of Tennyson's "Idylls."* Lincoln: Keyworth and Fry, 1973.

————. "The Purpose of an Epic List in 'The Coming of Arthur.' " *Victorian Poetry* 8 (1970): 339–41.

————. *Serial and Cyclical Characterisation in Tennyson's "Idylls."* Lincoln: Keyworth and Fry, 1973.

————. "Source and Symbol in 'Geraint and Enid': Tennyson's Doorm and Limours." *Victorian Poetry* 4 (1966): 131–32.

————. "A Study in Idyl: Tennyson's *The Coming of Arthur*." *Renaissance and Modern Studies* 14 (1970): 111–50.

————. "Tennyson and Geoffrey of Monmouth." *Notes and Queries*, n.s. 14 (1967): 52–53.

————. "Tennyson and Layamon." *Notes and Queries*, n.s. 15 (1968): 176–78.

————. "Tennyson and Nennius." *Notes and Queries*, n.s. 13 (1966): 341–42.

————. *Tennyson's Doppelgänger: Balin and Balan*. Tennyson Society Monograph no. 3. Lincoln: Tennyson Research Centre, 1971.

Green, Joyce. "Tennyson's Development during the 'Ten Years' Silence' (1832–1842)." *PMLA* 66 (1951): 662–97.

Gridley, Roy. "Confusion of the Seasons in Tennyson's 'The Last Tournament.' " *Victorian Newsletter*, no. 22 (1962), pp. 14–16.

Grob, Alan. "Tennyson's 'The Lotos-Eaters': Two Versions of Art." *Modern Philology* 62 (1964): 118–29.

Gunter, G. O. "Life and Death Symbols in Tennyson's 'Mariana.' " *South Atlantic Bulletin* 36 (1971): 64–67.

Gwynn, Frederick L. "Tennyson's 'Tithon,' 'Tears, Idle Tears,' and 'Tithonus.' " *PMLA* 67 (1952): 572–75.

Haight, Gordon S. "Tennyson's Merlin." *Studies in Philology* 44 (1947): 549–66.

Harrison, James. "Tennyson and Evolution." *Durham University Journal* 64 (1971): 26–31.

Harrison, Thomas P., Jr. "Tennyson's *Maud* and Shakespeare." *Shakespeare Association Bulletin* 17 (1942): 80–85.

Healy, Sister Emma Therese. "Virgil and Tennyson." *Kentucky Foreign Language Quarterly* 2 (1955): 20–25.

Hellstrom, Ward. *On the Poems of Tennyson.* Gainesville: University of Florida Press, 1972.

Hill, James L. "Tennyson's 'The Lady of Shalott': The Ambiguity of Commitment." *Centennial Review* 12 (1968): 415–29.

Hirsch, Gordon D. "Tennyson's *Commedia.*" *Victorian Poetry* 8 (1970): 93–106.

Hoge, James O. "Emily Tennyson's Narrative for Her Sons." *Texas Studies in Literature and Language* 14 (1972): 93–106.

Hornback, Bert G. "Tennyson's 'Break, Break, Break' Again." *Victorian Newsletter*, no. 33 (1968), pp. 47–48.

Hough, Graham. "Tears, Idle Tears." *Hopkins Review* 4, no. 3 (1951): 31–36.

House, Humphry. *All in Due Time*, pp. 122–39. London: Rupert Hart-Davis, 1955.

Hóvy, Richard B. "Tennyson's 'Locksley Hall': A Re-Interpretation." *Forum* (Houston) 4, no. 1 (1963): 24–30.

Howell, A. C. "Tennyson's 'Palace of Art'—An Interpretation." *Studies in Philology* 33 (1936): 507–22.

Hume, Robert D., and Olshin, Toby A. "Ambrosius in 'The Holy Grail': Source and Function." *Notes and Queries*, n.s. 16 (1969): 208–09.

Hunt, John Dixon. "The Symbolist Vision of *In Memoriam.*" *Victorian Poetry* 8 (1970): 187–98.

Hutton, R. H. "Tennyson." *Macmillan's* 27 (1872): 143–67.

James, D. G. "Wordsworth and Tennyson." Warton Lecture on English Poetry. *Proceedings of the British Academy* 36 (1950): 113–29.

Johnson, E. D. H. *The Alien Vision of Victorian Poetry: Sources of the Poetic Imagination in Tennyson, Browning, and Arnold.* Princeton Studies in English, no. 34. Princeton: Princeton University Press, 1952.

———. "*In Memoriam*: The Way of a Poet." *Victorian Studies* 2 (1958): 139–48.

———. "The Lily and the Rose: Symbolic Meaning in Tennyson's *Maud.*" *PMLA* 64 (1949): 1222–27.

Jones, Richard. *The Growth of "The Idylls of the King."* Philadelphia: J. B. Lippincott, 1895.

Joseph, Gerhard. "The Idea of Mortality in Tennyson's Classical and Arthurian Poems: 'Honor Comes with Mystery.'" *Modern Philology* 66 (1968): 136–45.

———. *Tennysonian Love: The Strange Diagonal.* Minneapolis: University of Minnesota Press, 1969.

———. "Tennyson's Concepts of Knowledge, Wisdom, and Pallas Athene." *Modern Philology* 69 (1972): 314–22.

———. "Tennyson's Death in Life in Lyric and Myth: 'Tears, Idle Tears' and 'Demeter and Persephone.'" *Victorian Newsletter*, no. 34 (1968), pp. 13–18.

Jump, John D., ed. *Tennyson: The Critical Heritage*. London: Routledge and
  Kegan Paul, 1967.
Kaplan, Fred. "Woven Paces and Waving Hands: Tennyson's Merlin as
  Fallen Artist." *Victorian Poetry* 7 (1969): 285–98.
Kay, Donald. " 'The Holy Grail' and Tennyson's Quest for Poetic
  Identity." *Arlington Quarterly* 2, no. 1 (1969): 58–70.
Kendall, J. L. "A Neglected Theme in Tennyson's *In Memoriam*." *Modern
  Language Notes* 76 (1961): 414–20.
Kermode, Frank. *The Romantic Image*. London: Routledge and Kegan
  Paul, 1957.
Killham, John, ed. *Critical Essays on the Poetry of Tennyson*. London:
  Routledge and Kegan Paul, 1960.
————. *Tennyson and "The Princess": Reflections of an Age*. London: Athlone
  Press, 1958.
————. "Tennyson and the Sinful Queen—A Corrected Impression."
  Notes and Queries, n.s. 5 (1958): 507–11.
————. "Tennyson's *Maud*—The Function of the Imagery." *Critical Essays
  on the Poetry of Tennyson*, edited by John Killham, pp. 219–35. London:
  Routledge and Kegan Paul, 1960.
Kincaid, James R. "Tennyson's 'Crossing the Bar': A Poem of Frustra-
  tion." *Victorian Poetry* 3 (1965): 57–61.
————. "Tennyson's Mariners and Spenser's Despair: The Argument of
  'The Lotos-Eaters.' " *Papers on Language and Literature* 5 (1969): 273–81.
Kingsley, Charles. "Tennyson." *Fraser's Magazine* 42 (September 1850):
  245–55.
Kissane, James. *Alfred Tennyson*. New York: Twayne, 1970.
————. "Tennyson: The Passion of the Past and the Curse of Time." *ELH*
  32 (1965): 85–109.
————. "Victorian Mythology." *Victorian Studies* 6 (1962): 5–28.
Knight, G. Wilson. "Excalibur: An Essay on Tennyson." *Neglected Powers:
  Essays on Nineteenth and Twentieth Century Literature*, pp. 419–29. New York:
  Barnes and Noble, 1971.
Korg, Jacob. "The Pattern of Fatality in Tennyson's Poetry." *Victorian
  Newsletter*, no. 14 (1958), pp. 8–11.
Kozicki, Henry. "Tennyson's *Idylls of the King* as Tragic Drama." *Victorian
  Poetry* 4 (1966): 15–20.
————. "Wave and Fire Imagery in Tennyson's *Idylls*." *Victorian Newsletter*,
  no. 43 (1973), pp. 21–23.
Kramer, Dale. "Metaphor and Meaning in 'Crossing the Bar.' " *Ball State
  University Forum* 10, no. 3 (1969): 44–47.
Langbaum, Robert. "The Dynamic Unity of *In Memoriam*." *The Modern
  Spirit: Essays on the Continuity of Nineteenth- and Twentieth-Century Literature*,
  pp. 51–75. New York: Oxford University Press, 1970.

————. *The Poetry of Experience: The Dramatic Monologue in Modern Literary Tradition.* New York: Random House, 1957.

Lawry, J. S. "Tennyson's 'The Epic': A Gesture of Recovered Faith." *Modern Language Notes* 74 (1959): 400–03.

Leggett, B. J. "Dante, Byron, and Tennyson's Ulysses." *Tennessee Studies in Literature* 15 (1970): 143–59.

Legris, Maurice. "Structure and Allegory in Tennyson's *Idylls of the King.*" *Humanities Association Bulletin* 16 (1965): 37–44.

LeMire, Eugene D. "Tennyson's Weeper in Context." *University of Windsor Review* 1 (1966): 196–205.

Lewin, Lois S. "The Blameless King? The Conceptual Flaw in Tennyson's Arthur." *Ball State University Forum* 10, no. 3 (1969): 32–41.

Litzinger, Boyd. "The Structure of Tennyson's 'The Last Tournament.' " *Victorian Poetry* 1 (1963): 53–60.

Lucas, F. L. *Tennyson.* Writers and Their Work, no. 83. London: Longmans, Green, 1957.

McKean, G. R. "Faith in Locksley Hall." *Dalhousie Review* 19 (1940): 472–78.

McLuhan, H. M. "Tennyson and Picturesque Poetry." *Essays in Criticism* 1 (1951): 262–82.

————. "Tennyson and the Romantic Epic." In *Critical Essays on the Poetry of Tennyson*, edited by John Killham, pp. 86–95. London: Routledge and Kegan Paul, 1960.

MacLaren, Malcolm. "Tennyson's Epicurean Lotos-Eaters." *Classical Journal* 56 (1961): 259–67.

Mann, Robert James. *Tennyson's "Maud" Vindicated: An Explanatory Essay.* London: Jarrold, n.d. [1856].

Marshall, George O., Jr. *A Tennyson Handbook.* New York: Twayne, 1963.

————. "Tennyson's 'Oh! That 'Twere Possible': A Link Between *In Memoriam* and *Maud.*" *PMLA* 78 (1963): 225–29.

————. "Tennyson's 'The Poet': Mis-seeing Shelley Plain." *Philological Quarterly* 40 (1961): 156–57.

Mason, Michael Y. "*In Memoriam*: The Dramatization of Sorrow." *Victorian Poetry* 10 (1972): 161–77.

Mattes, Eleanor B. "*In Memoriam*": *The Way of a Soul: A Study of Some Influences that Shaped Tennyson's Poem.* New York: Exposition Press, 1951.

Mayhead, Robin. "The Poetry of Tennyson." In *From Dickens to Hardy*, edited by Boris Ford, pp. 227–44. Baltimore: Penguin, 1958.

Mays, J. C. C. "*In Memoriam*: An Aspect of Form." *University of Toronto Quarterly* 35 (1965): 22–46.

Meinhold, George D. "The Idylls of the King and the Mabinogion." *Tennyson Society Research Bulletin* 1, no. 3 (1969): 61–63.

Mendilow, A. A. "Tennyson's Palace of the Sinful Muse." In *Studies in*

English Language and Literature, edited by Alice Shalvi and A. A. Mendilow, pp. 155–89. Jerusalem: The Hebrew University, 1966.

Metzger, Lore. "The Eternal Process: Some Parallels Between Goethe's *Faust* and Tennyson's *In Memoriam*." *Victorian Poetry* 1 (1963): 189–96.

Mill, John Stuart. Review of *Poems, Chiefly Lyrical. Westminster Review* 14 (January 1831): 210–24.

———. Review of *Poems, Chiefly Lyrical* and *Poems* (1833). *London Review* 1 (July, 1835): 402–24.

Miller, Betty. "Tennyson and the Sinful Queen." *Twentieth Century* 158 (1955): 355–63.

Millhauser, Milton. *Fire and Ice: The Influence of Science on Tennyson's Poetry.* Tennyson Society Monograph no. 4. Lincoln: Tennyson Research Centre, 1971.

———. "A Plurality of After-worlds: Isaac Taylor and Alfred Tennyson's Conception of Immortality." *Hartford Studies in Literature* 1 (1969): 37–49.

———. "Structure and Symbol in 'Crossing the Bar.' " *Victorian Poetry* 4 (1966): 34–39.

———. "Tennyson: Artifice and Image." *Journal of Aesthetics and Art Criticism* 14 (1956): 333–38.

———. "Tennyson, *Vestiges*, and the Dark Side of Science." *Victorian Newsletter*, no. 35 (1969), pp. 22–25.

———. "Tennyson's *Princess* and *Vestiges*." *PMLA* 69 (1954): 337–43.

Mitchell, Charles. "The Undying Will of Tennyson's Ulysses." *Victorian Poetry* 2 (1964): 87–95.

Miyoshi, Masao. *The Divided Self: A Perspective on the Literature of the Victorians.* New York: New York University Press, 1969.

———. "Narrative Structure and the Moral System: Three Tristram Poems." *Victorian Newsletter*, no. 35 (1969), pp. 5–10.

Moore, Carlisle. "Faith, Doubt, and Mystical Experience in *In Memoriam*." *Victorian Studies* 7 (1963): 155–69.

Muecke, Douglas C. *The Compass of Irony.* London: Methuen, 1969.

Nelson, James G. "Milton and Tennyson." *The Sublime Puritan: Milton and the Victorians*, pp. 106–25. Madison: University of Wisconsin Press, 1963.

Nicolson, Harold. *Tennyson: Aspects of His Life, Character, and Poetry.* London: Constable, 1923.

Noland, Richard W. "Tennyson and Hegel on War." *Victorian Newsletter*, no. 31 (1967), pp. 39–40.

Ostriker, Alicia. "The Three Modes in Tennyson's Prosody." *PMLA* 82 (1967): 273–84.

Packer, Lona Mosk. "Sun and Shadow: The Nature of Experience in Tennyson's 'The Lady of Shalott.' " *Victorian Newsletter*, no. 25 (1964), pp. 4–8.

Paden, W. D. *Tennyson in Egypt: A Study of the Imagery in His Earlier Work.*

University of Kansas Humanistic Studies, no. 27. Lawrence: University of Kansas Press, 1942.

Pallen, Condé Benoist. *The Meaning of "The Idylls of the King."* Reprinted New York: Haskell House, 1965.

Perrine, Laurence. "When Does Hope Mean Doubt? The Tone of 'Crossing the Bar.' " *Victorian Poetry* 4 (1966): 127–31.

Pettigrew, John. *Tennyson: The Early Poems.* Studies in English Literature, no. 41. London: Edward Arnold, 1970.

———. "Tennyson's 'Ulysses': A Reconciliation of Opposites." *Victorian Poetry* 1 (1963): 27–45.

Pipes, B. N., Jr. "A Slight Meteorological Disturbance: The Last Two Stanzas of Tennyson's 'The Poet.' " *Victorian Poetry* 1 (1963): 74–76.

Pitt, Valerie. *Tennyson Laureate.* London: Barrie and Rockliff, 1962.

Pitts, Gordon. "A Reading of Tennyson's 'Ulysses.' " *West Virginia University Bulletin: Philological Papers* 15 (1966): 36–42.

Poston, Lawrence III. "The Argument of the Geraint-Enid Books in *Idylls of the King.*" *Victorian Poetry* 2 (1964): 269–75.

———. " 'Pelleas and Ettarre': Tennyson's 'Troilus.' " *Victorian Poetry* 4 (1966): 199–204.

———. "The Two Provinces of Tennyson's *Idylls.*" *Criticism* 9 (1967): 372–82.

Potter, George R. "Tennyson and the Biological Theory of Mutability in Species." *Philological Quarterly* 16 (1937): 321–43.

Preyer, Robert. "Alfred Tennyson: The Poetry and Politics of Conservative Vision." *Victorian Studies* 9 (1966): 325–52.

———. "Tennyson as an Oracular Poet." *Modern Philology* 55 (1958): 239–51.

Priestley, F. E. L. "Control of Tone in Tennyson's *The Princess.*" *Langue et littérature: Actes du VIIIᵉ Congrès de la Fédération Internationale des Langues et Littératures Modernes.* Bibliothèque de la Faculté de Philosophie et Lettres de l'Université de Liège, Facs. 161, pp. 314–15. Paris: Société d'Édition "Les Belles Lettres," 1961.

———. "Tennyson's *Idylls.*" *University of Toronto Quarterly* 19 (1949): 35–49.

Pyre, J. F. A. *The Formation of Tennyson's Style: A Study, Primarily, of the Versification of the Early Poems.* University of Wisconsin Studies, no. 12. Madison: University of Wisconsin Press, 1921.

Quereshi, A. H. "The Waste Land Motif in Tennyson." *Humanities Association Bulletin* 18, no. 2 (1967): 20–30.

Rackin, Phyllis. "Recent Misreadings of 'Break, Break, Break' and Their Implications for Poetic Theory." *Journal of English and Germanic Philology* 65 (1966): 217–18.

Rader, Ralph Wilson. "The Composition of Tennyson's *Maud.*" *Modern Philology* 59 (1962): 265–69.

———. *Tennyson's Maud: The Biographical Genesis.* Perspectives in Criticism, no. 15. Berkeley and Los Angeles: University of California Press, 1963.

Ray, Gordon N. "Tennyson Reads Maud." In *Romantic and Victorian: Studies in Memory of William H. Marshall*, edited by W. Paul Elledge and Richard L. Hoffman, pp. 290–317. Rutherford: Fairleigh Dickinson University Press, 1971.

Reed, John R. "The Design of Tennyson's 'The Two Voices.' " *University of Toronto Quarterly* 37 (1968): 186–96.

———. *Perception and Design in Tennyson's "Idylls of the King."* Athens, Ohio University Press, 1969.

Reid, Margaret J. C. *The Arthurian Legend: Comparison of Treatment in Modern and Medieval Literature.* New York: Barnes and Noble, 1938.

Richardson, Joanna. *The Pre-Eminent Victorian: A Study of Tennyson.* London: Jonathan Cape, 1962.

Ricks, Christopher. " 'Peace and War' and 'Maud.' " *Notes and Queries*, n.s. 9 (1962): 230.

———. *Tennyson.* New York: Macmillan, 1972.

———. "Tennyson as a Love-Poet." *Malahat Review* 12 (1969): 73–88.

———. "Tennyson's Lucretius." *Library* 20 (1965): 63–64.

———. "Tennyson's Methods of Composition." *Proceedings of the British Academy* 52 (1966): 209–30.

———. "Two Early Poems by Tennyson." *Victorian Poetry* 3 (1965): 55–57.

———, ed. *The Poems of Tennyson.* London: Longmans, 1969.

Robson, W. W. "The Dilemma of Tennyson." *Listener* 57 (1957): 963–65. Reprinted in *Critical Essays*, pp. 191–99. New York: Barnes and Noble, 1967.

Roppen, Georg. "Alfred Tennyson." *Evolution and Poetic Belief: A Study in Some Victorian and Modern Writers*, pp. 66–112. Oslo: Oslo University Press, 1956.

———. " 'Ulysses' and Tennyson's Sea Quest." *English Studies* 40 (1959): 77–90.

Rosenberg, John D. "The Two Kingdoms of *In Memoriam*." *Journal of English and Germanic Philology* 58 (1959): 228–40.

Rutland, William R. "Tennyson and the Theory of Evolution." *Essays and Studies* 26 (1940): 7–29.

Ryals, Clyde deL. "The 'Fatal Woman' Symbol in Tennyson." *PMLA* 74 (1959): 438–43.

———. *From the Great Deep: Essays on "Idylls of the King."* Athens, Ohio: Ohio University Press, 1967.

———. "The 'Heavenly Friend': The 'New Mythus' of *In Memoriam*." *The Personalist* 43 (1962): 383–402.

———. "The Poet as Critic: Appraisals of Tennyson by His Contemporaries." *Tennessee Studies in Literature* 7 (1962): 113–25.

———. "Point of View in Tennyson's *Ulysses*." *Archiv fur der Studien der neueren Sprachen und Literaturen* 199 (1962): 232–34.

————. "Tennyson's *Maud.*" *Connotation* 1 (1962): 12–32.

————. "Tennyson's *The Lotus-Eaters* [sic]." *Revue des Langues Vivantes* 25 (1959): 474–86.

————. *Theme and Symbol in Tennyson's Poems to 1850.* Philadelphia: University of Pennsylvania Press, 1964.

————. "The 'Weird Seizures' in *The Princess.*" *Texas Studies in Literature and Language* 4 (1962): 268–75.

Sanders, Charles Richard. "Carlyle and Tennyson." *PMLA* 76 (1961): 82–97.

————. "Tennyson and the Human Hand." *Victorian Newsletter,* no. 11 (1957), pp. 5–14.

Schweik, Robert C. "The 'Peace or War' Passages in Tennyson's 'Maud.'" *Notes and Queries,* n.s. 7 (1960): 457–58.

Scott, P. G. *Tennyson's Enoch Arden: A Victorian Best-Seller.* Tennyson Society Monograph no. 2. Lincoln: Tennyson Research Centre, 1970.

Sendry, Joseph. "*In Memoriam* and *Lycidas.*" *PMLA* 82 (1967): 437–43.

————. "'The Palace of Art' Revisited." *Victorian Poetry* 4 (1966): 149–62.

Shannon, Edgar F., Jr. "Alfred Tennyson." *Victorian Newsletter,* no. 12 (1957), pp. 26–27.

————. "The Critical Reception of Tennyson's 'Maud.'" *PMLA* 68 (1953): 397–417.

————. "The History of a Poem: Tennyson's *Ode on the Death of the Duke of Wellington.*" *Studies in Bibliography* 13 (1960): 149–77.

————. *Tennyson and the Reviewers: A Study of His Literary Reputation and the Influence of the Critics upon His Poetry, 1827–1851.* Cambridge, Mass.: Harvard University Press, 1952.

Shaw, W. David. "Gareth's Four Antagonists: A Biblical Source." *Victorian Newsletter,* no. 34 (1968), pp. 34–35.

————. "The Idealist's Dilemma in *Idylls of the King.*" *Victorian Poetry* 5 (1967): 41–53.

————. "*Idylls of the King*: A Dialectical Reading." *Victorian Poetry* 7 (1969): 175–90.

————. "Imagination and Intellect in Tennyson's 'Lucretius.'" *Modern Language Quarterly* 33 (1972): 130–39.

————. "*In Memoriam* and the Rhetoric of Confession." *ELH* 38 (1971): 80–103.

————. "The Passion of the Past: Tennyson and Francis Grose." *ELN* 5 (1968): 269–77.

————. "The Transcendentalist Problem in Tennyson's Poetry of Debate." *Philological Quarterly* 46 (1967): 79–94.

————. "Victorian Poetics: An Approach through Genre." *Victorian Newsletter,* no. 39 (1971), pp. 1–4.

Shaw, W. David, and Gartlein, Carl W. "The Aurora: A Spiritual Metaphor in Tennyson." *Victorian Poetry* 3 (1965): 213–22.

Shmiefsky, Marvel. " 'In Memoriam': Its Seasonal Imagery Reconsidered." *Studies in English Literature* 7 (1967): 721–39.

Short, Clarice. "Tennyson and 'The Lover's Tale.' " *PMLA* 82 (1967): 78–84.

Sinfeld, Alan. *The Language of Tennyson's "In Memoriam."* New York: Barnes and Noble, 1971.

———. "Matter-Moulded Forms of Speech: Tennyson's Use of Language in *In Memoriam*." In *The Major Victorian Poets: Reconsiderations*, edited by Isobel Armstrong, pp. 51–67. Lincoln, Neb.: University of Nebraska Press, 1969.

Slinn, E. Warwick. "Deception and Artifice in *Idylls of the King*." *Victorian Poetry* 11 (1973): 1–14.

Smith, Elton Edward. "Tennyson Criticism 1923–1966: From Fragmentation to Tension in Polarity." *Victorian Newsletter*, no. 31 (1967), pp. 1–4.

———. *The Two Voices: A Tennyson Study*. Lincoln, Neb.: University of Nebraska Press, 1964.

Smith, R. B. "Sexual Ambivalence in Tennyson." *The College English Association Critic* 27, no. 9 (1965): 8–9.

Solimine, Joseph, Jr. "The Burkean Idea of the State in Tennyson's Poetry: The Vision in Crisis." *Huntington Library Quarterly* 30 (1967): 147–65.

———. "The *Idylls of the King*: The Rise, Decline, and Fall of the State." *The Personalist* 50 (1969): 105–16.

Solomon, Stanley J. "Tennyson's Paradoxical King." *Victorian Poetry* 1 (1963): 258–71.

Sonn, Carl Robinson. "Poetic Vision and Religious Certainty in Tennyson's Earlier Poetry." *Modern Philology* 57 (1959): 83–93.

Southam, B. C. *Tennyson*. London: Longmans, 1971.

Spitzer, Leo. " 'Tears, Idle Tears' Again." *Hopkins Review* 5, no. 3 (1952): 71–80.

Stange, G. Robert. "Tennyson's Garden of Art: A Study of *The Hesperides*." *PMLA* 67 (1952): 732–43.

———. "Tennyson's Mythology: A Study of 'Demeter and Persephone.' " *ELH* 21 (1954): 67–80.

Starzyk, Lawrence J. " 'That Promised Land': Poetry and Religion in the Early Victorian Period." *Victorian Studies* 16 (1973): 269–90.

Steane, J. B. *Tennyson*. London: Evans, 1966.

Stephen, Leslie. "Life of Tennyson." In *Studies of a Biographer*, 2: 196–240. London: G. P. Putnam's Sons, 1899.

Stevenson, Lionel. "The 'High-Born Maiden' Symbol in Tennyson." *PMLA* 63 (1948): 234–43.

———. "Tennyson, Browning, and a Romantic Fallacy." *University of Toronto Quarterly* 13 (1944): 175–95.

Stokes, Edward. "The Metrics of *Maud*." *Victorian Poetry* 2 (1964): 97–110.

Storch, R. F. "The Fugitive from the Ancestral Hearth: Tennyson's 'Ulysses.' " *Texas Studies in Literature and Language* 13 (1971): 281–97.

Sucksmith, H. P. "Tennyson on the Nature of His Own Poetic Genius: Some Recently Discovered Marginalia." *Renaissance and Modern Studies* 11 (1967): 84–89.

Sundell, Michael G. "Spiritual Confusion and Artistic Form in Victorian Poetry." *Victorian Newsletter*, no. 39 (1971), pp. 4–7.

Svaglic, Martin J. "A Framework for Tennyson's *In Memoriam*." *Journal of English and Germanic Philology* 61 (1962): 810–25.

Taafe, James G. "Circle Imagery in Tennyson's *In Memoriam*." *Victorian Poetry* 1 (1963): 123–31.

Templeman, William Darby. "A Consideration of the Fame of 'Locksley Hall.' " *Victorian Poetry* 1 (1963): 81–103.

———. "Tennyson's *Locksley Hall* and Thomas Carlyle." In *Booker Memorial Studies: Eight Essays on Victorian Literature in Memory of John Manning Booker*, edited by Hill Shine, pp. 34–59. Chapel Hill: University of North Carolina Press, 1950.

Tennyson, Sir Charles. *Alfred Tennyson*. New York: Macmillan, 1949.

———. "The Dream in Tennyson's Poetry." *Virginia Quarterly Review* 40 (1964): 228–48.

———. "The Idylls of the King." *Twentieth Century* 161 (1957): 277–86.

———. *Six Tennyson Essays*. London: Cassell, 1954.

———. "Tennyson: Mind and Method." *Tennyson Research Bulletin* 1 (November 1971): 127–36.

———. "Tennyson's 'Doubt and Prayer' Sonnet." *Victorian Poetry* 6 (1968): 1–3.

Tennyson, Sir Charles, and Fall, Christine. *Alfred Tennyson: An Annotated Bibliography*. Athens, Ga.: University of Georgia Press, 1967.

Tennyson, Hallam, Lord. *Alfred, Lord Tennyson: A Memoir*. 2 vols. New York: Macmillan, 1898.

Tillotson, Kathleen. "Tennyson's Serial Poem." *Mid-Victorian Studies*, pp. 80–109. London: Athlone Press, 1965.

Tobias, Richard. "Tennyson's Painted Shell." *Victorian Newsletter*, no. 39 (1971), pp. 7–10.

Turner, Paul. "Some Ancient Light on Tennyson's 'Oenone.' " *Journal of English and Germanic Philology* 61 (1962): 57–72.

———. "The Stupidest English Poet." *English Studies* 30 (1949): 1–12.

Walton, James. "Tennyson's Patrimony: From 'The Outcast' to 'Maud.' " *Texas Studies in Literature and Language* 11 (1969): 733–59.

Waterston, Elizabeth H. "Symbolism in Tennyson's Minor Poems." *University of Toronto Quarterly* 20 (1951): 369–80.

Weiner, S. Ronald. "The Chord of Self: Tennyson's *Maud*." *Literature and Psychology* 16 (1966): 175–83.

Whiting, George Wesley. "The Artist and Tennyson." *Rice University Studies* 50 (1964): 1–84.

Wiggins, Louise D. "Tennyson's Veiled Statue." *English Studies* 49 (1968): 444–45 [on *In Memoriam*, 103].

Wilkenfeld, R. B. "Tennyson's Camelot: The Kingdom of Folly." *University of Toronto Quarterly* 37 (1968): 281–94.

———. "The Shape of Two Voices." *Victorian Poetry* 4 (1966): 163–73.

Willey, Basil. "Tennyson." *More Nineteenth Century Studies: A Group of Honest Doubters*, pp. 53–105. London: Chatto and Windus, 1956.

Wilson, Charles. "Mirror of a Shire: Tennyson's Dialect Poems." *Durham University Journal*, n.s. 21 (1959): 22–28.

Wilson, Hugh H. "Tennyson: Unscholarly Arthurian." *Victorian Newsletter*, no. 32 (1967), pp. 5–11.

Wilson, J. [Christopher North]. Review of *Poems, Chiefly Lyrical*. *Blackwood's* 31 (1832): 721–41.

Zuckerman, Joanne P. "Tennyson's *In Memoriam* as Love Poetry." *Dalhousie Review* 51 (1971): 202–17.

Index